The Asbury Theological Seminary Series in Christian Revitalization Studies

This volume is published in collaboration with the Center for the Study of World Christian Revitalization Movements, a cooperative initiative of Asbury Theological Seminary faculty. Building on the work of the previous Wesleyan/ Holiness Studies Center at the Seminary, the Center provides a focus for research in the Wesleyan Holiness and other related Christian renewal movements, including Pietism and Pentecostal movements, which have had a world impact. The research seeks to develop analytical models of these movements, including their biblical and theological assessment. Using an interdisciplinary approach, the Center bridges relevant discourses in several areas in order to gain insights for effective Christian mission globally. It recognizes the need for conducting research that combines insights from the history of evangelical renewal and revival movements with anthropological and religious studies literature on revitalization movements. It also networks with similar or related research and study centers around the world, in addition to sponsoring its own research projects.

This title presents Dr. Yabbeju Rapaka's important research on the Indian Pentecostal Church of God (IPC) in the state of Andhra Pradesh, the first insider perspective on an indigenous church that features ministry among the "untouchables" – the poor and marginalized Dalit population of Andhra whose narrative has not heretofore been told. Drawing from a range of primary research methods, his study contributes to the research of this publication series by providing a comprehensive account of key ecclesial tradition which has been at the heart of the explosive growth of indigenous Pentecostal and charismatic Christianity sweeping the Indian subcontinent.

>J. Steven O'Malley
>General Editor
>The Asbury Theological Seminary Studies in Christian Revitalization

Dalit Pentecostalism

A Study of the Indian Pentecostal Church of God, 1932 to 2010

Asbury Theological Seminary Series in
World Christian Revitalization Movements in
Pentecostal/Charismatic Studies, No.

Yabbeju (Jabez) Rapaka

EMETH PRESS
www.emethpress.com

Dalit Pentecostalism: Study of the Indian Pentecostal Church of God, 1932 to 2010

Copyright © 2013
Printed in the United States of America on acid-free paper

All rights reserved. No part of this book may be reproduced, or stored in a retrieval system or transmitted in any form or by any means, electronic, mechanical, photocopying, recording, scanning or otherwise, except as permitted by the 1976 United States Copyright Act, or with the prior written permission of Emeth Press. Requests for permission should be addressed to: Emeth Press, P. O. Box 23961, Lexington, KY 40523-3961. http://www.emethpress.com.

Library of Congress Cataloging-in-Publication Data

Rapaka, Yabbeju.
  Dalit pentecostalism : a study of the Indian Pentecostal Church of God, 1932 to 2010 / Yabbeju Rapaka.
     pages cm. -- (Asbury theological seminary series in world Christian revitalization movements in Pentecostal/Charismatic studies ; no. 7)
  Includes bibliographical references.
  ISBN 978-1-60947-054-8 (alk. paper)
  1. Pentecostalism--India--Andhra Pradesh--History--20th century. 2. Pentecostalism--India--Andhra Pradesh--History--21st century. 3. Indian Pentecostal Church of God--History. 4. Dalits--India--Religion. 5. Andhra Pradesh (India)--Church history--20th century. 6. Andhra Pradesh (India)--Church history--21st century. I. Title.
  BR1644.5.I4R37 2013
  289.9'4095484--dc23
                                                2013013677

Cover photo: The first Indian Pentecostal Church, Eluru, India (the mother church of all the IPC churches); courtesy of the author

Map of India

Map of Andhra Pradesh

Dedication

This book is dedicated to my lovely wife, Gloria Rapaka, and my three wonderful children, Jeremiah W. Rapaka, Glorianna A. Rapaka, and Theresa O. Rapaka. For the last fifteen years, my wife has been a source of strength, support, and encouragement in all my endeavors. Gloria has made many sacrifices for me throughout my academic journey. She has unwaveringly supported my call, and her commitment and faithfulness to my academic and ministerial success are highly laudable. For this I am indescribably grateful to her. My children also gave me constant inspiration and support throughout my academic endeavors. Without their encouragement and prayers, I could have not completed this monograph. This book is also dedicated to my loving parents, Subba Rao and Sugunamma Rapaka, who instilled in me a passion for learning and higher education. I am indeed grateful to them for their love, support, and encouragement throughout my life's journey.

Contents

Abbreviations / xi

Foreword / xiii

Preface / xv

Chapter 1: Introduction / 1

Chapter 2: Dalit Reality and Dalit Contributions to Indian Christianity / 7

Chapter 3: Three Successive Stages of Indian Pentecostalism / 23

Chapter 4: Early History of the IPC in Andhra Pradesh (1932 to 1959) / 53

Chapter 5: Transition Years of the IPC in Andhra Pradesh (1960 to 1981) / 79

Chapter 6: Later History of the IPC in Andhra Pradesh (1982 to 2010) / 91

Chapter 7: Conclusion / 103

Chapter 8: Epilogue / 123

Appendix A / 129

Bibliography / 133

Abbreviations

ABM:	The American Baptist Mission or The American Baptist Missionary Union
AG:	The Assemblies of God
CBM:	The Canadian Baptist Mission
CMS:	The Church Missionary Society
COG:	The Church of God
CPM:	The Ceylon Pentecostal Mission
CSI:	The Church of South India
GDM:	The Godavari Delta Mission
IPC:	The Indian Pentecostal Church
LMS:	The London Missionary Society
NIDPCM:	The New International Dictionary of Pentecostal and Charismatic Movements
SPG:	The Society for the Propagation of the Gospel in Foreign Parts
UK:	The United Kingdom
US:	The United States
WME:	The World Missionary Evangelism

Foreword

With the exception of the vast literature concerning African Indigenous Churches, there has been a relative dearth of analytic research studies on indigenous church movements throughout the world. As a result, the present study by Dr. Yabbeju Rapaka on the Indian Pentecostal Church of God (IPC) in the Indian state of Andhra Pradesh is a most welcomed addition. It is especially important because Rapaka presents an insider Dalit perspective of this indigenous Pentecostal movement in India. This is a rare treat for outside scholars who have only had access to outsider views, usually limited to the perspectives of white Western observers. Before this study, we knew little, if anything, about Andhra "untouchables," and their religious beliefs and practices. This tome opens up a wide vista of new understandings about Indian Christianity, about Christianity in Andhra Pradesh, about Pentecostalism in the sub-continent, and about Dalit Christianity. Rapaka even addresses the biases of other Christians against these "Children of God."

The author also deals with historiographic misconceptions about the socially depressed. In the process, he codifies indigenous Christian growth from British colonialism through a period of new found nationalism and into descriptions of recent beliefs, practices, and structural configurations. Itself a split from the IPC in Kerala in 1932, the IPC in Andhra Pradesh from 1960-1981 experienced additional schisms, spawning World Missionary Evangelism and Manna Ministries. Rapaka laments that it still is dominated by more aggressive Malayalis from Kerala.

Drawing on primary research techniques, such as interviews of the movement's leaders and pastors, Rapaka attempts to reconstruct not only the history of the IPC in Andhra Pradesh, but also its impact on society. Clearly, the IPC has brought a social uplift to the poor, empowering them "spiritually, emotionally, and behaviorally," although not economically. With this volume, Dr. Rapaka has taken the first major step to rescue his fellow IPC Dalits from being marginalized and forgotten.

—Stanley M. Burgess, Ph.D.

Preface

Research for this monograph was originally undertaken for a Ph.D. at Regent University, Virginia Beach, Virginia, and the substance of the work first appeared in the dissertation entitled *The Indian Pentecostal Church of God in Andhra Pradesh, 1932 to 2010: A Study of Dalit Pentecostalism*. While pursuing doctoral studies at Regent, my preliminary research led me to *The New International Dictionary of Pentecostal and Charismatic Movements*, edited by Dr. Stanley Burgess. As I initially skimmed his monumental work, I was amazed to discover that no substantial article on the major indigenous Indian movement called "the Indian Pentecostal Church of God" was included. This unexpected discovery stimulated a desire in me to undertake the recording of the history of this important movement, and to thereby fill this gap in Pentecostal Christian historiography.

This subject is also of particular importance to me because I am a native of India, born and raised in the city of Eluru, where this movement was officially started and registered, and from where it then spread like wildfire throughout India. I was a member of the mother church of the Indian Pentecostal Church of God (IPC) in Eluru for several decades, until I emigrated from India to the United States in 1993 to pursue graduate and postgraduate degrees.

Additionally, no attempt has ever been made to provide an organized and comprehensive historical account of the origin and growth of the Indian Pentecostal Church of God in its home state of Andhra Pradesh either. The reasons for this neglect are two-fold. First, the pioneers and early leaders of the IPC and others who succeeded them failed to capture the history of their denomination because they lacked higher education (both secular and theological) and possessed an anti-intellectual attitude. Second, a culturally motivated bias has long existed against most adherents of the IPC, who are predominantly "Dalits," the subaltern people of Indian society. This unfortunate situation made me feel compelled to plunge into undertaking the needed and neglected research, to embark on an interesting adventure to narrate and interpret the historical development of the Indian Pentecostal Church of God (IPC), an indigenous Pentecostal movement in India.

The completed work is the culmination of the shared efforts of many scholars. Several faculty members of Regent University's School of Divinity offered invaluable advice and support during every stage of the preparation of this monograph. I extend my heartfelt gratitude first to Dr. Stanley Burgess. His continual encouragement was a source of strength throughout this research process, especially in the selection of my topic, in locating the appropriate resources, and in writing this historical document. His in-depth knowledge of Indian Pentecostal history also contributed immensely to the success of this work. I am also indebted to Dr. Ruth Burgess for her helpful advice on conducting oral history interviews for this research and for her incalculable periodic inputs. I also want to extend my gratitude to Dr. Eric Newberg, who met with me regularly to steer my research in the right direction. I am also appreciative of the sage advice offered by Dr. Roger Hedlund, who encouraged me to focus my attention on the contributions of the subaltern people of India—the Dalits—to the history of the IPC in Andhra. Finally, I want to extend my gratitude to the Pentecostal leaders, especially Geddam Rathnam Purushotham, Godi Samuel, Komanapalli Ernest, Deekollu John Sunder Rao, Pachigalla Spurgeon Raju, and Plathaneth Noel Samuel, and the constituents of the Indian Pentecostal Church in Andhra Pradesh, who provided rare and invaluable historical information for this research through oral history. Without their contributions, this monograph never could have materialized.

Throughout this monograph I have used the full names of the Indian people discussed in this study when they are available, and their initials when their full names are unavailable. However, it is important (and will be useful to the understanding of the reader) to note here, that the majority of people in Andhra usually use their surnames first, but generally refer to them by their initials, due to tradition. They sometimes use their parent's or grandparent's given name between their own surnames and given names. For example: in the name Kanumala Peturu Devasahayam (K.P. Devasahayam), *Kanumala* is the surname, *Peturu* is his father's name, and *Devasahayam* is his given name.

Many of the high caste people intentionally use their caste names (such as Sharma, Setti, Chowdary, Raju, Reddy, et cetera) after their given names to display their higher caste status in society. However, for the low caste people and the Dalits (who do not fit in the caste strata at all), displaying the caste name after the given name is not advantageous because of the stigma of social segregation and prejudice that still exists today, not only in Andhra, but also throughout India.

Chapter 1

Introduction

The Pentecostal-charismatic movement is a fast-growing, global Christian tradition, second in number only to Roman Catholicism.[1] The explosive growth of this movement today is centered in Asia, Africa, and Latin America. The rapid growth of indigenous Christianity in these regions belongs to Pentecostal and charismatic Christianity, which holds considerable appeal to the poor, marginalized, and disfranchised.

India is the bastion of indigenous Pentecostal and charismatic movements in South Asia. The fifth largest body of Pentecostal-charismatics in the world in the 21st century is found in India. Its rapid growth has reached over 33.5 million adherents, divided among 27.3 million Neocharismatics, 5 million charismatics, and 1.2 million classical Pentecostals.[2]

One of the largest indigenous[3] Pentecostal movements in India is the Indian Pentecostal Church of God (IPC) with 900,000 adherents, 86,000 of which belong to the IPC in the state of Andhra Pradesh. It is, therefore, ironic that the majority of works dealing with the history of Indian Christianity overlook the presence of the Indian Pentecostal Church of God in Andhra Pradesh. The aim of this monograph is to remedy this omission by narrating and interpreting the history of the IPC in the region of Andhra Pradesh, as seen from an indigenous Indian perspective.

Map 1- Map of India

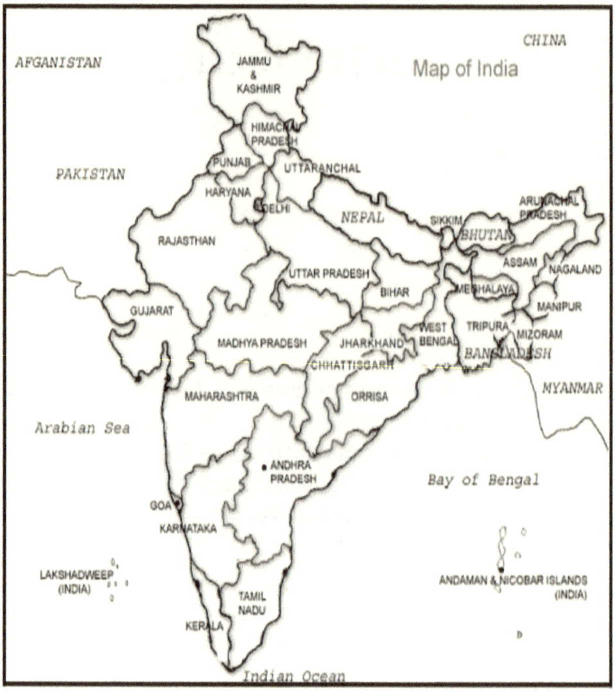

Problem

The immediate problem confronting the historical researcher of this subject is the dearth of published research on the Indian Pentecostal Church of God in Andhra Pradesh. This scarcity raises an important preliminary question: What has caused researchers to ignore the history of the Andhra IPC? This monograph postulates that there are two primary reasons for this historical neglect. The first is that the leaders of the IPC in Andhra Pradesh failed to recognize any need to compose histories of their denomination since its inception in 1932 because, for the most part, these leaders were not highly-educated in either secular or theological fields. Early Pentecostal pioneers and leaders also generally embraced an anti-intellectual bias. The second reason for the neglect could stem from a culturally-motivated bias. Historical research on the Indian Pentecostal Church of God by historians Pothen Thottumkal Abraham, Thackil Chacko George, Thomson K. Mathew, Kunjappan C. Varghese, and others has focused mainly on the history of the IPC in the state of Kerala, and on Kulathumoolackal Eapen Abraham (K.E. Abraham), a founder of the IPC.[4] They apparently did not recognize the relevance of the history of the Andhra IPC and its Dalit pioneers and leaders. Such neglect is likely due to an ingrained culturally motivated bias against the Dalit constituents of the IPC in Andhra. Dalits in Indian society have continually faced discrimination because of historical cultural marginalization and entrenched social prejudice and their omission from the history of the IPC may be no exception.

A general view of the plight of the Dalits in India is given in this section to demonstrate how their cultural and social marginalization developed. The Dalit reality is further discussed in Chapter Two. Preliminary information is offered to establish the vital connection between the Dalits and the IPC. In fact, the majority of Christians in India (including Pentecostals) are from a Dalit background.[5]

Who, then, are these Dalit people? What is their actual status in modern Indian society? Dalits are the deprived and dispossessed segment of Indian society. They are the oppressed and crushed victims of the Indian caste system who are considered polluted and treated as untouchables. Dalits are restricted from drawing water from wells and tanks and entering temples or residences of higher caste people. Their ability to own land is limited. Many reside in isolated areas sequestered from the rest of the population. Dalit people not only face social discrimination, but also the near constant threat of physical violence, including murder.

The plight of Dalit Christians is really no better than that of other Dalits. Conversion to Christianity by the Dalit masses has not brought much change in their economic conditions or their historically-entrenched social and cultural status. Three hundred years of Protestant missionary activity in India has seen most Dalit Christians remain in the same conditions of historic cultural deprivation, still bearing the stigma of social prejudice. The Christians of Dalit origin remain mostly among the economically poor and unjustly oppressed. Not only do upper caste Hindus discriminate against and victimize them, but also their own Indian government. The government provides benefits to the poor based on constitutional provisions, but benefits are actually only allotted to Dalits belonging to the Hindu and Sikh religions. Meanwhile, the government denies the same benefits to Dalits belonging to other faiths, like Islam and Christianity.[6]

Dalit Pentecostals face a situation not much different from that of other Dalit Christians. They suffer the same social injustice and face social discrimination from Hindus and even fellow Christians belonging to the upper castes. Dalit Pentecostals also encounter opposition from Christians of mainline churches because they disapprove of their theological orientation and charismatic spiritual practices (expressive worship, speaking in tongues, prayer for healing, and prophetic utterances).

The following primary questions concerning Dalit Pentecostals in Andhra Pradesh are addressed in this monograph: Who were the key players in the origin and growth of the IPC? What role did Dalits play in the indigenous Pentecostal movement in Andhra Pradesh? How was the IPC contextualized regarding the conditions of social marginalization and the poverty of the Dalits in Andhra Pradesh? This monograph attempts to narrate and interpret the historical development of the IPC. It also incorporates an inquiry into the contributions of the Dalits to IPC's formation and expansion, as well as the impact that the IPC has had on them.

Organization of the Study

This study is divided into eight chapters. Chapter one introduces the importance of this study. Chapter two focuses on the Indian caste system's origin and development, socio-economic conditions of Dalits in Indian society, and Dalit contributions to Indian Christianity. Chapter three examines the successive stages of Indian Pentecostalism. Chapter four narrates the IPC's early history beginning in 1932 and proceeding to 1959, documenting its origin and expansion in Andhra Pradesh. Chapter five covers the transitional period of the IPC from 1960 to 1981, focusing on several key individuals who played a significant role in the schism of the IPC. Chapter six narrates the major contributions of second generation leaders and significant issues and events occurring from 1982 to 2010. Chapter seven analyzes and interprets the findings, and chapter eight summarizes and concludes the monograph.

Notes

[1]David Barrett & Todd Johnson, "Annual Statistical Table on Global Missions: 1999" *International Bulletin of Missionary Research* 23 (January, 1999): 24.

[2]David B. Barrett & Todd Johnson, "Global Statistics" in Stanley M. Burgess, ed., *The New International Dictionary of Pentecostal and Charismatic Movements* (Grand Rapids: Zondervan, 2002), 284-302.

According to Vinson Synan, the classical Pentecostals can be defined as those who believe the teaching that the gift of tongues is the sign of receiving the subsequent second blessing, or baptism in the Holy Spirit. *The Holiness-Pentecostal Tradition: Charismatic Movements in the Twentieth Century* (Grand Rapids: Wm. B. Eerdmans Publishing Co., 1997), xi.

Donald Gee describes the charismatics as those who are outside a denominational and/or confessional Pentecostal framework and who believe in the phenomena or experience of infilling/empowerment with the Holy Spirit generally termed as baptism in the Holy Spirit. Burgess, ed., *NIDPCM*, 477.

Neocharismatics believe in Pentecostal-like experiences, i.e., receiving and exercising the gifts of the Holy Spirit. They should be viewed as part of a broader category which includes the vast numbers of independent and indigenous churches and groups that cannot be classified as either Pentecostal or Charismatic. Burgess, ed., *NIDPCM*, 928.

[3] Indigenous church can be defined as "a group of believers, who live out their life including their socialized Christian activity in the patterns of the local society and for whom any transformation of that society comes out of the felt needs, under the guidance of the Holy Spirit and Scriptures." William Smalley, "Cultural Implica-

tions of an Indigenous Church," in Ralph Winter, *Perspectives on the World Christian Movement* (Pasadena: William Carey Library, 1981), 497. According to Roger Hedlund, "indigenous Christianity" or "Little Tradition" Churches in India have their own structures and cultural expressions which are frequently outside the orbit of the traditional Churches or "Great Tradition" Churches that are largely the product of foreign missionary effort." *Quest for Identity: India's Churches of Indiegenous Origin: The "Little Tradition" in Indian Christianity* (Delhi and Chennai: ISPCK/MIIS, 2000), 3.

4Thackil Chacko George, "The Growth of the Pentecostal Churches in South India" (master's thesis, Fuller Theological Seminary, 1975). Thomson K. Mathew, "A Study in the History of the Pentecostal Movement in South India" (master's thesis, Yale University Divinity School, 1975). Abraham Thottumkal Pothen, "The India Pentecostal Church of God and Its Contribution to Church Growth" (master's thesis, Fuller Theological Seminary, 1988). Kunjappan C. Varghese, "Reformation Brings Revival: A Historical Study of K.E. Abraham and His Contributions in the Founding of the Indian Pentecostal Church of God" (Ph.D. diss., Trinity International University, 1999).

5 Estimates place the figure at around 80 percent of the Indian church being comprised of Dalits. Roger Hedlund, ed., *Christianity is Indian: The Emergence of an Indigenous Community* (Delhi: ISPCK, 2004), 452.

6Azariah Masilamani, *A Pastor's Search for Dalit Theology* (Delhi: ISPCK, 2000), 22-23.

Chapter 2

Dalit Reality and Dalit Contribution to Indian Christianity

Introduction

Social injustice exists in every society, whether in the form of racism in the United States, ethnic cleansing in Eastern Europe, tribalism in Africa, or the caste system in India. Out of every six people in the world today, one is an Indian, and out of every six Indians, one is an untouchable, or a Dalit. There are an estimated 165 million Dalits currently living in India.[1] They continue to suffer fear, poverty, humiliation, and torture under India's 3,500 year old caste system, a stigma in civilized society. Despite their low social status in India, these marginalized Dalits played a pivotal role in shaping Indian Christianity, including Pentecostalism. This section provides the caste system's historical and religious roots and Indian society's Dalit segregation through the centuries. It details the Dalits' social and economic conditions and also addresses their contributions to Christianity in India.

Historical Roots of the Caste System and the Dalits

The term "Dalit" was first coined by Bhimrao Ramji Ambedkar, himself a Dalit and one of the architects of the Indian Constitution. The term comes from the Sanskrit word *dal*, meaning "burst, split, broken or torn asunder, downtrodden, scattered, crushed and destroyed." Dalits are the oppressed, the deprived, the dispossessed, and the marginalized section of Indian society.[2] Among the names given to them are *Harijan* (children of God, by Mahatma Gandhi); *Avarnas* (casteless); *Panchamas* (fifth caste); *Chandalas* (worst of the earth); *Depressed Classes* (during British Colonial days); and *Scheduled Castes* (the Indian Constitution's discriminating designation).

Pre-Aryan People—the Dravidians

On the Indo-Pakistan subcontinent over 4,000 years ago, a civilization existed called the Indus (or Sindhu Valley) from its major river of the same name (*"Sindhu"* in Sanskrit). It extended beyond the limits of the valley to cover a 1,600 kilometer area from East to West (Alamgirpur to Sutkagendor) and 1,100 kilometers from North to South (Ropar to Bhagatrov).[3]

The excavations at Indus sites, such as Harappa, Mohenjo-daro (Pakistan), Kalibangan, Lothal, and Surkotada (India), reveal the highly advanced architecture and rigorous town planning of the Indus people. The art of making stone and metal sculptures, pottery, terracotta figurines, and seals was highly developed. These people were known to be literate by clear inscriptions on seals of a cleverly organized system of weights and measures and by their arithmetic proficiency. Their civilization represented a Bronze Age, objects of which were found in the excavations, including knives, saws, sickles, chisels, razors, pins, tweezers, and fish-hooks. Agriculture was their economy's backbone. The Indus, Ravi, Ghaggar, Satluj, and Hogavo rivers flowed on the outskirts of Mohenjo-daro, Harappa, Kalibangan, Ropar, and Lothal, providing adequate water for growing wheat, barley, bananas, melons, and peas. Cotton, their most remarkable agricultural achievement, was also cultivated.

The Indus people had a wide variety of religious practices. A figure surrounded by animals was depicted on seals, indicating the worship of Siva in the form of *Pasupati*, the Lord of Animals. Mother goddess worship was also practiced. They adored trees and streams, believing the spirits of ancestors resided there. Their burial practices indicated that they believed in a life hereafter. Mirrors, antimony rods, pearl shells, and pots were placed with dead bodies. The people lived in well-built cities, possessing a relatively mature culture with a high standard of art and craftsmanship, as established by Indus Valley archeological evidence. Three thousand years before Christ, they developed a system of pictorial writing.[4]

Ernest Mackay wrote about the Dravidians, a pre-Aryan race that settled in the Indus Valley and built Mohenjo-daro and Harappa. Their cities flourished a thousand years before any Aryan-speakers invaded India, starting about 1500 B.C. Their languages were Tamil, Telugu, Kannada, and Malayalam. Pre-Aryan Dravidian descendants can still be found in India today, particularly South India.

Invasion of the Aryans

When the Aryans in northwestern India invaded the Indus Valley, the Indus civilization ended. The Vedic civilization was inaugurated, bringing in their culture and Aryan language (Sanskrit). Religious practices, like the worship of Indra (the war-god) and Agni (the fire-god), came too. They composed Vedic hymns, the beginning of the Rig Veda. They had frequent armed struggles with the Dravidians. They occupied the Dravidians' land and took their possessions. The Aryans considered themselves noble and honorable, and called the Dravidians "*Dasas*" or "*Dasyas*" (slaves). The Dravidians were absorbed into their community as Sudras. Therefore, *dasa* is applied to the lowest of the four castes, the Sudras.[5] Later, Portuguese traders applied the word *casta* (family or race) to the Hindu social system. *Varna* (color in Sanskrit) refers to the system of caste or to a group of *Jatis* (races). It was used to distinquish between light-skinned Aryans and dark-skinned aboriginal Dravidians.[6]

Religious Roots of the Caste System

Hindus believe God originated the caste system. One of their sacred texts, the Rig-Veda, (India's earliest literary source, circa 1,000 B.C.) describes how human stratification began. *Purusha,* a cosmic giant, sacrificed parts of his body to create mankind. "When they divided the *Purusha*...The *Brahmin* was his mouth, his two arms were made the *rajanya* or *kshatriya* (warrior), his two thighs are *vaisya* (trader and agriculturist), from his feet the *sudra* (servile class)..." (Rig-Veda, X 90:11-12). The mouth of *Purusha* became the priestly class. The arms were the warriors and landowners and his thighs became the merchants or traders. His feet produced the slaves or servants. This fourfold division is called *Chaturvarna* (four castes). No place is allocated for Dalits, who were therefore placed below the lowest caste.

The *Upanishads* (circa 800 B.C.) compare the outcastes (Dalits) to dogs or swine. The *Chandogya Upanishad* states, "accordingly, those who are of pleasant conduct here—the prospect is, indeed, that they will enter a pleasant womb, either the womb of a Brahmin, or the womb of a Kshatriya or the womb of a Vaisya. But those who are of stinking conduct here—the prospect is, indeed, they will enter a stinking womb—either the womb of a dog, or the womb of a swine or the womb of an outcaste (*chandala*)."[7]

The ancient Hindu Law book, *Manu Smruti* (Ordinance of Manu) accepted only three castes: the Brahmin, Kshatriya, and Vaisya. It degraded the state of the Sudras, who have only one birth. "But a Sudra, whether bought or unbought, he may compel to do servile work; for he was created by the self-existent to be a slave of a Brahmin. A Sudra, though emancipated by his master, is not released from servitude; since that is innate in him, who can set him free from it?" (*Manu Dharma Sastra*, VIII, 413-414).[8] The *Manu Smruti* completely removed the human identity of the Dalits, because it said hat there is no fifth caste. It did not allow Sudras or Dalits to possess any wealth other than dogs and donkeys. "The dwelling of Chandalas and Cavpacas (*sapaka*) ought to be outside of the village, they should be deprived of dishes (*apapatra*), their property consists of dogs and asses. Their clothes should be the garments of the dead, and their ornaments should be of iron, and their food should be in broken dishes and they must constantly wander about (*Manu Smruti* 10.51, 52)."[9] Hindu law books did not allow a Sudra or a Dalit to approach the sacred texts, even pronouncing a curse on them if they did so. "If he listens intentionally to the Vedas, his ears shall be filled with lead. If he recites them, his tongue shall be cut out. If he remembers them, his body shall be split in twain (*Manu Smruti* 12.4)."

Hinduism's great epics and sacred texts are the *Ramayana* and the *Mahabharata*. Both advocate the caste system and promote segregation of the Dalits. Hindu society venerated and deified their heroes, Rama and Krishna, as gods. The Mahabharata epic (circa 1000 B.C.) contains a celebrated tale about Ekalavya, a tribal boy who is an outcaste. The greatest archer was Dronacharya, a Brahmin, and guru of one of the five Pandava kings. The tribal boy saw the young princes learning archery and warfare from him and wanted to join them. He was threatened with death if he came in their vicinity, so he hid and watched them train. While practicing in front of an image symbolizing Dronachraya, he repeated the guru's instructions and soon mastered archery.

One time Dronacharya saw a deer bolting at lightning speed being shot. While looking for the arrow's source, he discovered a ragged Dalit boy who came and bowed before him. It was Ekalavya. He confessed that no guru had trained him. Dronacharya cunningly asked him to pay *guru-dakshina* (a gift offered to a teacher in gratitude). Ekalavya offered himself as the guru's slave. But Dronacharya asked for his right thumb, knowing that without it he could not perform archery. The boy calmly said that a guru is equal to a god and he would gladly do what the guru wished. He cut off his thumb, laying it at Dronacharya's feet. In this way, Dronacharya kept him from practicing archery for the rest of his life.[10] It is not legal, according to *Varna dharma* (caste duty), for a Dalit to practice archery, being reserved only for Kshatriyas.

The Ramayana was another Hindu sacred text (composed circa 400 B.C.), in which Valmiki, the author, tells a story about a Sudra named Sambuka during the reign of Rama. Only the three upper castes were allowed to do *tapasya* (penance and meditation). However, Sambuka, the Sudra, undertook religious meditation to attain divinity. A Brahmin boy of fifteen died and the Sudra was made responsible for his death. The bereaved father complained to Rama, and after learning the cause of the death, Rama went in search of the Sudra. On meeting the Sudra, Rama said to him, "You are blessed. Tell me in which caste you have been born. I am Rama, son of Dasaratha. Out of curiosity, I have asked you this question. Tell me the truth; are you a Brahmin, Kshatriya or Sudra?" The Sudra replied, "O, king! I am born of the Sudra Caste. I want to attain divinity by such penance. When I want to attain divinity, I won't tell lies. I am a Sudra by caste and my name is Sambuka. As soon as the ascetic (Sudra) uttered those words, Rama drew forth his sword and severed Sambuka's head." Later, Rama asked the gods to restore the Brahmin boy to life, and he was told that he had already been revived the moment the Sudra was killed. This is how the Sudras, the fourth caste, became degraded, not to mention the Dalits or outcastes.[11] These stories clearly depict that the marginalization of Dalits is rooted in Hindu ethos and promoted by its sacred texts.

Social and Economic Conditions of the Dalits in India

India's caste system considers each person a member of the particular caste into which he or she was born, and he or she remains so until death. The ranking of that caste and differences in status are traditionally justified by the Hindu religious doctrine called *Karma*, the belief that a person's place in life is determined by his or her deeds in previous lifetimes.

Article 17 of the Constitution of India (the Fundamental Rights) clearly states that untouchability is prohibited. "Untouchability is abolished and its practice in any form is forbidden. The enforcement of any disability arising out of untouchability shall be an offense punishable in accordance with law." Yet the practice still continues to dominate Indian society and still determines the socio-economic and religious standing of those at the bottom of the caste system.

A case in point is the present situation in Tamilnadu in the 21st century. Twenty-two villages practice untouchability in the Tirunelveli District. In Vennilingapuram, Kammavoor, Rukmaniammalpuram, and other surrounding villages, the two-tumbler system is very much prevalent. Teashop owners use two different sets of stainless steel tumblers. Non-Dalits and Thevars (high caste Hindus) are served from a set of tumblers set aside just for them. Dalits are served from another set of tumblers or disposable plastic cups. The Dalits understandably prefer making tea at home.

Dalits in these villages have no land of their own. They have to work in the Thevars' fields. The Dalits do not want to antagonize Thevars by addressing the issue or they could lose their livelihood or even their lives.[12] Dalit children are forced to sit in the back of the classroom in many places. In urban areas, Dalits live in segregated colonies or on the outskirts of villages, away from high caste Hindus. Most live in thatched-roof huts with no electricity, no safe drinking water and no medical facilities, and miles from the nearest water source.[13]

The majority of Dalits live at, or below, poverty level, lacking opportunity for better education or employment. Many work as manual scavengers, removers of human waste and dead animals, street sweepers, and cobblers. Dalit children are often sold as maidservants or domestic help to pay off debts owed to high caste landowners and creditors. Millions of Dalit men, women, and children work ten to twelve hours a day in the paddy fields as agricultural laborers for less than a dollar (15 to 35 rupees, equal to 38 to 88 US cents), or for a few kilograms of rice.[14]

According to the Human Rights Watch, one irony of the caste system is that no high caste person practices untouchability when it comes to sex. Dalit girls have been forced to become prostitutes for high caste patrons and village priests (Brahmins). Later they are auctioned off to a brothel house in cities like Bombay, Calcutta, and Delhi. Dalit women are raped or sexually abused by high caste landlords as a form of retaliation, and by police in pursuit of their male relatives. There is widespread violence against the Dalits by the high castes. Police refuse to register cases against culprits. They do not prosecute those who commit atrocities, such as murder, rape, exploitative labor practices, and forced displacement of Dalits from their lands and homes, because many in the police department belong to a high caste or enjoy their patronage. The Indian government and the police are required to protect the Dalits under the provisions made by *the Scheduled Castes and Scheduled Tribes Prevention of Atrocities Act, 1989* and *the Scheduled Castes and Scheduled Tribes Preventions of Atrocities Rules, 1995*. Instead, the police arrest Dalit men and women, torture them, and sometimes even beat them to death while they are in custody.

In the state of Andhra Pradesh, Brahmins comprise 3 percent of the population and are ritually placed at the top of the caste pyramid. Historically, they have dominated social, cultural, and economic life. The other dominant castes in Andhra Pradesh are the Kammas, Reddys, and Kapus, who own large areas of land throughout Andhra and many are affluent. The Reddys and Kammas comprise 6.5 percent and 4.8 percent of the state's population respectively. They are the two main politically dominant communities. Most leading politicians are Kammas and Reddys and many hold leadership positions in government. The control of these castes over agrarian resources, such as land and water, has been the most important source of their economic and political power. Since they are the major land-owning communities and occupants of important positions of a village, they have traditionally controlled village political life.[15] Kammas dominate the Krishana and Guntur Districts, a fine farming community. Reddys are also big landowners and are the majority in the Cudappah and Chittoor Districts. Kapus, another dominant caste of the cultivated, are in great numbers in the East and West Godavari Districts.[16] Therefore, these three castes dominate political, agricultural, educational, and governmental sectors with many being lawyers, doctors, engineers, educators, landlords, and government officials.

At the bottom of the social order are the Dalits. The 2001 Indian Census puts the total population of Dalits in Andhra Pradesh at 12.3 million, almost 16.5 percent of the state's total population. Nearly 85 percent of Dalits live in rural areas. Malas and Madigas are the two dominant Dalit communities in Andhra Pradesh. Madigas are estimated at 3.5 million and Malas at about 3 million. They are landless and laborers to the rich and the farming communities of Kamma and Reddy. Malas are mainly employed as agricultural laborers or weavers and very few are independent farmers. Madigas are primarily leather workers who manufacture leather articles necessary for daily use. There is not much intermarriage between the two Dalit castes. The structure of Hindu society is the source of the obvious inequality in Andhra Pradesh. Status and identity are determined purely by caste and wealth.

Dalits in Andhra Pradesh have to live in constant subordination to upper caste Hindus. They have to stand in a bending position in front of an upper caste landlord and may not hold up their heads. They are not allowed to wear neat dresses or sandals or to use umbrellas. Dalits are denied access to public places, including temples, and are denied entry into the upper caste Hindu's streets. Dalit children are forbidden to sit with the children of the dominant caste.[17]

Dalit Contributions to Christianity in India

Despite their low social status and their struggle for justice, equality, and dignity, Dalits contributed immensely to the formation and spread of Protestant Christianity throughout India. They can be seen as the real pioneers of Indian Christianity. However, their zeal for evangelism and their efforts regarding the growth of the Indian Church have been overlooked in the annals of Indian Church history. In the following section, some of the key Dalits who played a major role in shaping Chrisianity in India are highlighted.

Ditt of Shahabdike and the United Presbyterian Church

A great awakening took place in Punjab (1870) among the people called the *Churas* (Dalits) through the efforts of a hide dealer named Ditt, born in Shahabdike (1843) in the Sialkot District. He was converted to Christianity through Nattu, a Hindu convert of the Jat caste. After he was baptized in Sialkot (June 1873) by Samuel Martin, a missionary of the United Presbyterian Church of North America, he refused to stay in a protected mission compound. He returned to his hometown where he faced severe opposition from not only his fellow villagers, but also his own relatives. Opposition did not deter his zeal to witness about his new faith in Christ to his family members and others. Within three months (August 1873), he took his wife, his daughter, and two of his neighbors to Sialkot for baptism. They had to walk thirty miles to be baptized by Martin. Ditt worked buying hides from different places, which took him to many villages. Wherever he went, Ditt witnessed to people about Christ. Eleven years after his baptism (1884), he had won more then 500 people from his community to Christ. By 1900, half the people of his community were converted to Christianity, and by 1915, almost all the *Churas* (Dalits) of the Sialkot District had accepted Christ.[18] According to Donald McGavran, the efforts of Ditt, a Dalit, produced one *lakh* (100,000) converts to Christianity.[19]

Vethamanikam of Mailady and the London Missionary Society

Vethamanikam was a Dalit born in Mailady, who belonged to the Sambavar caste in Travancore (present-day Kerala). He took a pilgrimage to the temple of Chidambaram in search of truth. On his return, he stopped at Tanjore to visit his sister and heard the gospel while standing by a church. The church missionary gave him a booklet, and after he read it, great joy and satisfaction filled him. He said, "My Lord and Savior Jesus Christ! He touched my heart and it melted before God. A light from heaven shone upon my darkness and I did not want to leave the place." His search for truth ended when he found the true Savior.

Vethamanikam was baptized in water, continued his stay in Tanjore for further guidance, and then returned home. When he reached his village, Vethamanikam began to preach the good news that he had learned. Many listened and several hundred people became Christians and joined the church. This band of believers met regularly, led by Vethamanikam. The Hindu community gave him severe opposition and persecution and excommunicated him from his caste. His life and property were suddenly in danger but he did not abandon his mission from God. Instead, he sought God for protection and guidance. He prayed:

> O Thou dear Lord! When I worshipped idols which have not life, Thou didst pass by the rich, the learned, the honorable people, and didst choose me to be Thine. Now teach me, O Lord, what I should do. Put me in Thy right path, and let me know what I should do in this difficulty. Is it Thy will that the light which has begun to shine here should be quenched?[20]

God answered his prayers with William Ringeltaube, a missionary from the London Missionary Society whom He had already prepared. Ringeltaube came to Mailady (April 25, 1806) to work with Vethamanikam, who handed the work over to him. A group of believers already prepared for baptism awaited Ringeltaube, who baptized them and made Vethamanikam their catechist. When Ringeltaube left later for health reasons (1816), he put Vethamanikam in charge of the whole ministry work. Charles Mead, another missionary, arrived next in Mailady (December 1817) and assumed the work. James Massey's research reveals that both the Sambavar community and the Nadars (Shanars), another Dalit community, responded to the gospel because of the efforts of Vethamanikam. This was followed by a revival movement among both communities (1819).

Dalits played a crucial role in the spread of Christianity not only in the states of Punjab and Kerala, but also in the state of Andhra Pradesh. They were involved in various Protestant mission organizations, such as the American Baptist Missionary Union, the Church Missionary Society, the Society for the Propagation of the Gospel in Foreign Parts, and the Canadian

Baptist Mission. The following paragraphs highlight the contributions of a few notable Dalits to Christianity in Andhra Pradesh.

Veeragenthala Periah of Tallakondapud and the American Baptist Missionary Union

The American Baptist Missionary Union started its work in Visakhapatnam (1836) with their first missionary to the Telugu people, Samuel Stearns Day. He later came to Madras (1837) and then went to Nellore (1840), where Reverend Van Husen joined him (1840) to serve among the Telugus. The first convert was baptized two years later (September 1842). Husen then had to leave India for health reasons. By 1844, the mission had only eight church members.[21] Day also had to return to the U.S. (1846) because of failed health. When he recovered his health, he returned to Nellore with Lyman Jewett and his wife (1848). Jewett baptized a Telugu for the first time in 1852.

On two occasions, the mission board in the United States proposed shutting down the Telugu mission (1853, 1862). The insistence and determination of Jewett and S. F. Smith enabled the Telugu mission to continue. Day's health failed again (1853), so he left Andhra Pradesh permanently. The following year Jewett baptized Kanakiah, who became the mission's first ordained pastor. Jewett returned to the U.S. on furlough (1862) and two years later returned to India with John E. Clough. Clough later settled in Ongole (1866) and worked there among the Dalit leather workers. The following January, twenty-eight people from the Madiga caste were baptized and a church was soon established. By the end of the year, the Ongole church increased to seventy-five members.

The church at Ongole was established through the efforts of Veeragenthala Periah of Tallakondapud. He was a relative of Vongole Abraham, a Dalit convert of the Madiga caste from Ongole, who settled in Eluru. When Periah visited his relative Abraham in Eluru, he met a missionary working there named F.W.N. Alexander. Then Periah visited William Bowden in Palakol. He was told to wait until the missionaries came to his own district. Instead, Periah walked forty miles to Ongole to seek out missionaries and met a local lady in the street named Mrs. Shilling. She told him about Jesus Christ from chapter three of the gospel of John, and he became a Christian. Before long, because of his zeal to win souls, his wife, Nagamma, and his friends also became Christians. This passion stayed with him until his death (1897). He learned about Clough of the American Baptist Telugu Mission who was working in Nellore. Periah then enlisted him to start a mission work in Ongole, and a church was established (January 1, 1867).

The work of the American Baptist Mission began to grow through Clough's efforts. Growth in church membership was explosive at Ongole following a year long famine (1876 to 1877). Clough took a contract for fifteen months to dig the three and a half mile Buckingham Canal in order to provide employment for his church members and many other poor people. The laborers who worked on the canal were reached with the gospel during this time. When the project ended, 9,606 people had been baptized in the Gundlakamma River (1879). It was estimated that the largest number baptized by Clough in any one day was 2,222.[22] Consequently, the church membership at Ongole rose to 12,204. The American Baptist Church began to spread later in the Guntur District with the Dalit mass movements (1878 to 1879, 1890 to 1891). The Dalits were primarily from the Madiga caste around Ongole and Cumbum of the old Guntur District. Interestingly, the number of converts in the American Baptist Missionary Union was estimated at 30,000 when it celebrated its Jubilee (1886), almost all of whom were Dalits of the Madiga caste. Today the Baptist church is still known as the Madiga religion. According to Clough, "if Vongole Abraham had not settled in the north of Andhradesa (Eluru) and become a man of Christian character, his kinsman (Veeragenthala Periah) might never have become converted and the mass movement in Andhradesa might have never happened."[23]

The mission founded a theological seminary at Ramayapatnam, forty-five miles north of Nellore (1872). Clough raised 65,000 dollars in the U.S. for the seminary (endowment fund-50,000 dollars, building fund-15,000 dollars). A high school was also started in Ongole (1880) which developed into a college (1894). "In 1894, there were connected with American Baptist Missionary Union 38 foreign missionaries, 54,968 church members and about 4,000 scholars."[24] The mission's spectacular evangelization success was widely known, even in the West. It started with 28 converts (1867), climbed to 10,000 (1879), then 65,000 (1899) and later reached 140,000 (1956).

The work of American Baptists is still fruitful in many parts of Andhra Pradesh. They extended their work from Nellore to Ongole and other places in nearby districts, including Ramayapatnam, Eluru, Atmakuru, Udayagiri, Kavali, Kanegiri, Dhonakonda, Podali, Bapatla, Narsarao Pet, Vinukonda, Sathenapalli, Gurujala, Kurnool, Cumbum, and Markapuram.[25] The American Baptist Church in Andhra Pradesh is now called the "Samavesham of Telugu Baptist Churches."

Pagolu Venkayya of Raghavapuram and the Church Missionary Society

Bishop Corrie (the first Madras bishop) longed to see the gospel reach to the Telugu country. After Corrie died (1840), a letter was sent to England requesting men to help since 2,000 pounds had been raised to open a mission school in Machilipatnam. The letter ended up with Robert Noble of Cambridge and Henry Fox of Oxford. They gladly consented to the request. As a result, the Church Missionary Society (CMS) launched its work in Machilipatnam in Andhra Pradesh (1841) with these two notable pioneers. After they arrived in Andhra (October 28, 1841), Noble devoted himself to

Christian education and Fox to evangelistic efforts. Fox tirelessly worked among the Telugus, going from village to village, living in tents six months of the year, and preaching the gospel among the Dalits (Mala and Madiga castes). Then he fell seriously ill and had to return to England. He died at age thirty and made this now famous statement on his deathbed: "If I had to live over again, I would do the same." Many mission stations were established and thousands of Hindus embraced Christianity in spite of the short duration of his missionary work in Andhra.

Noble started a school in Machilipatnam (1843) with two pupils that soon grew to ninety pupils. However, every time a pupil was baptized, there was a community uproar, causing some students to withdraw. A greater tumult occurred when Rathnam, a high caste Brahmin (the first Brahmin convert) and Bhushanam, a high caste Sudra, broke from the caste system and joined Christianity, forcing them to take refuge in Noble's house. Because of this uproar, the school enrollment plunged from ninety to four. It managed to recover before long, however, and developed into a college. Then a terrible hurricane and flood devastated the country (1864). Many lost their lives, including thirty-three girls in Noble's school who were swept away in the floodwaters. The death toll reached 35,000 in this great tragedy. Not long after the flood, a plague broke out. Noble fell seriously ill and died a few days later. "In 1893 the CMS Telugu mission had 14 European missionaries, 11,025 native Christians, 1,802 communicants and 2,961 scholars."[26] When Noble College celebrated the Jubilee (November 13, 1893), the enrollment of the school was more than 500. Today, Noble College is still a prestigious and famous college in Andhra Pradesh with 3000 in attendance. A. Ruben, former treasurer of the Andhra IPC and a Dalit, was vice-principal and professor of commerce at Noble College.

The efforts of a particular Dalit, Pagolu Venkayya, are worth mentioning during the time of Reverend John Darling, a missionary from the Church Missionary Society. Venkayya was a Mala outcast and highway robber from the village of Raghavapuram (thirty miles from Vijayawada) in the Krishna District of Andhra Pradesh. He became a Christian (1849) through Darling's efforts. Darling concentrated his first seven years of mission work among the high caste Hindus, but not one person became a Christian. According to Bishop Pickett, "his eyes were upon the high caste Hindus, and he had preached to them and had personally sought out individually among them with constant diligence, but lack of interest discouraged him."[27] Venkayya heard of a missionary who said, "Idols are no gods. A carpenter makes them and a painter paints them." Venkayya began to pray, "O great God, what art Thou? Where art Thou?" Later he dreamed about a man of singular beauty looking on him kindly who said he was his friend. He visited a Hindu festival next at Vijayawada. Pilgrims bathed there in the sacred waters, but Venkayya protested that the water could never wash away sin. A Brahmin priest overheard him and directed him to Darling's house. That same day, Darling had poured out his heart in desperate prayer and told God he was ready to give up if no one showed up. Then he saw Venkayya with five other men, and received them thankfully. Venkayya heard the gospel and gave his life to Christ.

At Venkayya's invitation, Darling visited Raghavapuram and baptized sixteen people (March 9, 1859). Venkayya led 700 people to Christ in twelve years. By the time he died in 1891, 2,945 souls had been won to Christ in the Krishna District. In 1859, the Church Missionary Society had 200 converts and by 1891, there were 10,000 believers in Andhra Pradesh.[28] Venkayya's death did not end the ripple effect of his passionate evangelism, which spread to other districts in Andhra Pradesh. It is estimated that over 800,000 Malas and Madigas, and many thousands from other castes, became Christians (1931). By 1938, at least 1,100,000 people in the Madras Province had come to Christ. By the end of the same year, over 70,000 from at least fifty different castes, including high caste Hindus, had turned to Christ. Venkayya not only led eleven *lakhs* (over 1 million) of his Dalit community to Christ, but he also started a movement among the privileged classes.[29]

Nonchar of Rudravaram and the Society for the Propagation of the Gospel in Foreign Parts

The Society for the Propagation of the Gospel in Foreign Parts (SPG) began its mission work at Cuddapah (1842) when W. Howell and several families left the London Missionary Society and joined the Church of England. John Clay was appointed the first Telugu missionary of the society (1854). The following year, the society's headquarters were moved from Cuddapah to Mutyalapad. The SPG began a work there after a Dalit named Nonchar attempted to enter a Hindu temple located in the high caste area of Rudravaram village. The temple priest and the village head imprisoned him because Dalits were forbidden to enter any temple. Only high caste Hindus were allowed to enter.

Meanwhile, two young Christians from Tanjavur were appointed to serve the Christians in the British military in the Rudravaram area where Nonchar was imprisoned. They happened to meet him in prison and discovered why he was confined. With the help of the authorities, the Christians rescued him from prison. Nonchar took the men to his village where they witnessed to the people, and thirty villagers came to know Jesus as their Savior. Then, at the request of the young men, Clay was sent to Andhra by the Madras SPG.

Spencer and Higgins joined Clay later and carried on the work. Many Dalit weavers and village laborers, including Malas, became Christians, and the number of adherents grew to 1,146 (1859). Then new mission centers were established in Kalasapad (1861), Kurnool (1875), and Nandyal (1883), where a training college for native agents was founded. Indeed, by 1893 "there were connected with the SPG Mission 5 European missionaries, 6,431 native Christians, 2,117 communicants, and 2,008 scholars."[30]

Thalluri Marayya (Thomas Gabriel) of Kolleru Lanka and the Canadian Baptist Mission

Robert Philip of Ontario, Canada, expressed the desire of the Canadian churches to become involved in missions in his letter to the American Baptist Union in Boston, Massachusetts (1865 to 1866). As a result, the Baptist Missionary Union was created as an auxiliary for Canadian churches (1866). A.V. Timpany and his wife arrived at Madras (April 16, 1868) with the support of the Baptist Churches in Canada. They then moved to Nellore where they lived with Zavet and his wife, an American Baptist missionary couple. The Timpanys worked with Clough, who was working in Ongole as the missionary of the American Baptists. As soon as they could speak Telugu, they came to Ramayapatnam (1869) to establish the Canadian Baptist Mission there.

Another missionary family, John McLaurin and his wife (sister of A.V. Timpany's wife), arrived in Madras during this time (January 18, 1870), and traveled to Ramayapatnam. Meanwhile, Clough fell ill in Ongole and McLaurin had to take his place for a short time. After Clough returned, McLaurin started the Canadian Baptist Telugu Mission in Kakinada (1874). He worked with Thalluri Marayya (later called Thalluri Thomas Gabriel), a Dalit, who was born in 1837. Gabriel was educated in mission schools of Godavari Delta Mission (Narsapuram) and the Lutheran Mission (Rajahmundry). He later secured a job in the telegraph department at Dowlaswaram, near Rajahmundry. During his stay there, he attended the Lutheran Church, where his name was changed from Thalluri Marayya to Thalluri Thomas Gabriel. Later, his job transferred him to Kakinada and then to Bombay in 1867.[31] While traveling to Bombay, he contracted smallpox and was hospitalized in Madras, where he came into contact with Das Antirvedi, who baptized him in water. In the meantime, his transfer orders to Bombay were revoked. Upon his return to Kakinada, he realized that there was no mission work there (unlike Narsapuram and Rajahmundry), so he resigned from his job with the telegraph department to start a mission.

Thomas Gabriel started Kolleru Mission (1870), an independent mission work among his kinsmen in Kolleru Lanka. To support his work, he started a small business refining skins. While the work of evangelism progressed, he faced financial challenges and he sought financial assistance from the Baptist mission in Madras. On his way there, he came to Ramayapatnam and met McLaurin (June 17, 1871) and shared his burden with him for the Kolleru mission and for making Kakinada a mission center. After failing to receive financial assistance from the Baptist missionaries, Thomas Gabriel returned to Kolleru Lanka to continue his work. However, he stayed in touch with McLaurin and Timpany. McLaurin sent Thomas Gabriel's proposal later to the Canadian Baptist Foreign Mission Society. At the same time, the Canadian Baptist Union Auxiliary decided to start its own work and had given its consent to McLaurin (October 28, 1873). Therefore, McLaurin went to Kakinada because of the Dalit Thomas Gabriel (March 12, 1874).

The work of the Canadian Baptist Mission later spread to other places, like Bimilipatnam (1875), Srikakulam and Tuni (1878), and Bobbili (1879). A theological seminary was started at Samalkot to train natives (1882). The mission progressed to fourteen foreign missionaries, about 3,000 communicants, and seventy-five students in the theological seminary (1893). Today there are 300 Canadian Baptist churches throughout the state of Andhra Pradesh, from Avanigadda to Sompeta. It is now known as the Andhra Baptist Church.

Summary

Despite the marginalization, social injustice, inequality, ostracism, and humiliation that Dalits constantly faced in Indian society, they played a major role in the expansion of Indian Christianity. The preceding brief case histories help to provide living proof of direct Dalit contributions to the formation and spread of Christianity in India. As Bishop Picket commented, the real founders of the churches in Sialkot, Travancore, and the Krishna districts were not Ringeltaube, Gordon, Martin, or Darling, but the Dalits: Ditt, Venkayya, and Vethamanikam.

Notes

[1] Narendra Jadhav, *Untouchables: My Family's Triumphant Journey Out of the Caste System in Modern India* (New York: Scribner, 2003), 1.

[2] George Oommen, "The Emerging Dalit Theology: A Historical Appraisal," *Indian Church History Review* 34:1 (June 2000): 19.

[3] A.L. Basham, *A Cultural History of India* (London: Oxford University Press, 1975), 11.

[4] Sir John Marshall, "Harappa and Mohenjo-daro" in Gregory L. Possehl, *Ancient Cities of the Indus* (New Delhi : Vikas, 1979), 181. Cited in James Massey, *Roots of Dalit History, Christianity, Theology and Spirituality* (Delhi: ISPCK, 1996), 12.

[5] Basham, *A Cultural History of India*, 20, 23.

[6] Benjamin Khan, *Dalit Christian Movement and Christian Theology* (Indore: Sat Prachar Press, 1995), 23.

[7] Robert Ernest Hume, *The Thirteen Principal Upanishads*, (London: Oxford University Press, 1951), 233. Cited in Massey, *Roots of Dalit History, Christianity, Theology and Spirituality*, 22.

[8] Arvind Nirmal, ed., *A Reader in Dalit Theology* (Madras: Gurukul Lutheran Theological College, 1990), 53.

⁹ James Massey, *Roots of Dalit History, Christianity, Theology and Spirituality*, (Delhi: ISPCK, 1996), 22-23.
¹⁰ V. Devasahayam, *Doing Dalit Theology in Biblical Key* (Madras: Gurukul Lutheran Theological College, 1997), 20-21.
¹¹ Makhan Lal Sen, *Ramayana* (Calcutta: Oriental Publications, 1989), 699-702. Cited in Massey, *Roots of Dalit History, Christianity, Theology and Spirituality*, 22-23.
¹² "Untouchability through the drinking glass in TN," accessed October 7, 2008. Online: http://www.rediff.com/cms/print.jsp?docpath=news/2008/oct/07tn.htm.
¹³ Human Rights Watch, *Broken People*. (New York, 1999), 2.
¹⁴ Human Rights Watch, *Broken People*, 2.
¹⁵ K. Srinivasulu, *Caste, Class and Social Articulation in Andhra Pradesh* (Hyderabad: Osmania University, 2002), 3. Accessed May 21, 2010. Online: http://www.odi.org.uk/resources/download/1998.pdf
¹⁶ B.V. Subbamma, *New Patterns for Discipling Hindus* (Pasadena: William Carey Library, 1970), 4.
¹⁷ K.Y. Ratnam, *The Dalit Movement and Democrization in Andhra Pradesh* (Washington: East-West Center, 2008), 9-10. Accessed May 21, 2010. Online: http://www.ciaonet.org/wps/ewc/0016466/f_0016466_14236.pdf
¹⁸ J. Waskom Pickett, *Christian Mass Movements in India* (New York: Abingdon Press. 1993), 46-49. Cited in Massey, *Roots of Dalit History, Christianity, Theology and Spirituality*, 55.
¹⁹ Donald McGavran, *The Founders of the Indian Church* (Chennai: Church Growth Association of India, 1998), 5.
²⁰ Massey, *Roots of Dalit History, Christianity, Theology and Spirituality*, 57.
²¹ K. B. Simon, *The Andhra Churches* (Bezwada: A.G. Press, 1942), 5.
²² J. Edwin Orr, *Evangelical Awakening in India in the Early Twentieth Century* (New Delhi: Christian Literature Institute, 1970), 43-45.
²³ Orr, *Evangelical Awakening in India in the Early Twentieth Century*, 43.
²⁴ Badley Smith, *History of Christianity in India; with its Prospects: A Sketch* (Madras: SPCK Press, 1895), 91.
²⁵ Sam Mathews Kakkhukuzhil, "An Assessment of the Dawn and Growth of the Indigenous Penteocostal Movement in the State of Andhra Pradesh" (master's thesis, SAICS, 1990), 24.
²⁶ Smith, *History of Christianity in India; with its Prospects: A Sketch*, 93.
²⁷ Pickett, *Christian Mass Movements in India*, 149.
²⁸ Orr, *Evangelical Awakening in India in the Early Twentieth Century*, 43.
²⁹ McGavran, *The Founders of the Indian Church*, 46-49.
³⁰ Smith, *History of Christianity in India; with its Prospects: A Sketch*, 93.
³¹ Victor Palla, *Origins, Growth and Development of Christianity in the Srikakulam District of Andhra Pradesh, India* (unpublished document, n.d.), 37.

Chapter 3

Three Successive Stages of Indian Pentecostalism

Introduction

This chapter covers three successive stages of progressive understanding of the work of the Holy Spirit in India. These stages reflect a shift from early charismatic manifestations in various revivals in India to doctrinal emphasis on the baptism of the Holy Spirit in Indian Pentecostalism.

Three separate bodies of water can be identified which all meet at Cape Comorin on the southern tip of India: the Arabian Sea, the Bay of Bengal, and the Indian Ocean. But they cannot be separated from one another. The Pentecostal movement in India resembles this situation. It can be analyzed in three successive stages: antecedent revivals, Western Pentecostal missionary invasion, and consolidation of the indigenous Pentecostal church and native leadership. Although these three separate stages can be differentiated, they are too intertwined with each other to be separated.

In the first stage, "Proto-Pentecostalism," the antecedent revivals occurred in India. Charismatic "phenomena" involving manifestations of the Holy Spirit were experienced in these revivals, but they had not yet been formulated into doctrine. In the second stage, "Colonial Pentecostalism," the doctrine of the baptism of the Holy Spirit was formulated with a Western interpretation. In the third stage, "Indigenous Pentecostalism" was consolidated or emerged when the Indian Pentecostal Church (IPC) and the Ceylon Pentecostal Mission (CPM) were formed as native Pentecostal leaders resisted foreign domination. Therefore, contrary to popular opinion, the origin of the Pentecostal movement in India can be traced back directly to earlier revivals in India, but not to the arrival of Western Pentecostal missionaries impacted by the Azusa Revival in the United States in the early 1900s.

Proto-Pentecostal Phenomena in Antecedent Revivals in India

The next section focuses on various revivals in which charismatic manifestations of the Holy Spirit ("proto-Pentecostal phenomenon") were evident, which was the situation preceding the Pentecostal movement in India. "Proto-Pentecostalism" can be defined as the Holy Spirit spontaneously manifested in His power and presence. This stage was characterized by believers experiencing visions, dreams, prophecies, falling under the influence of the Holy Spirit, as well as speaking in tongues.

Pentecostal-like Revival in Tinnevelly or Tirunelveli (1860 to 1865)

The first recorded revival that had Pentecostal characteristics took place (1860 to 1865) in the state of Tinnevelly (Tirunelveli, present-day Tamilnadu). It occurred among the Shanars, a people of the low caste (Dalits), under the leadership of John Christian Aroolappen. He was a native evangelist trained as an Anglican catechist by Carl T. E. Rhenius, a Prussian missionary sent by the Church Missionary Society (1814), and by Anthony Norris Groves, an independent missionary who arrived from England (1833). Rhenius emphasized self-support and self-propagation for the Indian Church. Groves introduced the millennial eschatology of the Plymouth Brethren, which included an imminent Parousia, hope for the outpouring of the Holy Spirit, and spiritual gifts.

News of the revivals in the United States, England, and Ulster (1857 to 1859)[1] reached India. Aroolappen read about these revivals and they greatly influenced him. He prayed earnestly for similar revival in his native land. He was surprised when a great revival broke out in Tirunelveli (March 4, 1860). Aroolappen recorded in his diary,

> In the month of June some of our people praised the Lord by unknown tongues, with their interpretation....My son and a daughter and three others went to visit their own relations, in three villages, who are under the Church Missionary Society, and they also received the Holy Ghost. Some prophesy and some speak by unknown tongues with their interpretations (August 8, 1860).[2]

In his article, "Pentecostal Phenomena and Revivals in India: Implications for Indigenous Church Leadership," Gary B. McGee cites that

> The phenomena in the revival included prophecy, glossolalia, glossographia, and interpretation of tongues, as well as intense conviction of sin among nominal Christians, dreams, visions, signs in the heavens, and people falling down and/or shaking. Other noted features were restoration of the offices of apostle and

prophet, evangelism, conversions of unbelievers, prayer for the sick, and concern for the poor.[3]

After the revival, believers shared their experience and faith with non-believers. CMS missionary Ashton Dibb reported that in Aroolappen's church, "there was a baptism of the Holy Spirit which filled the members with a holy enthusiasm; and caused them to go everywhere preaching the gospel, in demonstration of the Spirit and of power."[4]

Aroolappen followed the pattern of the New Testament apostles and evangelists and traveled "by faith" to many places, preaching the gospel in many Syrian churches. He awakened the people to a deeper spiritual life. As a faith preacher, he did not depend on Western money and had no salary or pledged support. As a result, many indigenous missionaries and evangelists, including Ammal Vedanayagam, David (known as "Tamil David"), and David Fenn emulated his example. Dibb further comments that "it is indeed a new era in Indian Missions, that of lay converts going forth without purse or script to preach the gospel of Christ to their fellow-country men, and that with a zeal and life we had hardly thought them capable of."[5] Dibb's comments reveal two things about the common attitude of western missionaries towards evangelization of India. First, up to this point, missionaries thought Indian Christians needed a sound English education in Western culture and theology before they could make any attempt to evangelize their people in their own vernacular. Second, they believed that God providently entrusted India to British rule to ensure its evangelization.

Revival in Travancore (1873 to 1881)

A decade after the Tirunelveli Revival began, Aroolappen traveled to Travancore (southernmost region of present-day Kerala). He brought the revival message not only to CMS churches, but also to Syrian churches there. A revival then took place that lasted about nine years. Two prominent leaders of this revival were Koodarapallil Thommen and Yusthus (Justus) Joseph, who had been converted from a high caste Brahmin family under the ministry of CMS missionary Joseph Peet. Justus later became a CMS priest. A.C. George writes in "Pentecostal Beginnings in Travancore, South India" that thousands of people were attracted to Justus Joseph's ministry because of its charismatic nature, including visions, prophecies, revelations, and the like. Thommen, another leader, claimed to have received a divine revelation of the *Parousia* (the second Coming of Christ)[6] and he predicted that Christ would return within six years (1881). The CMS branded him a heretic when his prophecy was not fulfilled. As a consequence, the revival church Justus founded (1875) began to decline, and his followers came to be called the "Six Years Party" (or "Five and a Half Years Party").[7] Nevertheless, the revival church started by Justus continued into the twentieth century, albeit in diminished proportions. These examples alone show that Pentecostal-like revivals in India preceded the Western Pentecostal movement by at least forty years.

According to McGee, at the beginning of this revival missionaries applauded what they viewed as positive aspects in the movement, but later were suspicious because of the glossolalia and other proto-Pentecostal spiritual phenomena.

> They also detected lingering traces of heathen culture in the lack of emotional restraint among the participants. Complaints also included Anglican criticisms of independent and unordained clergy, the establishing of the prophetic office, the pronouncing of controversial predictions, and the growth of schismatic congregations.[8]

The reason for this criticism was that the missionaries' thinking was influenced by Western enlightenment. The missionaries failed to contextualize the gospel, instead imposing Western culture and thought on Indian Christianity. They also tried to interpret the proto-Pentecostal phenomenon in Indian revivals within the Western framework.

George pointed out in his article, "Pentecostal Beginnings in Travancore, South India," that:

> The second half of the nineteenth century witnessed powerful revivals in India: one in 1860, another in 1873 and a third in 1895. In all of these revivals people experienced the outpouring of the Holy Spirit with diverse manifestations including glossolalia. However, the recipients of these experiences did not know that they were speaking in unknown tongues as a result of the baptism in the Holy Spirit as taught in the book of Acts.[9]

He believed this ignorance was due to the fact that the Bible was a foreign book to many Indian believers because they were illiterate. They had little or no teaching on spiritual matters and biblical doctrines from their clergy, including the person and work of the Holy Spirit, the third person of the Trinity. However, George seems to be reading back into history by imposing the classical Pentecostal view on proto-Penecostal revivals and interpreting the revivals from that perspective. Indian Christians had a definite manifestation of the Holy Spirit, but they could not understand what it really meant because they had not yet been indoctrinated. When they were taught, they began to understand the Holy Spirit's work as it became clearer to them. Through the process of reflection, they later began to interpret and develop the doctrine of the baptism of the Holy Spirit.

There were three major factors George suggested that contributed to these powerful revivals. The first factor was New Testament-style preaching by native preachers. Then came availability of the Bible in two major South Indian languages: the Tamil Bible (1715) translated by Birtholomaeus Ziegenbalg (the first Protestant missionary to India), and the Malayam Bible (1841) translated by Benjamin Baily. These translations brought new life into the hearts of the Christians and new understanding of Christianity. Lastly, the Syrian Christian congregations were tired of "dead" ritualism and mere formalism, characterized by traditions, ceremonies, and festivals honoring the saints of the church. George seems biased, however, in his assessment of Syrian Christians who had a different understanding of the baptism of the Holy Spirit. The Syrians believed in the baptism of the Holy Spirit, but equated it with *theosis*. *Theosis*, or to become god, is not losing the essence of human nature, or human participation in the essence or nature of God, but it is participating in God by divine energies or grace.

Revival in Mukti Mission in Pune (1905 to 1907)

The Mukti Revival in India was more akin to Pentecostalism. It was led by Sarasvati Mary Ramabai (known as "Pandita" Ramabai), who was born in an upper caste Hindu Brahmin family. Her father was both a Sanskrit and Indian literature scholar who decided to give Ramabai a classical Hindu education. She lost her parents to famine when she was sixteen and married Bipin Medhavi from a Sudra (low caste) family (1880). They had a daughter named Manoramabai (1881). Ramabai was twenty-three when her husband died of cholera (1882). She went to England for further studies the following year, where she and her daughter "Mano," (age two) were baptized in the Church of England.[10] Ramabai visited the United States (1886) at the invitation of the American Episcopal Church, spending over two years there. While in the U.S., she formed the Ramabai Association and published her book, *The High-Caste Indian Woman* (1887).

When she returned to India, she started a home and school called *Sharada Sadan* ("Home of Learning") for child widows (1889). When bubonic plague and famine struck, she expanded her mission (late 1890s). She accommodated not only high caste Hindu child widows, but also all widows and orphans regardless of caste or creed, especially from Madhya Pradesh and Gujarat. Ramabai founded *Mukti Sadan* ("Home of Salvation or Liberation") at Kedgaon, near Poona (1899). It soon became a haven for hundreds of child widows and orphans and a place for education, vocational training, and religious outreach.

The revival started with a simple prayer meeting which grew into a revival at the mission (1905). At four-thirty each morning, seventy women at the mission met for prayer, asking God for "the true conversion of all the Indian Christians, including themselves and for a special outpouring of the Holy Spirit on all Christians of every land."[11] They prayed in this manner for six months and several women experienced the baptism of the Holy Spirit at the mission (June 29, 1905). "The Lord graciously sent a glorious Holy Ghost revival among us, and also in many schools and churches. The results of this have been most satisfactory."[12] Some were "slain in the Spirit" and others experienced a burning sensation. The revival continued into 1906 and 1907. Methodist missionaries Minnie Abrams and Albert Norton were said to have been baptized in the Holy Spirit at the mission during this time. Abrams wrote *The Baptism of the Holy Ghost and Fire* about this experience

(1906). During the same time period, several girls at the mission received a call to preach the gospel and others experienced glossolalia. Ramabai wrote about the revival (1907),

> I have seen not only the most ignorant of our people coming under the power of revival, but the most refined and very highly educated English men and women, who have given their lives for God's service in this country, coming under the power of God, so that they lose all control over their bodies, and are shaken like reeds, stammering words in various unknown tongues as the Spirit teaches them to speak, and gradually get to a place where they are in unbroken communion with God.[13]

Sister Geraldine, an Anglican sister of St. Mary the Virgin at Wantage, described the revival (based on letters received from Ramabai's daughter) as "a marvelous Pentecostal outpouring of the Holy Spirit." Mano said the revival "was manifestly God Himself working. No stirring address was delivered at the meeting; nor had there been any special effort to bring conviction of sin."[14] Mano further reported that a large number of girls and women were converted and many received the cleansing and fullness of the spirit for life and service. An excerpt from the *India Alliance*, a paper of the Christian Missionary Alliance, reported that

> Some of the gifts which have been scarcely heard of in the church for many centuries, are now being given by the Holy Ghost to simple, unlearned members of the body of Christ and communities are being stirred and transformed by the wonderful grace of God. Healing, the gifts of tongues, visions, and dreams, discernment of spirits, the power to prophesy and to pray the prayer of faith, all have a place in the present revival.[15]

These same kinds of proto-Pentecostal charismatic manifestations were not only evident in the Mukti Revival, but had also been part of earlier revivals in India.

Ramabai never insisted that "speaking in tongues" (*glossalalia*) was the initial physical evidence of the baptism of the Holy Spirit (as Pentecostals teach), but she believed the physical manifestations, including speaking in tongues, were indications of the working of the Holy Spirit. Even though they were not granted as fully to her as to others, she never sought to restrain them.[16] In *Mukti Prayer Bell*, she writes, "Love, perfect divine love, is the only and most necessary sign of the baptism of the Holy Spirit. But other gifts, such as the power to heal, to speak with tongues, and to prophesy are not to be discarded. Indeed we should seek from God such gifts as they will enable us to preach the gospel of Jesus Christ with power and draw men unto him."[17] Her view of the initial sign of reception of the baptism of the Holy Spirit was analogous to John Wesley's view of sanctification or Christian perfection. In *Plain Account of Christian Perfection*, he equated Christian perfection to perfect love. He spoke of perfection as the mind of Christ, a total devotion to God, and love of God and neighbor.

Even though Ramabai did not emphasize speaking in tongues as the initial physical evidence of the baptism of the Holy Spirit, she did believe in a three-stage baptism of the Holy Spirit: justification, sanctification, and the baptism of the Holy Spirit.[18] One letter by a Mukti worker reported that:

> Even young girls are stricken down with the spirit of repentance. They cannot eat, sleep or work till they go to the bottom of things. They seek the peace of pardon [*justification, stage one*] and immediately begin to seek sanctification [*stage two*] and and the baptism of the Holy Spirit [*stage three*]. They repent, restore, confess, and finally come into such joy that it knows no bounds. They call it a baptism of fire. They say that when the Holy Spirit comes upon them the burning within them is almost unbearable.[19]

These three stages are also mentioned in a letter received by Sister Geraldine from Mano:

> I told how the Holy Spirit had begun to work in the hearts of the girls in a most marvelous way and how His working led to agony on account of sin, confession [*stage one*] and restoration [*stage two*] and then intense joy. Perhaps, I did not mention the joy, for I remember that I wrote that letter at the very beginning of this Revival; and for the first few days hardly any joy was seen, but a sense of awe pervaded the atmosphere, and there was deep sorrow for sin. Then came the joy and the baptism of the Holy Ghost and Fire; [*stage three*] and what seems to be a special anointing for the Ministry of Intercession.[20]

Belief in a three-stage baptism of the Holy Spirit at Mukti became the precursor to the Pentecostal movement in India. Mukti stands as a proto-Pentecostal movement in India, because it taught and practiced the doctrine of the baptism of the Holy Spirit. However, it differed from the later Pentecostal movement because it did not accept "speaking with tongues" as the initial physical evidence of the baptism of the Holy Spirit. Still, it was very close to the view of the present Pentecostal movement in India.

Howard Snyder argues that the Mukti movement can also be termed a post-holiness movement in India. The practice of a three-stage baptism of the Holy Spirit at Mukti could be viewed as a direct influence of the movement on Pandita Ramabai. He further contends that a Holiness Movement influence was in India because of the efforts of Methodist missionary Bishop John Thoburn, and of William Taylor, a missionary and church planter (1870s and 1880s).[21] And also John Inskip, a prominent holiness evangelist and founder of the National Association for the Promotion of Holiness, conducted a series of evangelistic and holiness meetings in India (1880). He held them in cooperation with William Bramwell Osborn, an American Methodist evangelist,[22] who went to India with Taylor (1875). Inskip preached the Methodist doctrine of entire sanctification as "the baptism of the Holy Spirit."[23] Ramabai reported that she experienced a deeper work of the Holy Spirit (April 1895) at the Holiness camp meeting established by Osborn at Lanuli (or Lanowli, between Bombay and Pune). Ramabai learned of this new experience while reading the autobiography of African Methodist Episcopal Holiness preacher and former slave, Amanda Berry Smith. She was a missionary in India at the same time as Inskip (1880s).

However, Allan Anderson takes a different stance. Ramabai understood that the Mukti Mission was the Holy Spirit's means of raising up an independent and indigenous Indian Christianity. He writes that *The Apostolic Faith* (the Azusa Revival periodical) mentioned the news of this revival in its November, 1906 issue, saying: "Hallelujah! God is sending the Pentecost to India. He is no respecter of persons." The report neither mentioned native Indian missionaries nor the famous Pandita Ramabai by name. Anderson contends that the Indian natives who were simply taught of God were responsible for the outpouring of the Spirit. The gifts of the Spirit were given to simple, unlearned members of the body of Christ.

The Mukti Revival also had other far-reaching consequences, according to Anderson. He points out, in *The Origins of Pentecostalism and Its Global Spread in the Early Twentieth Century,* that the Mukti Revival penetrated other parts of the world untouched by the Azusa Revival, especially South America. Willis Hoover, an American Methodist revivalist in Valparaiso, Chile, heard about the Mukti Mission (1907) through a pamphlet by his wife's former classmate, Minnie Abrams (who worked with Pandita Ramabai). Hoover inquired about the Pentecostal revivals in other places, including Venezuela and Norway. Then revival broke out in his church (1909), resulting in his expulsion from the Methodist Church (1910). Eventually this led to the formation of Chilean Pentecostalism.[24]

McGee, in "Latter Rain Falling in the East: Early-Twentieth Century Pentecostalism in India and the Debate over Speaking in Tongues," aptly comments that the revival at Mukti (1905 to 1907) challenges the common view that modern Pentecostalism traces it origins back to Azusa. Before news of the Azusa Revival first reached India, a Pentecostal revival was already underway on the Indian subcontinent.

Revivals in Andhra Pradesh (1905 to 1906)

These revivals were not limited to Kerala, Tamilnadu, and Maharashtra. The state of Andhra Pradesh also witnessed some powerful proto-Pentecostal revivals in various places, such as Aki(vi)du, Nellore, Ongole, and Bimilipatnam near Visakhapatnam. In these revivals the charismatic manifestations, including visions, trances, shaking, and tongues, were common occurances. Most of these revivals took place among the Dalits. In this section, some of the revivals are briefly discussed.

Revival in the Aki(vi)du Area. The first recorded revival in Andhra Pradesh occurred in the Aki(vi)du area (August 1905). Evangelist S.E. Morrow went to Peddukapavaram where his ministry brought the deep conviction of sin in the hearts of many, followed by confessions. The revival spread later to Siddapuram and Atmakuru. Ten months after the outbreak in the Aki(vi)du area, E.S. Bowden, a missionary of the Godavari Delta Mission, reported a revival in Chettipet. The Chettipet Revival started simultaneously at Aki(vi)du and Yellamanchili (Sunday, August 11, 1905). "Many Hindus gathered in the doorways for six weeks. The meetings lasted from five to ten hours. There was no order of service, no leader, no sermon in any meeting, except the divine order of the Spirit as He led."[25] This revival followed a prayer meeting where Dr. Brown (Secretary of the Foreign Missions board), LaFlamme, and Craig (the Canadian missionaries) were burdened to tears in an upper room on Brunswick Avenue in Toronto for an awakening among the Telugu people.

Revival in Nellore. Another revival in Andhra began in Nellore. David Downie attended one of the prayer meetings in New York's Bowery Theater during the American Awakening (1858). He received a call to India after he heard a missionary address by Alexander Duff, and ended up spending forty years in Andhra as a missionary. According to Downie, one evening (1906) at Nellore's Chambers Hall, it was agreed that the Telugu church should pray every evening until a revival broke out. They met for prayer for ten days. Suddenly one evening in church, while someone was praying, the power of the Spirit descended.

> There was a rumbling noise like distant thunder and a simultaneous, agonizing cry went up from the whole congregation. Some were sobbing; some crying out and all were confessing their sins....Some of the girls went into trances as though speaking to some unseen one, were unconscious of anything around them. There were no human leaders. The Spirit of God led.[26]

Following this revival, quarrels were settled and restitution was made of things stolen and wrongs done. Valuable possessions, especially jewelry, were surrendered as freewill offerings to God (jewelry was and is of special value in India).

Revival in Ongole. Ongole was another center of revival in Andhra Pradesh during this time. American Baptist missionary James Baker, who spent forty years in Andhra Pradesh, recalled the awakening. A missionary had sent some Telugu leaflets to Ongole describing the great Welsh Revival. These became catalysts for a revival among the area preachers. Dr. Boggs (an American Baptist missionary) preached Sunday morning at the usual April quarterly meeting for all the field workers. The next morning they observed the Lord's Supper, followed by a season of prayer.

> Suddenly without warning the usual stoical mindedness of our Indian assembly was broken as by an earthquake. Every one present was shaken. One of the most quiet of the field workers arose, striking his breast, cried in Telugu in a loud voice 'Perishudatma! Perishudatma! (Holy Spirit, Holy Spirit). Many others followed.[27]

Later, Welsh missionary William Powell, who had been in the midst of the Welsh Revival, told of God's dealings with the people in his native land one Sunday evening. When they bowed for prayer, suddenly the spirit of confession broke forth and swept through the assembly of nearly 1000 (July 1906). The noise was so tremendous that non-Christians in nearby places came running to see what the trouble was. This revival in Ongole lasted a year and a half.

Revival in Kurnool. A great famine threatened the Kurnool District of Andhra Pradesh (1906). Then typhoid, smallpox, and cholera ravaged the area and many died. Baptist missionary William Arthur Stanton was stricken with smallpox and his wife had a nervous breakdown. Christians met in chapels and school houses for prayer and sought God for deliverance. Non-Christians joined them, hoping their God could save them. Stanton wrote that the revival came unexpectedly like the rushing of a mighty wind and like a fire from heaven. A regular quarterly meeting was turned into a revival meeting lasting two weeks. All day and far into the night all the people prayed in a loud voice and cried out to God for mercy. Many wept and confessed their sins. Some experienced visions and trances and some seemed possessed. People's lives were burned, cleansed, quickened, and transformed by divine power.[28] This revival, not confined to Kurnool, swept over the entire Telugu mission like wildfire.

When the Canadian Baptists heard that the American Baptist Churches in Nellore and Ongole were visited by the Spirit of God, they began to seek a similar experience with expectation. Revival began next in the girls' school at Kakinada (August 14, 1906) by a sudden visitation by the Holy Spirit in overwhelming power and lasted seven weeks. Classes and work had to stand still for days. Food and rest were almost forgotten while God dealt with souls. The Spirit of God brought hidden things to the surface and people began to confess and discard their long-cherished sins openly with tears and lamentations. Stolen property was restored and estranged lives were reconciled through the power of the Spirit. Non-believers who came to witness all these proceedings were converted.

Revival in Bimilipatnam. The fire of revival spread to other places also, including Ramachandrapuram, Yellamanchili, and Bimilipatnam near Visakhapatnam. A band of Christians touched by the revival went on an evangelistic tour and visited various congregations. The team spent three weeks in Bimilipatnam, where "the Spirit came like a flood during the meetings and there was an occasional outburst of joyous laughing and clapping when some victory was gained. One woman went into a trance-like state and seemed to give messages directly from God, visions of the Crucified One."[29]

Following the revival awakening in Andhra Pradesh (1906), the Canadian Baptist Mission, the American Baptist Mission, the American Lutheran Church, and the Anglican Church experienced numerical growth in their churches. The Canadian Mission had 5,924 members and 8,276 adherents in 1904. By 1914, they had 9,482 members and 13,909 adherents. The American Baptist Church had 54,649 communicants (1905), then increased to 56,001 (1907) and later to 56,525 (1908). The American Lutheran Church membership grew from 18,964 to 40,198 in the Guntur area. In the Godavari District, baptized membership rose from 11,938 to 16,953 (1905 to 1910).

Clearly the charismatic manifestation of the Holy Spirit occurred spontaneously in India before the Azusa Revival even began, and before the

Western Pentecostal missionaries ever arrived under the ministry of mainline Protestant missionaries. Neither the Protestant missionaries nor the Indian Christians had any idea about the work and manifestations of the Holy Spirit. A missionary with the American Board of Commissioners for Foreign Missions in Madura wrote to Rufus Anderson, "We commenced a prayer meeting, but the excitement soon became uncontrollable and we were obliged to stop and address ourselves to individuals. The next day we cautioned the people to avoid, as far as possible, giving way to their feelings."[30] Stanton states that these charismatic (or proto-Pentecostal) phenomena, such as visions, trances, speaking to some unseen one (tongues), prophecies, and occasional outbursts of joyous laughing are not only strange, but also disturbing to Western Protestant missionaries. The main intent of these missionaries was to encourage people to commit their lives to Christ. When they witnessed the charismatic phenomenon among them, they considered the work of the Holy Spirit as practices of the heathen. One primary reason for this misunderstanding was that the missionaries were bound by denominational and theological limitations concerning the activities of the Holy Spirit.

Indians responded positively to the gospel that missionaries preached because of their deep hunger for spiritual things. The gospel offered them a message of hope and forgiveness of sins and a new beginning. When there was a spontaneous outbreak of the Spirit's manifestation, they could not understand the proto-Pentecostal phenomenon that they experienced in their midst as the work of the Holy Spirit. However, they were attracted to the charismatic manifestions, including visions, dreams, and healings. They did not understand because of ignorance and lack of biblical teaching on the person and work of the Holy Spirit.

Dalit Contributions during the Era of Antecedent Pentecostal-like Revivals

The efforts of Aroolappen, from the Dalit background, should not be ignored in this period. His tireless efforts in preaching the revival messages, not only in the CMS churches but also in the Syrian churches, brought a great revival in both Tirunelveli and Travancore States. During this period, another prominant leader of Dalit masses, Vedanayagam Samuel Azariah, came to Dornakal as a missionary of the Indian Missionary Society of Tirunelveli. Under his leadership, a folk religious movment occurred there during the time of the Andhra Awakening (early 1900s). Azariah was born (August 17, 1874) at Vellalanvillai village in the Tirunelveli district, Tamilnadu. His father, Velayudam, was converted from Hinduism and took the name "Thomas Vedanayagam." He later became a pastor and continued his pastoral ministry for over twenty years.

Azariah completed his bachelor's degree in Madras Christian College and later was elected Secretary of the YMCA for South India (1895), rendering his services in that capacity for thirteen years. He married Anbu Mariammal (1889) during that time. After making a trip to Jaffna in Ceylon with Sherwood Eddy (1902), he was inspired to start a missionary society, and he founded the Indian Missionary Society (1903). He then took a daring step and went to Dornakal as a missionary to work among the poor and the outcastes, including the Lambadis and other tribal groups (1909). He became the first Indian bishop of the Anglican Church (1912). Bishop Azariah was one of the guest speakers at the Edinburgh Missionary Conference (1910), Tranquebar Conference (1919), the National Christian Council of India, Burma, and Ceylon (1929 to 1945) and the World Missionary Conference at Tambaram, India (1938).[31] He built a magnificent cathedral called "The Cathedral Church of the Epiphany of Our Lord" (1939). By implementing the methods developed in the earlier Tinnevelli Revival, Azariah baptized three thousand people a year for thirty years. Because of his efforts, the Christian community in the Dornakal Diocese increased from 77,000 (1919) to 230,000 (1943).[32] After a long and illustrious ministry work in Dornakal, Azariah died at the age of seventy (January 1, 1945).

Colonial Pentecostalism and Invasion of Western Pentecostal Missionaries

During this stage, Western Pentecostal missionaries came to India intending to preach the Pentecostal message and establish Western Pentecostal denominations. In so doing, Pentecostal missionaries suffered hardships, including illness, loss of children and spouses, and alienation from their own families. However, they, like their predecessors (mainline Protestant missionaries), generally maintained the colonial mentality, dominated the native leaders, and tried to import the Western brand of Pentecostalism. The Indians saw them as opportunists who worked with local leaders to advance their own agenda. Robert Cook fit the role of a typical colonizer, like many other Western missionaries. He worked with native leaders and Dalits, but considered himself superior as a white man. In his works, *A Quarter Century of Divine Leading in India* and *Half a Century of Divine Leading and 37 Years of Apostolic Achievements in South India*, Cook portrayed himself as a bearer of light to "dark India." He highlighted what he accomplished in India through his missionary work but ignored efforts of local leaders, especially Dalits. V.V. Thomas points out that Cook did not acknowledge the efforts of those Dalit leaders who worked with him (Vellikara Matthai or Choti and Poikayil Yohannan). However, he did mention his Syrian associates, like K.E. Abraham. Cook worked with the Dalits and they rallied around him, but he did not consider them equal to Syrians or to his own status as a missionary.[33]

The native leaders were resilient in consolidating their Pentecostal work and chartering their own denominations, in order to combat the colonial attitude and withstand competition from Western Pentecostal missionaries.

On the other hand, a positive result from the arrival of foreign missionaries was that the work of the Holy Spirit and the doctrine of Holy Spirit baptism were further explained to Indian Christians who had already witnessed the Spirit's charismatic manifestations in their midst through earlier revivals.

George Berg was the first Pentecostal missionary to come to India, followed by Robert Cook. Both Berg and Cook preached the message of Pentecost, emphasizing the baptism of the Holy Spirit with the initial evidence of speaking in tongues as a doctrine. There were numerous instances of people speaking in tongues in the various earlier revivals in India, but they could not articulate it as doctrine until the arrival of Berg.[34]

Berg was an American of German descent and pastor of a Protestant church in Chicago, Illinois. He received the baptism of the Holy Spirit at the Azusa Revival during a time when he lived only twenty-five miles away. He had heard false reports about the new phenomenon which stirred his interest in it (June 1906). He visited Azusa Street to see for himself because of a deep hunger to know more about God (July 1906). He understood that there was something more beyond sanctification. God touched him in the revival but he was still confused about speaking in tongues. He returned to Azusa (September 13, 1906) and waited until he received Spirit baptism and spoke in other tongues.[35]

When Berg came to India, he arrived in Bangalore (February 28, 1908) and initially made it the center of his missionary work. He later visited Kerala with Miss Bouncil and Miss Aldy Winkle to preach at the Brethren convention held at Thrikkannamangal (1909). Since Berg was not affiliated with any formal organization, the Brethren did not find it difficult to invite him to speak at their convention. Bouncil and Winkle originally came to India as Brethren missionaries from England. They then experienced the baptism of the Holy Spirit through the work of Thomas Barrett of Norway[36] who also visited India not long after Berg's arrival (1908). During the time of the Azusa Revival, Barrett was traveling in the U.S. raising funds to build his home church in Oslo. While he was in the U.S., he received the baptism of the Holy Spirit and stopped his fundraising efforts to return home with the message of the Pentecostal outpouring. Many in Norway received the baptism through his ministry. Later he visited India, spending nine months there.

Berg visited Kerala again (1910) to preach at the Brethren convention at Kottarkkara on the significance of speaking in tongues. He soon faced stiff opposition from the Brethren because of his topic. On his third visit to Kerala (1911) he came into contact with native Indian missionary Charles (Robert) Cumine, a Tamil-speaking Anglo-Indian from Kolar, near Bangalore. He also met local Christian leaders Paruttupara Ummachan (from Thuvayoor, near Adur), Umman Mammen, and Pandalam Mattai. Berg worked along with these native workers in South India. When he traveled to Kerala (1913) for the last time, Cook and Cumine accompanied him. They conducted meetings in various places, including Punthala, Kidangnoor, Elanthoor and Punalur. As a result of Berg's work, along with the help of native workers, a Pentecostal church was formed in Thuvayoor. Most of the members of the church were from a Dalit background. Berg and Cook were co-workers at the beginning but separated later because of a disagreement, most likely over a leadership issue due to a power struggle. They then continued their independent ministries. Berg finally left India permanently (1914) because of the First World War, when the British forced him to return to the United States since he was of German origin.

Cook attended the first worldwide Pentecostal conference at Los Angeles, California (1912) where Berg talked about India and opportunities available for ministry there. Cook and his wife decided to come to India with Berg (October 1913), where he briefly worked in the Tinnevelly District (Tamilnadu). During the First World War, Cook had to temporarily move to Bangalore where the British had a cantonment because missionaries were safer there. He went next to Kerala with Cumine on an evangelistic trip (Winter 1916). Cook concentrated his work among the Dalits in Thuvayoor and later in Suranadu and Punalur. Most of his followers came from a Dalit background. As the war intensified, Cook, Bouncil, and Winkle left India, like many other missionaries. During this interval, Bouncil died in England and Berg in America. Cook returned to India (1921) and continued the work Berg had left behind.[37]

Prior to his return, Cook affiliated with the Assemblies of God in the U.S. (1919) after six years of independent work in Travancore and continued with them until 1926. He primarily joined the Assemblies of God because the British Government passed an ordinance that all missionaries should affiliate with an organization. Cook had no choice but to join in order to meet the requirement, even though he desired to remain independent. Some of the Assemblies of God missionaries who came to India were Mary Chapman (1916), Susan Rice Chester (1922), Martha Kucera (1925), and John H. Burgess (1926). The efforts of these missionaries are briefly mentioned next.

After the Assemblies of God was first formed in Arkansas (1914), Chapman was sent to South India. She stayed at Dodaballpur in Mysore State (present-day Karnataka State, January 13, 1916).[38] She later stayed in Madras (1921) and traveled to many places in South India proclaiming the Pentecostal message. Chapman traveled to Kerala (1921) where three men from there visited her and invited her to minister in Travancore.[39] She made periodic trips and encouraged the workers there. She moved later to Kerala (1924) after a great flood and started several new missions in the southern part of Travancore. She sought Cook's support because of his experience and popularity in the Indian mission field. She concentrated her work among the Dalits in Mavelikara and the Syrians without seeing much growth. Chapman died (November 27, 1926) a few months after handing her work over to Burgess, who came to Travancore in 1926.[40] Her sudden death and the formation of the South Indian Pentecostal Church of God (1924) were a formidable challenge to the Assemblies of God.

Margaret Clark was another Assemblies of God missionary who worked in Bombay, Maharashtra State. During a convention in Sharampur (1918), the first Indian Assemblies of God was formed due to her efforts. After two years it became affiliated with the Assemblies of God in the U.S. under the banner of the North India Assemblies of God.[41]

Chester came to India as an Assemblies of God missionary and ministered in Travancore. The extent of her work is not known. When she died (Feburary 17, 1924), Chapman took over and continued her work. Kucera was another Assemblies of God missionary who came to Travancore (1925 or 1926). She worked with Cook and the Assemblies of God among the poor and the needy in the central and southern parts of Travancore.[42]

Burgess came to central Travancore in South India (1926) and worked with Chapman. He established the first Assemblies of God Bible School (Bethel Bible School) in Mavelikara less than a year after his arrival in Kerala (1927). It was later moved to Punalur (1940). Bethel Bible School is considered the oldest Assemblies of God Bible School in the world outside of the U.S.[43]

Cook founded a new denomination (1921) known as the "Malankara Full Gospel Church" (*Malankara Poorna Suvishesha Sabha*) and continued his ties with the Assemblies of God. He moved to Kerala permanently (1922) to continue his mission work. Dalits continued to be attracted to his ministry. Prominent among them were two Dalit leaders, Matthai (or Choti) and Yohannan who invited Cook to preach to their followers. They helped him to minister among the Dalits and to get acquainted with the Syrian Christians.

Cook went on furlough (1923) and, in the meantime, Syrian Christians entered the Pentecostal movement. In the beginning they were not interested in the movement, not due to doctrinal considerations, but because it was basically a Dalit movement. In the early period of its history in Kerala, Pentecostalism took root mainly among the Dalit community, along with a few Syrians who were poor, like the way it emerged in the United States among the oppressed Black community and the poor Whites.[44] Most Syrian Christians did not want to associate with the Dalits and their movement, i.e., Pentecostalism. However, they slowly joined the movement after they saw that Kulathumoolackal Eapen Abraham (K.E. Abraham) had accepted the Pentecostal faith. Abraham and A.J. John embraced Pentecostalism (1923 or 1924) along with K.C. Cheriyan and P.V. John (1924). They dominated the Pentecostal movement and became leaders of it in Kerala. They bypassed Dalit leaders Choti and Yohannan, who had helped Cook spread the Pentecostal faith in Kerala. These Dalit leaders and their followers had hoped to achieve higher social status in Pentecostalism. They anticipated a change in status through their affiliation with the Pentecostal movement and their association with Syrians. However, when the caste-minded Syrian Christians entered Pentecostalism, the efforts of Dalit leaders to climb the social ladder remained just a dream.

While Cook was on furlough, K.E. Abraham worked with Chapman of the Assemblies of God. This affiliation abruptly ended when Chapman and Abraham disagreed over a church property, leading to their separation. Meanwhile, Cook returned to India (1926) and severed his ties with the Assemblies of God. The "South India Pentecostal Church of God," founded by K.E. Abraham, and the "Malankara Full Gospel Church," founded by Cook, were merged to establish a new Pentecostal denomination called the "Malankara Pentecostal Church (October 6, 1926)." However, this merger did not last long. Abraham and other Indian Pentecostal leaders got into serious conflict (1930), both with Cook and among themselves, over questions regarding leadership positions, financial matters and affiliation with Western missionary societies. According to V.V. Thomas, a main reason for the split was that Abraham wanted to have an exclusively Syrian-controlled Pentecostal church.[45] He also wanted to attract many Syrians from other churches into the Pentecostal movement.

Dalits were always treated as inferior by Syrians, who have a deep-rooted consciousness regarding their caste as being socially elevated. They have been treated similarly to other higher castes in their community. According to George Oommen, Syrian Christians generally considered themselves as an ethnically defined caste group of very high social status, equal to Brahmans. The Dalits who converted to Christianity during this period were harassed in an organized way by the higher caste Christians and were not accepted into the fellowship of the Syrian Christians. Syrian Christians practiced untouchability toward the Dalits by not allowing them to sit on the chairs in the Syrian churches, forcing them to sit in an area assigned for them on the floor. This attitude of discrimination therefore distanced the Dalits from the Syrian Christians. Dalits had expected social acceptance and economic mobility when they joined mainstream Christianity, but Syrian Christians were not interested in spreading the gospel to the Dalits, or accepting them as co-equal Christians.[46]

Abraham continued to carry this caste-consciousness even after he became a Pentecostal. The same attitude caused Dalit leaders Choti and Yohannan to leave the Pentecostal movement in the early days of Indian Pentecostalism. Even today there are no Dalit leaders at the top level in Kerala, only Syrians. Michael Bergunder's comments echo that, in regard to caste, the Pentecostal movement practiced discrimination similar to the established churches from the very beginning.[47]

T.S. Samuel Kutty expressed the same view in his work, *The Place and Contributions of Dalits in Select Pentecostal Churches in India*. Abraham did not want Pentecostalism to be identified as a Dalit movment, but rather as a new and true form of Christianity which emerged from among the upper caste Christians. When the upper caste Christians began to join the Pentecostal church, Syrian Christian leaders wanted to avoid close affinity with the Dalits, particularly in Abraham's church (the IPC in Kerala), with the intention of painting a picture of Pentecostalism as an upper caste Syrian movement. According to Kutty, after 1930, Dalits flowed into the Pentecostal church, primarily in Cook's church, once he separated from Abraham. Abraham and others concentrated primarily among the upper castes, the Syrians.[48] He wrote in his autobiography that when people from the Dalit community came to Pentecostalism, he stayed in their huts, ate with them, and thereby led them to Christ more effectively. Perhaps he was not totally sincere in his attitude toward the Dalits, because he always attached great importance to his Syrian Christian identity, according to George Oommen.[49]

After Cook separated from Abraham, he went to Nilgiris in Madras State (1936) where he met J.H. Ingram, the representative of the Church of God (Cleveland, Tennessee). Ingram invited Cook to speak at a general meeting of his churches at Malankara. This relationship eventually paved the way for the Church of God in India, when fifty-one of Cook's churches, along with their pastors and representatives, decided to join the U.S. Church of God. Approximately forty-three of these were Dalit churches. The Indian Church of God was officially registered by Cook at Coimbatore (1949). The next year Cook retired from missionary work and returned to the U.S. (1950).[50]

According to Bergunder, out of this conflict between Cook and Abraham, four Pentecostal denominations came into existence in Kerala (1930s). Two had direct links with Western missions: the Assemblies of God and the Church of God. The remaining two were independent and indigenous organizations: the "Ceylon Pentecostal Mission," (presently known as the "Pentecostal Mission")[51] and the "Indian Pentecostal Church of God."[52] As a consequence, Bergunder wrote that, "This historical genesis shows that the emerging Pentecostal movement in India could hardly be rendered as the missionary history of Western Pentecostal denominations."[53] The same conclusion is echoed by Abraham in his book entitled *The Early Years of IPC* (1955).

It is thought by many people that the Indian Pentecostal Church of God was formed after the break with Cook. This error stems from their lack of information about the early history of this movement. Abraham's book shows that this movement (the Indian Pentecostal Church) was already in existence under the name "South India Pentecostal Church." Cook had worked in association with the movement for over three years. From the beginning of 1930, Cook de-affiliated with this alliance.[54]

In his earlier presidential address to the workers of the IPC (1939), Abraham stated that those who had recently joined the fellowship might be surprised to learn that the movement had started fifteen years ago. "Many think that this movement began after we left the relationship with Pastor Cook. It is not so! This movement was founded fifteen years ago by those ministers and congregations who accepted Pentecostal truth and decided to minister independently in central Travancore."[55] Paulson Pulikottil comments that, in these statements, Abraham, one founder of the IPC, had struggled to make it clear that their denomination had come into existence even before he came into contact with the Pentecostal missionaries and established Pentecostal churches in India.[56]

Dalit Contributions during the Era of Colonial Pentecostalism

During the second stage, the contributions made by two prominant Dalit leaders, Matthai (or Choti) and Yohannan, to Pentecostalism were incalculable. They stirred up the Dalits to accept this new variety of Christianity which was different from that of the mainline denominations.

Vellikara Matthai or Choti. He came from a Dalit family and had originally belonged to the Anglican Church. He met Robert Cook while on his way for treatment in Trivandrum (1922) when he went to visit A.K. Varghese, who was translating Cook's messages in various places. Choti requested prayer for healing from Cook. Later, he visited Cook again and explained that he was not healed. Cook anointed him with oil and prayed for him a second time, and this time he was instantly healed. After this incident, Choti invited him to preach to his followers at Kumbanadu. Cook accepted the invitation "with much joy and my longing desire was at last realized; i.e., to preach among these untouchables."[57] He acknowledged that God had used Choti "marvelously" in developing relationships with the Dalits, and in granting his followers freedom to embrace Pentecostalism. Kutty points out that, when Choti experienced the gift of healing in Cook's ministry, it might have influenced him to persuade his Dalit followers to consider an alternative (Pentecostalism) for their spiritual and social empowerment. Hence, Choti, a Dalit, played a major role in bringing Cook to Kumbanadu so that the Dalits could embrace the Pentecostal doctrine of the baptism of the Holy Spirit.

Poikayil Yohannan. He was from the Paraya caste (a Dalit caste) and belonged to the Mar Thoma church. He was attracted to the preaching of the CMS missionaries and later became an evangelist with the CMS. However, he did not stay long with that mission because of caste discrimination. He joined the Brethren Church, which attracted many from the Dalit communities because of its radical stance regarding caste practice. Yohannan became a chief advocate of this movement. However, his association with the Brethren movement was short-lived when he realized that there was caste discrimination in the Brethren movement also, especially from the Syrian Brethren. He formed his own organization for the Dalits known as *Prathyaksha Raksha Daiva Sabha* (Church of God for Visible Salvation) to challenge the Syrian domination within the mainline and Brethren churches. Robert Cook met Yohannan at Kumbanadu (1922) and was invited to preach to his followers at Eraviperoor. Cook writes that "John (Yohannan) was an influential man amongst the low castes or untouchables. The same was an earnest Christian and had 5,000 followers in the whole of Travancore. God had used him in bringing thousand out of heathen darkness to Jesus Christ"[58] Through the efforts of Yohannan, many Dalits accepted Cook's Pentecostal message and began to embrace Pentecostalism.

Indigenous Pentecostalism and Consolidation of Native Leadership

During this stage, native leaders P. Ramankutty (also known as Paul—a Dalit), K.E. Abraham, Plathaneth Matthew Samuel (P.M. Samuel), and K.C. Cheriyan (the three Syrians) and a few others grasped that the Pentecostal doctrine of the baptism of the Holy Spirit was the work of the Holy Spirit. On that premise, they built their organizations and churches, along with emphasis on the importance of the Word of God, fasting and prayer, healing (including exorcisms), and the believer's separation from the world (holy living) within the Indian context. These indigenous leaders successfully rose above the domination of Western Pentecostal missionaries to found indigenous Pentecostal denominations, namely the Ceylon Pentecostal Mission and the Indian Pentecostal Church.

The founders of the IPC, Abraham, Samuel, and Cheriyan, not only had their roots in the Syrian church, but also had ties with the Brethren movement and the Ceylon Pentecostal Mission. Therefore, the next section briefly discusses the IPC leaders' connection with these three different groups.

Syrian Background of IPC Leaders

The three Indian Pentecostal Church founders, Samuel, Abraham, and Cheriyan, came from the Syrian Christian Community. These Syrian Christian leaders left the Syrian church and later formed the "South Indian Pentecostal Church of God." This national Pentecostal movement began to grow and spread to other places, including Hyderabad (Andhra Pradesh), Mysore (Karnataka), Madras (Tamilnadu) and some places in North India. Then the leaders of the "South Indian Pentecostal Church of God" changed its name to "The Indian Pentecostal Church of God" (May, 1934). Finally, the IPC was registered at Eluru in December, 1935.[59] According to Pulikottil, the IPC is considered to be the first indigenous Pentecostal denomination in India.[60]

However, Pulikottil apparently was not aware that the Ceylon Pentecostal Church should be considered the first indigenous Pentecostal denomination in British India. Even though it was officially registered in Colombo (1924), the Ceylon Pentecostal Church was actually founded by Paul, a Dalit (1923), before Abraham became a Pentecostal or received the baptism of the Holy Spirit. Abraham received the baptism of the Holy Spirit by the laying of hands of Dalit evangelist C. Manaseh (1924).[61] Even though Abraham started the South Indian Pentecostal Church in 1924, it was not officially registered as an organization with the government of Travancore at Aranmula until December, 1933.

It appears that Pentecostal historians in India intentionally avoided including in Pentecostal historiography not only the Dalit pioneers Choti and Yohannan, but also Ramankutty (or Paul), founder of the Ceylon Pentecostal Church, with the intention of portraying the Pentecostal movement as having begun among the upper castes and the Syrians. They overlooked the fact that it was Paul, a Dalit, who was instrumental in helping Samuel receive the baptism of the Holy Spirit at Lunav (September 20, 1929). Moreover, he also ordained Abraham as a minister at Kumbanadu (March 6, 1930). Paul was invited by Samuel to preach at a convention held at Keekozhoor (January 23 to 26, 1930). After the convention, while on his way to Ceylon, he was invited to Kumbanadu to ordain Abraham.[62] Therefore, it was not a missionary from the West (Berg or Cook), but Paul, a Dalit and the founder of the first indigenous Pentecostal organization, who ordained Abraham.

The Indian Pentecostal Church also seems to be connected with the Syrian Christian Community, which claims its origin in 52 C.E., when Saint Thomas (one of the twelve original apostles) came to India. *The Acts of Thomas*, an apocryphal work, is one of the earliest written records about Saint Thomas and his missionary activities in India. It is usually dated between 180 C.E. and 230 C.E. Bardesanes, a Syrian native of Edessa in Mesopotomia, is considered the author.[63] According to the Saint Thomas tradition, the Apostle Thomas came by sea and first landed at Malankara near Cranganore (circa 52 C.E.). He went there to construct a palace for Gondophares, an Indian king. Thomas agreed to undertake the project in winter, not the normal summer building season. However, he gave the poor the royal funds instead of building a palace. When the king learned of it, he seized Thomas and imprisoned him. Meanwhile, the king's brother, Gad, died and then miraculously came back to life, recounting a marvelous vision of the splendor of the celestial palace Thomas had promised. Thomas was soon released and he then baptized both Gondophares and Gad.[64]

When Thomas came to India, he led several Hindu Brahmins to Christ. On the Malabar Coast, he met Hindu priests sprinkling water from the river on the people, believing it was sacred and would wash away their sins. Their customs astonished him and he felt pity for their innocence and ignorance. He made a challenge to the priests to which they agreed. If a groove would remain in the place where they collected the water from the river, and if it did not fall back when they threw the water in mid-air, then he would follow their gods. Otherwise, the priests would follow Christ, whom Thomas was serving. The Hindu priests tried a number of times to meet the challenge without success. To their surprise, Thomas performed the miracle against the law of gravity. The priests fell at his feet to worship him, but Thomas protested their error and pointed them to Christ. As a result, many of the high caste Hindu Brahmin priests became Christians.

Thomas later planted seven churches on the Malabar Coast. They were in the various centers of his missionary work: Cranganore (Malankara), Palur (Palayur), Parur (Kottakavu), Kokkamangalam, Niranam, Chayal (Nilakal), and Quilor (Kollam).⁶⁵ From there he went to the East Coast and planted more churches. Then he was speared to death by high caste Hindu Brahmin priests (72 C.E.) who feared that he would convert the rest of the Brahmin priests if they did not stop him. His tomb is believed to still exist to this day at San Thome Cathedral in Mylapore, Tamilnadu.

However, the presence of the Apostle Thomas in India is highly debatable. There are two schools of thought regarding this apocryphal work. The old school completely rejects the whole episode as unhistorical, while more recent thought accepts the idea of St. Thomas' apostolate to India. The modern school seeks to establish the existence of both King Gondophares and his brother Gad as historical and not simply mythological figures. They point out the fact that coins of Gondophares inscribed in the Indian Pali language were found in Afghanistan by Masson (1834). An inscription of Gondophares was also discovered in Takht-i-Bahi, dated in the twenty-sixth year of his reign.⁶⁶ Moreover, the modern school has made further attempts to prove St. Thomas' presence by early ecclesiastical writings and liturgical documents and by the testimony of the Church fathers. For example, Ephraim, a famous Christian poet who lived in the fourth century, mentioned the removal of Thomas' relics from India to Edessa in his Nisibene hymns. Gregory Nazianzen also linked Thomas with India in his *Against Arians*.⁶⁷ The Syntaxarum of the Church of Constantinople supports the mission of Thomas to India.

But Eusebius gives a rival account, stating that the Apostle Bartholomew went to India in the first century, accomplishing much of what has been ascribed to Thomas. Bartholomew is believed to have preached and founded a church at Kalyan near Bombay (A.D. 55 to 62). It is said that he left a copy there of the gospel of Matthew written in Hebrew which was later taken by Pantaenus to Alexandria.⁶⁸ However, some have argued that Eusebius might have mistaken the Indian name of Mar Thomas for Bar Thomas.

Abraham's parents, Eapen and Anna Tharakan, belonged to the Jacobite Syrian Church⁶⁹ which St. Thomas started, and raised him to become a Syrian Orthodox priest. According to Kunjappan Varghese, Abraham left the Syrian Church because it followed many heathen practices that had come in through Hindu influence. Syncretism, festivals, and ritualistic liturgy took a pre-eminent place. The Syrian Church became nominal and the work of the Holy Spirit and teaching of the Word of God no longer had importance. After Abraham departed, being a former Syrian leader, he concentrated his work in central Travancore among the Syrian Christians. He preached the Pentecostal message among them and, as a result, many small Pentecostal congregations were formed.

Samuel's parents also belonged to the Mar Thoma Church. Samuel experienced his conversion in the Syrian Church (1920). He was also trained to become a Syrian Orthodox priest in their seminary in Kottayam. He left the Syrian Church when he came into contact with the Brethren, and received water baptism by Kunjappi Upadesi (1926).

Cheriyan's family belonged to the Syrian Orthodox Church. Cheriyan was converted by Muttampackal Kochukunju, an evangelist of the Mar Thoma Church. He also taught in the Syrian church-run school and was very active in Syrian Church activities. Later, he left the Syrian Church (early 1920s) like Abraham and Samuel. This is the connection between the first IPC leaders and the Syrian Orthodox Church.

Brethren Background of IPC Leaders

The Brethren movement began after people met for Bible study and prayer meetings (1820s). The first group met in Dublin, Ireland (1827) while similar groups also met in England. About 700 people came together under the leadership of V.W. Newton and John Nelson Darby. Another Brethren group was formed in Bristol under the leadership of George Muller and Henry Baker.

The Brethren ministry in India began in Bihar, which is located in North India. E.C. Stuart worked there with the cooperation of Anthony Groves (1833). Later William Bowden, George Beer, and John Parnal worked with Groves in Andhra Pradesh. Then Silas Fox, a Canadian missionary, came to work in the southern part of Andhra Pradesh. Fox was assisted by Agrippa, an Andhra native. Paul V. Gupta, founder of Hindustan Bible Institute (HBI), became a Christian through Fox's ministry (1937).[70]

When the Brethren missionaries came to India, many in the established churches were attracted to their preaching. The Brethren assembly witnessed high rates of growth under the able leadership of foreign missionaries, such as Volbrech Nagal and J.C. Gergson, and local Indian leaders, including K.V. Simon and P.E. Mammen in Kerala. Simon was a member of the Mar Thoma Syrian church, but was expelled from the church because he received baptism by immersion. His inspiring messages and writings stirred many in the Syrian Church. Hundreds of Syrian Christians, including Abraham, became members of the Brethren Church because of Simon's dynamic ministry. He was a respected leader, preacher, theologian, and author.

After Abraham left the Syrian church, he joined the Brethren assembly and associated with Simon. After reading Simon's book on baptism, Abraham received water baptism by him. Simon and Abraham later conducted many evangelistic meetings together and baptized hundred of converts. Then Abraham heard about the baptism of the Holy Spirit and speaking in unknown tongues. He began to study the Bible and pray for this baptism. He also learned from A.C. Mathai, an evangelist from Pandalam, that speaking in tongues would be the initial sign of Spirit baptism. Abraham was fasting and praying with C. Manaseh, a Dalit evangelist from Trivandrum (1924), when he experienced the baptism of the Holy Spirit with speaking in tongues. Abraham describes his dramatic experience:

> While we were praying, Brother Manaseh laid his hand upon my head and prayed. All of a sudden I experienced the passing of a current through my body

by the power of the Holy Spirit and my body began to shiver. This power gradually took me and I came completely under the spell of the Holy Spirit....my tongue so moved that I was unable to praise God in my mother tongue. The whole day was spent in the presence of the Holy Spirit. The same thing repeated on the next day....I began to weep and cry before the Lord and asked him to sanctify me by his precious blood. Then I saw a vision that Jesus was hanging on the cross. For hours that vision was before my eyes and I was continually speaking in tongues.
When I was going through the above experience, I was completely conscious.[71]

When his fellow members of the Brethren Church learned of his new experience, they began to ridicule and isolate him, resulting in his departure from the Brethren assembly. Not long after he left, he started his own ministry called the "South Indian Pentecostal Church of God."

According to Varghese, Abraham Malpan and later his son, Mar Thomas Athanasius, began to bring reformation in the Jacobite Syrian Church. This resulted in the formation of the Mar Thoma Syrian Church (1889), with an emphasis on missions, Bible study, and a burden for preaching the gospel. Malpan's interaction with Protestant missionaries also paved the way for the genesis of the Brethren movement, because the Mar Thoma Church was open to the missionaries who emphasized the importance of the Word of God. K.V. Simon was very much impacted by Malpan's reformation ideas. Consequently, he left the Mar Thoma Church and soon became a prominent leader of the Brethren movement. Later, Malpan and Simon influenced Abraham, resulting in revival and formation of the Indian Pentecostal Church of God.[72]

Cheriyan also had a Brethren connection. After he left the Syrian Church, he joined the Brethren movement and received water baptism by Abraham (1921). Later, when Abraham embraced the Pentecostal movement, Cheriyan followed him and received the baptism of the Holy Spirit (1924). Similarly, Plathaneth Matthew Samuel was a Brethren believer until he came into contact with the Pentecostal movement during a visit to Madras. He experienced Spirit baptism in Ceylon under the leadership of P. Paul (1929). Not long after he returned to India, he began to work with Abraham. Therefore, these IPC leaders not only had Syrian roots, but also links with the Brethren movement.

Dalit Contributions during the Era of Indigenous Pentecostalism -- IPC Leaders and Their Links with the Ceylon Pentecostal Church

As stated earlier, Manaseh, a Dalit, played a key role in helping K.E. Abraham receive the baptism of the Holy Spirit. Paul (Ramankutty), another prominent Dalit leader, contributed immensely to the work of the IPC and its founders. The Ceylon Pentecostal Mission was started in 1923 by Paul, a Dalit from central Kerala. He was born to a Hindu family in Engdiyur (1881) in the Trichur District of Kerala and moved to Ceylon in search of a job at age fourteen. He was hired by a wealthy man named Dr. Asarappa, who had converted from Hinduism to Christianity through the CMS. Ramankutty learned about Christianity through his family and became a follower of Jesus Christ at age eighteen (1899), following a vision he had of Him. Then he began to pray and meditate on Jesus secretly. He had another vision of Jesus when he was twenty-two. After that, he felt he could no longer remain a crypto-Christian, so he began to follow Christ openly. Before long he was baptized and his name was changed to Paul. Then he worked as a catechist in the CMS. It was not long before he received the baptism of the Holy Spirit, after which he left the CMS.[73]

Paul entered full-time ministry later and witnessed miraculous events in his early ministry. Adam, a leper, was cured instantaneously, and a dead person came back to life when Paul prayed over him. Soon people began to recognize Paul as a man of God and joined his newly-formed fellowship, the Ceylon Pentecostal Mission (CPM), including Alwin R. DeAlwis and his family. DeAlwis was a college professor from an affluent background. He was a great thinker, writer, and orator. Paul recognized his talent and ordained him as a pastor. He soon became Paul's immediate assistant in ministry. DeAlwis was very instrumental in the establishment of the Ceylon Pentecostal Mission (1923), which was eventually registered in Colombo (1924), according to historian G.P.V. Somaratna.[74]

Abraham joined the CPM after he parted ways with Cook. When Paul visited Travancore (1929), he went on an extensive preaching tour with Abraham and established many churches. Abraham wrote in *Yesuchristhuvinte Eliya Dasan* that during this tour, he and his co-workers invited Paul to conduct an ordination service for them, which he agreed to do. After Abraham was ordained as pastor at Kumbanadu, Paul suggested that Abraham should ordain the rest of the workers of the South India Pentecostal Church of God.[75] Abraham left the CPM after working with Paul for three years (1933) because he was unwilling to submit to the leadership of Paul and DeAlwis. He may have had reservations as a caste-minded Syrian in submitting to Dalit leadership.

Abraham appeared to be an opportunist when he joined the CPM. When he and Cook parted ways (1930), many Dalits followed Cook, while the Syrians went with Abraham. He might have joined the Ceylon Pentecostal Church to compete with Cook and attract at least a few Dalits to his fold. Another reason for joining may have been to give the impression that he was not biased against Dalits. However, Abraham's attitude may not have been sincere toward them, because he always gave importance to his Syrian background. Moreover, he wanted the Pentecostal Church to be dominated by Syrians in the first place.

Samuel also had a close connection with Paul. Samuel received the baptism of the Holy Spirit under his leadership. Paul invited him to Ceylon to participate in a Pentecostal convention at Lunav. Samuel wrote in his autobiography that Paul, DeAlwis, and his wife, Freeda, fasted and prayed for him that he might receive the baptism of the Holy Spirit, which he did before long (September 20, 1929). He wrote of his experience:

> I was encircled by a power and my body became so uncontrollable that I fell on the ground. I woke up after a long time, at that time I saw a vision. In my vision I saw a huge tank full of blood. I saw that I was fighting the waves caused by the blood. Suddenly a spark came and completely burnt my body. Then I saw the Lord. With all His glory, He came and stood beside me and smiled. My joy knew no limits and I smiled back at him. My Lord spoke to me in many languages and I replied Him back. Thus I was there for nearly 2 hours and people beside me told me later that I spoke in eight languages. I could not forget this incident and I thank God for baptizing me with the Holy Spirit.[76]

It, therefore, becomes obvious that the IPC leaders, especially Abraham and Samuel, had a close association with Paul and the Ceylon Pentecostal Church he founded. Both worked and traveled together with Paul, and he was a frequent speaker at their conventions. Therefore, both Abraham and Samuel's ministries were benefitted by the Dalit Paul in one way or another.

Summary

Indian Pentecostalism can be traced back directly to proto-Pentecostal revivals that occurred spontaneously among the Dalits throughout India in the second half of the nineteenth and the early twentieth centuries. In these revivals, Indian believers experienced charismatic manifestations. However, they could not fully grasp the work of the Holy Spirit in their midst due to a lack of scriptural teaching on the matter. During the first stage, Aroolappen and Azariah made a significant contribution to the religious awakening among the Dalits. Later, with the arrival of Western Pentecostal missionaries, the Indian Christians were introduced to the doctrine of the baptism of the Holy Spirit and were taught that the charismatic manifestations were the result of being baptized in the Holy Spirit. Cook worked in the second period with prominent Dalit leaders Matthai and Yohannan, who contributed immensely to the growth of Indian Pentecostalism in its early years. During the third stage, Indian leaders started their own indigenous denominations based on the doctrine of Holy Spirit baptism. They included the Indian Pentecostal Church, founded by Abraham, Samuel, and Cheriyan (former Syrian Christians), and the Ceylon Pentecostal Mission, founded by Paul (Ramankutty), who played a significant role in the lives and ministry of the early IPC leaders.

Notes

[1] The 1857-1858 revival began in Hamilton, Ontario, Canada, where Phoebe Palmer was conducting meetings on the Higher Life. It soon spread throughout

North America and impacted the urban cities of the North. The revival broke out in spontaneous prayer meetings wherever it appeared. Holiness teaching was emphasized in these prayer meetings which transcended denominational barriers, just like Palmer's Tuesday Meetings. The revival quickly spread to England through American Holiness evangelists like James Caughey, Walter and Phoebe Palmer, and Charles Finney in 1859. The Holiness message took root throughout Europe because of this revival. D. William Faupel, *The Everlasting Gospel: The Significance of Eschatology in the Development of Pentecostal Thought* (London: Sheffield Academic Press, 1996), 70-72.

[2] G. H. Lang, ed., *The History and Diaries of an Indian Christian* (London: Thynne, 1939, 23-28, and 114-145. Cited in McGee, "Pentecostal Phenomena and Revivals in India: Implications for Indigenous Church Leadership," *International Bulletin of Missionary Research* 20 (July 1996): 113.

[3] Burgess, ed., *NIDPCM*, 118.

[4] Anthony Norris Groves, *Memoir of Anthony Norris Groves, Compiled Chiefly from His Journals and Letters*, (London: James Nisbet, 1869), 616. Cited in McGee, "Pentecostal Phenomena and Revivals in India: Implications for Indigenous Church Leadership," *International Bulletin of Missionary Research* 20 (July 1996): 113.

[5] Ashton Dibb, "The Revival in North Tinnevelly," *Church Missionary Record* 5 (August 1860): 178.

[6] One of the main doctrines espoused by most of the early Pentecostals was the imminent return of Christ. This had its roots in the teaching of John Nelson Darby, founder of the Plymouth Brethren, who based his view on 1 Thessalonians 4:16-17. Faupel, *The Everlasting Gospel: The Significance of Eschatology in the Development of Pentecostal Thought*, 29.

[7] Burgess, ed., *NIDPCM*, 119. Cited in A.C. George in "Pentecostal Beginnings in Travancore, South India," *Asian Journal of Pentecostal Studies* 4:2 (July 2001): 223.

[8] W.S. Hunt, *Anglican Church in Travancore and Cochin, 1816-1916* (Kottayam, Kerala: Church Missionary Society Press, 1920), 160-68. Cited in McGee, "Pentecostal Phenomena and Revivals in India: Implications for Indigenous Church Leadership," *International Bulletin of Missionary Research* 20 (July 1996): 114.

[9] L. Sam, *Pastor A.C. Samuel: A Brief Biography* (Trivandrum: Bethel Assembly Publication, 1983), 10. Cited in A.C. George, "Pentecostal Beginnings in Travancore, South India," *Asian Journal of Pentecostal Studies* 4:2 (July 2001): 221.

[10] Howard A. Snyder, "Holiness Heritage: The Case of Pandita Ramabai," *Wesleyan Theological Journal* 40 (Fall 2005): 31.

[11] Ramabai, *A Testimony of Our Inexhaustible Treasure in Pandita Ramabai Through Her Own Words* (New Delhi: Oxford Press, 2000), 320.

[12] Ramabai, *A Testimony of Our Inexhaustible Treasure*, 320.

[13] Burgess, *NIDPCM*, 1018.

[14] Amritlal B. Shah, *Letters of Pandita Ramabai* (Bombay: Maharashtra State Board for Literature and Culture, 1977), xxxxi; 390f.

[15] *Apostolic Faith*, 1:3 (November 1906): 1.

[16] Helen S. Dyer, *Pandita Ramabai* (New York: Fleming H. Revell Company, 1900), 119.

[17] Ramabai, *Mukti Prayer Bell*, (September 1907): 11.

[18] The early Pentecostals adhered to the following doctrinal themes: justification, sanctification, healing, the Second Coming of Jesus Christ, and the baptism of the Holy Spirit. For the classical Pentecostal, these five cardinal doctrines constitute the

"Full Gospel." Faupel, *The Everlasting Gospel*, 28-30, See also: Donald Dayton, *Theological Roots of Pentecostalism* (Metuchen: Scarecrow Press, 1987), 30.

[19] Dyer, *Ramabai*, 119.

[20] Shah, *Letters of Pandita Ramabai*, 391.

[21] W. McDonald and John E. Searles, *The Life of Rev. John S. Inskip, President of the National Association for the Promotion of Holiness* (Salem: Allegheny Publications, 1986), 328-342.

[22] Padmini Sengupta, *Pandita Ramabai Saraswati: Her Life and Work* (Bombay: Asia Publishing Company, 1970), 232. See also: Nicol MacNicol, *What Liberates a Woman? The Story of Pandita Ramabai, A Builder of Modern India* (New Delhi: Nivedit Good Books, 1996), 142.

[23] McDonald and Searles, *The Life of Rev. John S. Inskip, President of the National Association for the Promotion of Holiness*, 329-341. Cited in Snyder, "Holiness Heritage: The Case of Pandita Ramabai," *Wesleyan Theological Journal* 20:2 (2005): 38. See also: McGee, "Latter Rain Falling in the East: Early Twentieth-Century Pentecostalism in India and the Debate over Speaking in Tongues," *Church History* 68:3 (1999): 651.

[24] Allan Anderson, "The Origins of Pentecostalism and Its Global Spread in the Early Twentieth Century," 18. Accessed 23 May 2006. Online: http://www.ocms.ac.uk/docs/Allan%20Anderson%20lectue20041005.pdf

[25] Orr, *Evangelical Awakenings in India: In the Early Twentieth Century*, 74-75.

[26] Orr, *Evangelical Awakenings in India: In the Early Twentieth Century*, 76.

[27] Orr, *Evangelical Awakenings in India: In the Early Twentieth Century*, 79.

[28] William A. Stanton, *The Awakening of India: Forty Years Among the Telugus* (Portland: Falmouth Publishing House, 1950), 63-64.

[29] Orr, *Evangelical Awakenings in India: In the Early Twentieth Century*, 85.

[30] Rufus Anderson, *History of the Mission of the American Board of Commissioners for Foreign Mission in India* (Boston: Congregational Publishing Society, 1874), 380.

[31] Carol Graham, *Azariah of Dornakal* (Delhi: ISPCK, 1972), 92-103. Cited in Joseph Raju Kothapalli, "A Survey On the Origin and Growth of Dornakal Diocese of the Church of South India with Respect to its Expansion in the District of Khammam" (masters thesis, COTR Seminary, 2001), 38.

[32] Sherwood Eddy, *Pathfinders of the World Missionary Crusade* (New York: Abingdon-Cokesbury Press, 1945), p. 153. Cited in Joseph Raju "A Survey On the Origin and Growth of Dornakal Diocese of the Church of South India with Respect to its Expansion in the District of Khammam," 40.

[33] V.V. Thomas, *Dalit Pentecostalism: Spirituality of the Empowered Poor* (Bangalore: Asian Trading Corporation, 2008), 235.

[34] Thomas, *Dalit Pentecostalism: Spirituality of the Empowered Poor*, 133.

[35] George Berg, "Baptized with the Holy Ghost," in *The Apostolic Faith* (December 1906): 3.

[36] Thomas Barrett was invited by a pastor in Connoor, Tamil Nadu, and he conducted revival meetings there where Bouncil and Winkle received the baptism of the Holy Spirit. They left the Brethren movement and joined the Pentecostal movement. Bouncil had the gift of healing which she used in the ministry. It helped the growth of their missionary activities. She and Winkle worked together with Berg in central Travancore for some time. Because of her work, groups of believers were filled with the Holy Spirit in various places in South Travancore, including Paraneeyam, Eyeranipuram, Planthoppu and Kulchal. Her work was extended to the

Tiruneleveli and Shenkottal districts of the Tamil Nadu. Matthew, "A Study in the History of the Pentecostal Movement in South India," 39.

37 Matthew, "A Study in the History of the Pentecostal Movement in South India," 37-40.

38 George, "The Growth of the Pentecostal Churches in South India," 13.

39 Mary W. Chapman, *Pentecostal Evangel* (December 16, 1916): 2.

40 John H. Burgess, "South India—John and Bernice Burgess, 11-18-80"

41 Pothen, "The India Pentecostal Church of God and Its Contribution to Church Growth," 14.

42 Information on Susan Rice Chester and Martha Kucera was taken from the files of the World Missions office of the AG in Springfield, Missouri, USA. Cited in Thomas, *Dalit Pentecostalism: Spirituality of the Empowered Poor*, 196-197.

43 Gary B. McGee, *People of the Spirit: The Assemblies of God* (Springfield: Gospel Publishing House, 2004), 491.

44 Thomas, *Dalit Pentecostalism: Spirituality of the Empowered Poor*, 193. Thomas points out that before high caste-minded Syrians came into Pentecostalism, the economically poor Syrians and Dalits maintained a 'brotherly' attitude toward one another in the movement's early days. Both the Dalits (majority group) and the poor Syrians (minority group) were able to sit and eat and fellowship together. However, it did not last very long, similar to the situation of racial and social unity which originally prevailed at Azusa between the Blacks and the Whites that also did not last, although William Seymour had hoped it would.

45 Thomas, *Dalit Pentecostalism: Spirituality of the Empowered Poor*, 207.

46 George Oommen, "Growth of Pentecostalism in Central Kerala from 1921-47: A Paradigm for Pentecostal Growth of Churches in North India," *Indian Church History Review* 35:2 (December 2001): 132-133.

47 Bergunder, *The South Indian Pentecostal Movement in the Twentieth Century*, 30.

48 T.S. Samuel Kutty, *The Place and Contributions of Dalits in Select Pentecostal Churches in India* (Delhi: ISPCK, 2000), 64.

49 Oommen, "Growth of Pentecostalism in Central Kerala from 1921-47: A Paradigm for Pentecostal Growth of Churches in North India," *Indian Church History Review* 35:2 (December 2001): 138.

50 B. Sobhanan, ed. *A History of the Christian Mission in South India* (Thiruvananthapuram: Kerala Historical Society, 1996), 191-193.

51 In the early 2000s, the Pentecostal Mission had 848 churches worldwide, including Australia, Papua New Guinea, Trinidad, Tobago, Mexico, Colombia, the Middle East, Kenya, Seychelles, Canada, the USA, the UK, France, Switzerland, Malaysia, Singapore, Nepal and India (708 branches there) with 3,984 full-time workers under the leadership of C.K. Lazarus. Hedlund, *Christianity is Indian: The Emergence of an Indigenous Community*, 433-434.

52 The Indian Pentecostal Church of God has an estimated 4000 churches, with 3,491 full-time ministers, spread throughout not only India but also other countries, including Australia, the USA, and the Middle East.

53 Michael Bergunder, "Constructing Indian Pentecostalism: On Issues of Methodology and Representation" in Allan Anderson, ed., *Asian and Pentecostal: The Charismatic Face of Christianity in Asia* (Baguio City: Regnum Books International, 2005), 193.

⁵⁴ Paulson Pulikottil, "As East and West Met in God's Own Country: Encounter of Western Pentecostalism with Native Pentecostalism in Kerala," 8. Accessed November 23, 2006. Online: http://www.pctii.org/cyberj/cyberj10/paulson.html.

⁵⁵ Pulikottil, "As East and West Met in God's Own Country," 9.

⁵⁶ Pulikottil, "As East and West Met in God's Own Country," 8.

⁵⁷ Robert F. Cook, *Half a Century of Divine Leading: 37 Years of Apostolic Achievements in South India*, 100. Cited in Kutty, *The Place and Contributions of Dalits in Select Pentecostal Churches in India*, 74.

⁵⁸ Cook, *Half a Century of Divine Leading*, 120-121. Cited in Kutty, *The Place and Contributions of Dalits in Select Pentecostal Churches in India*, 77.

⁵⁹ *Hand Book: The Indian Pentecostal Church of God* (Kumbanad: IPC General Council Office, 1999), 4-6.

⁶⁰ Pulikottil, "As East and West Met in God's Own Country," 3.

⁶¹ Habel Varghese, *K.E. Abraham: An Apostle From Modern India* (Tiruvalla: Rhema Publishers International, 2000), 33. However, some sources (including Michael Bergunder and Paulson Pulikottil) cite that K.E. Abraham received the baptism of the Holy Spirit on April 22, 1923. But even if Abraham was baptized in the Holy Spirit and became a Pentecostal in 1923, one still can argue that the Ceylon Pentecostal Church was started before the formation of the South Indian Pentecostal Church. The Ceylon Pentecostal Church was formed in 1923 and the South Indian Pentecostal Church in 1924. Each was officially registered as an organization in 1924 and 1933 respectively. Hence, the CPM must be considered the first indigenous Pentecostal denomination in British India.

⁶² Matthew, "A Study in the History of the Pentecostal Movement in South India," 66.

⁶³ C.V. Cheriyan, *A History of Christianity in Kerala: From the Mission of St. Thomas to the Arrival of Vasco Da Gama, A.D 52-1498* (Kottayam: the CMS Press, 1973), 2.

⁶⁴ Cheriyan, *A History of Christianity in Kerala*, 6.

⁶⁵ Herman D'Souza, *In the Steps of St. Thomas* (Madras: The Associated Printers Limited., 1952), 34.

⁶⁶ A. E. Medlycott, *India and The Apostle Thomas: An Inquiry, With a Critical Analysis of the Act A Thomae* (London: David Nutt, 1905), 1-3, and 13.

⁶⁷ "Peter indeed may have belonged to Judaea; but what had Paul in common with gentiles, Luke with Achaia, Andrew with Epirus, John with Ephesus, Thomas with India, Mark with Italy?" Gregory Nazianzen, *Contra Arianos Et de Seipso Oratio* 23.11.

⁶⁸ V. Titus Varghese, *Glimpses of the History of the Christian Churches in India* (Madras: The Christian Literature Society, 1983), 10.

⁶⁹ The Syrian Church consists of two distinct groups: the "Jacobite Syrian Church" (also known as the "Syrian Orthodox Church") and the reformed group, the "Mar Thoma Church" (also known as the "St. Thomas Church"). In 1843, Mar Matthew Athanasius, nephew of Abraham Malpan, was appointed the new Metropolitan (head) of the Jacobite Syrian Church by the Patriarch Elias; however, the Metropolitan presiding at that time, Dionysius IV (who was consecrated by Mar Philoxenus of Thozhiyoor), was not willing to vacate the See. In 1852, Athanasius was finally recognized as the legitimate Metropolitan by the Travancore State Government. In 1865, Jacobite priest Joseph Kathanar (who took the title of Mar Dionysius V) was appointed the Metropolitan by the Patriarch, who vigorously fought to oust Athanasius. The power struggle continued between the two Metropolitans until the latter's death in 1877, when a split occurred in the Jacobite Syrian Church. His cousin, Mar

Thomas Athanasius, became his successor, and under his leadership a group separated officially from the Jacobite Syrian Church and formed the Mar Thoma Church. C.P. Matthew and M.M. Thomas, *The Indian Churches of Saint Thomas* (Delhi: DJVP/ISPCK, 2006), 85-92.

[70] Varghese, "Reformation Brings Revival," 99.

[71] K.E. Abraham, *A Humble Servant of Jesus Christ: Autobiography of Pastor K.E. Abraham* (Kumbanadu: K.E. Abraham Foundation, 1983), 66-67.

[72] Varghese, "Reformation Brings Revival," 95-98.

[73] Paulson Pulikottil, "Emergence of Indian Pentecostalism," *Dharma Deepika* 6:2 (December 2002): 52.

[74] Hedlund, *Christianity is Indian*, 429-431.

[75] K.E. Abraham, *Yesuchristhuvinte Eliya Dasan* (Kumbanadu: Pentecostal Young People's Association, 1965), 179-180. Cited in Varghese, "Reformation Brings Revival," 168. See also: Matthew "A Study in the History of the Pentecostal Movement in South India," 66.

[76] Matthew Samuel Plathaneth, *Autobiography of Apostle P.M. Samuel* (Vijayawada: Zion Printing House, 1980), 9-10.

which they registered later with the Indian government at Eluru in Andhra Pradesh (1935).

Events that Led to the Formation of the IPC in Andhra Pradesh

Samuel felt a call to go to Andhra Pradesh while attending a special fasting and prayer meeting (1932).

> In the month of August, fasting and prayers were organized in Travancore. Pastor K.E. Abraham and others were in prayer. Before these meetings, I had received an invitation from Ceylon. They booked a ticket for me and I was about to start. Two days passed away. On the third day, God called me by my name, "Samuel, Samuel, go to Andhra Pradesh and preach the Pentecostal truth."[2]

As Samuel was contemplating his call to Andhra Pradesh, he unexpectedly received an invitation from Thullimalli Peter Gurupadam, a Dalit from Machilipatnam (Bandaru), urging him to come to Andhra Pradesh.

> I saw a post-man coming to me. He gave me a letter and I opened it and knew that it was from Brother Gurupadam, Machilipatnam, Andhra Pradesh. Once we met in Madras during conventions. Bro. Gurupadam compelled me in his letter to go to Machilipatnam. In that letter I read, 'You have spread the Pentecostal truth in the regions of Tamilnadu and Kerala. But Andhra Pradesh is totally neglected.' At last I decided to go to Andhra Pradesh as per the command of God and He sent a messenger, Mr. Gurupadam.[3]

That same year, Samuel left Travancore for Machilipatnam. The church at Travancore collected money for his ticket, but he only received enough to reach the Madras Central Railway Station. While he was walking on the platform there, not knowing what to do, a person from Karnataka suddenly came and took him to a nearby restaurant. After Samuel enjoyed a nice dinner, they returned to the station where the train for Machilipatnam was already on the platform. But Samuel had no ticket and no money to purchase one. When the train was about to move, he boldly jumped onto the train by faith. The same person who took him to the restaurant rushed to him and placed a ticket in his hand, along with some money, as the train began to leave.

Samuel reached Machilipatnam and stayed with Gurupadam. He participated in gospel meetings Gurupadam arranged and later traveled to Gudivada, Eluru, and other surrounding villages to conduct revival meetings. Samuel and R. Coal started preaching the Pentecostal message in Eluru. According to Pachigalla Lazarus Paramjyothi (P.L. Paramjyothi), Samuel left Andhra Pradesh (1932) after he preached the Pentecostal message in various churches. Then he returned to Andhra Pradesh (1934) to continue his work.

Later Abraham and Poozhicalayil Thomas Chacko (P.T. Chacko) reached Eluru (1935) after their preaching tour in North India and met Samuel, who had just returned from his tour of Tamilnadu. They registered an organization called "The Indian Pentecostal Church of God" with the Government of India under the Societies Act XXI of 1860, registration number 9/1935-1936 (December 9, 1935).[4] Samuel, Abraham, and Chacko were assisted in the registration process by Bathina Samuel Lukeson (B.S. Lukeson), a clerk in the registrar's office, and Kancherla Reuben John, a superintendent in the Irrigation Department, and all three shared the registration expenses. Both Lukeson and John were Dalits from Eluru. Samuel was chosen to be the president, Cheriyan, vice-president, and Chacko, secretary.[5] Samuel, therefore, co-founded the IPC, along with Abraham, and this was the genesis of the Indian Pentecostal Church of God denomination in India. Samuel writes in his autobiography:

> I (*P.M. Samuel*) was ordained by God as His apostle and I was sent on His service to Tamilnadu in 1930. God spoke to me and ordered me to spread the gospel in the east side where there were few Christian churches. Pastor *K.E. Abraham* was working in the midst of people who speak Malayalam (Kerala). Pastor *Cheriyan* was sent to the Kannada-speaking people. *We started* the Indian Pentecostal Church of God in 1934 and we gave this new name out of great enthusiasm for the revival and glory of our Lord. It was registered in 1935. Before registration, it was known as the Indian Pentecostal Church of South India (italics mine).[6]

Chacko later moved to Eluru with his family (1936) and worked with Samuel. The following year Samuel purchased a building in Eluru (1937) with funds received by Cheriyan and Abraham from Swedish believers when they went to Sweden on a mission trip. Samuel named the church the "Indian Pentecostal Church of God," making it the first church of the IPC. This church in Eluru became the mother church to all other IPC churches, both in India and other parts of the world.

Nevertheless, Eluru never became the national headquarters of the IPC, despite the fact that the denomination was officially started and registered there among the Telugus in the state of Andhra Pradesh. Regional feelings, power struggles, church politics, and the dominance of the Keralites interfered. Instead, Kumbanadu, in the state of Kerala, became the national headquarters of the IPC, because the founders of the IPC were from Kerala. Abraham had a reputation among a majority of IPC pastors of being dictatorial and authoritative in his leadership. Quarrels and disagreements occurred between Samuel, Abraham and Cheriyan.[7] Consequently, Samuel settled in Vijayawada (1940), about sixty kilometers from Eluru, and made it the state headquarters for the IPC in Andhra Pradesh.

Despite the later location of its headquarters, the IPC officially began in Eluru with one church, and in the early 2000s it had nearly 4,000 churches in India and abroad, including the Gulf countries, the United States, Canada, and Australia. In the state of Andhra Pradesh alone, the IPC had 660 churches with nearly 86,000 believers.[8] In spite of the deaths of first and second generation leaders, the IPC in Andhra Pradesh still experiences numerical growth. A new church is being pioneered about every six days.[9]

The popular opinion in the IPC is that P.M. Samuel was the first to bring the Pentecostal message to Andhra Pradesh. Although it cannot be denied that he was the founder of the IPC in Andhra Pradesh, he was not the first one to introduce Pentecostalism there. Lam Jeevaratnam, a Dalit from Andhra Pradesh, pioneered the Andhra Pentecostal movement when he began his Pentecostal work in the state (1926) before Samuel came there initially (1932).[10] Jeevaratnam was born in Medukonduru (February 27, 1890). His parents, Samuel and Harriet, belonged to the Lutheran Church. His father was a senior pastor of the Lutheran Church in Guntur. Jeevaratnam lost both his father and mother at an early age. He was enrolled in the United Lutheran Christian Mission Boarding School. In the seventh grade, his skill in drawing was noticed by the school warden who encouraged him to develop it. He completed two years of drawing classes in Madras after which he was employed as a drawing teacher by a Baptist Mission high school in Nellore. He married Kanaka Rathnam from the Canadian Baptist Mission (February, 13, 1914). Jeevaratnam's unusual drawing skills enabled him to draw with both hands simultaneously, and also with his nose, mouth and toes. He gave a performance of his artistic talent before the Deccan Maharajah and the Prince of Wales (1920). Indian princes soon learned of his talent and encouraged him to go to England. He had the opportunity to present his artistic talent before King George V and Queen Mary at Buckingham Palace.[11] During his twenty-five minute audience with the King, Jeevaratnam drew the portraits of both the King and the Queen on a small piece of paper and presented it to His Majesty at the end of the interview. Both George and Mary were astonished at his extraordinary artistic drawing talent.

Jeevaratnam received an offer of approximately 50 pounds a week from Manhattan, New York, to paint for Broadway. In the meantime, he came across an evangelistic meeting of the British Assemblies of God in Leeds where he was converted to Christ (1925). He later went to Hampstead Bible School in London, where he received the baptism of the Holy Spirit. He left England and returned to India (1926). Jeevaratham began a Pentecostal Church in Gudivada, itinerated as a healing evangelist throughout India, and traveled extensively in Europe and the United States (1937 to 1938, 1949 to 1950). He founded the Eastern Full Gospel Mission (1935). Jeevaratnam established a high school and childrens' home to provide an education for Dalit children. He also planted about fifty churches in Andhra Pradesh. Upon his demise (March 17, 1960), his children were disinterested in ministry. They handed over the churches he had established to various denominations, including the Salvation Army, the Baptists, the Lutherans, and independent Pentecostal organizations. They kept the Gudivada church. Jeevaratnam's eldest daughter-in-law, Victoria, watched over that church until she passed away. Currently, his granddaughter, Lam Pramada, is the pastor of the church.

Lester Sumrall reported that, "In Jeevaratnam's meetings, the dumb spoke, the ears of the deaf were opened, the lame walked, severe internal pains vanished, and the blind received their sight."[12] In his book, *Pioneers of Faith*, he further states that Jeevaratnam had "an unusual discernment of the presence of demon power and the knowledge of how to deal with it. In India, he was often called, 'Lam, the devil chaser,' because he stayed with his calling."

One of the healings he performed in his ministry included that of Neelam Sundaramma, sister of Gurupadam's wife, who was very sick. Jeevaratnam went to Machilipatnam to pray for her. He requested a glass of water and prayed that it would turn into the blood of Jesus. While he was praying, Dutt, the oldest son of Gurupadam, did not close his eyes because he was skeptical. Suddenly he saw a drop of blood fall into the glass and the water turned red. Jeevaratnam gave the water to Sundaramma and she was healed instantly. Before he gave it to her, Dutt asked him to leave a little bit of the water for him. Jeevaratnam did so and Dutt drank it to satisfy his curiosity.[13]

Jeevaratnam did an exorcism on an Anglo-Indian lady who was brought to him. She was very beautiful but was possessed by evil spirits. A young man wanted to marry her, but when he could not get her, he performed black magic against her. Then no one was able to control her. She would run away from Jeevaratnam and would scream and shout and climb trees. He would command her to come down. Finally he drew a circle and asked her to stay within it, which she did for three days. If she accidentally touched the line, she would scream that she was burning. The third day Jeevaratnam prayed and cast the demons out of her. He later wrote two booklets on exorcism: "The Divine Healing" and "Concerning the Demons."

Not only Jeevaratnam, but also Gurupadam, K. Mann Singh, and V.R. Egbert were instrumental in sharing the Pentecostal faith in Andhra Pradesh before the arrival of Samuel there. However, their efforts in spreading the Pentecostal faith were overshadowed by Samuel's aggressive church planting efforts. The next person who significantly promoted the Pentecostal faith in Andhra Pradesh after Jeevaratnam was Gurupadam. He was born in Dandiganipudi (1895) near Gudivada to a Dalit family. His father, Sathyanandam, and his mother, Isabel, belonged to the CSI Church. Gurupadam lost his father at an early age. His mother came to Machilipatnam and settled in Ananda Pet. Gurupadam graduated from Noble High School and later obtained a B.A. degree from Andhra Christian College in Guntur. Upon completion of his education, he obtained employment as a clerk in the Cooperative Department (Agriculture). He married Alice Rathnam, who worked as a teacher in Lady Ampthill High School in Machilipatnam. Gurupadam owned five acres of land in Ananda Pet. He conducted Pentecostal meetings there, inviting preachers such as Mann Singh, Murugeshan, and Jeevaratnam. He promoted the Pentecostal faith, including the baptism of the Holy Spirit and speaking in tongues, through these meetings.

One time Kartar Singh (a disciple of Sadhu Sunder Singh) preached in the meetings that Gurupadam had arranged (1920s). People in the meeting were filled with the Holy Spirit and spoke in other tongues. A mob from the CSI background came and threw stones at them, thus disturbing the meeting. The mob considered the manifestations in the meetings to be a nuisance and nonsense, since they were not accustomed to the concept of Spirit baptism. They also threw stones at Gurupadam's house. Kartar Singh later took Gurupadam through Ananda Pet, pointing out certain houses to him, and he told him that God was going to pour out judgment on those houses. They were the homes of the troublemakers who threw the stones. Subsequent to Singh's pronouncement, the houses were laid in ruins and still remain in desolate condition, filled with thistles and bushes.[14]

Gurupadam belonged to the CSI but he promoted the Pentecostal faith in Andhra Pradesh through the Pentecostal meetings he conducted in Machilipatnam. He was consequently excommunicated from the CSI, but the CSI leadership later restored him to their fold. Gurupadam translated and published Oral Roberts' magazine "Abundant Life" (*Samrudhi Jeevam*) in Telugu, and continued to do so until his death. His daughter, Nanduri Indira Vandanam, then continued the publication. He also translated books written by Roberts, including his autobiography, into Telugu. Prior to Samuel's arrival, Jeevaratnam, Gurupadam and Mann Singh worked as a team promoting the Pentecostal faith. Moreover, when Samuel came to Andhra Pradesh (1932), Gurupadam provided accommodations and took care of his basic needs.

Gurupadam introduced Samuel to Jeevaratnam since they were related (Gurupadam's daughter Victoria married Rabel Jeeva, Jeevaratnam's oldest son). Samuel worked with these men for some time. He then went to conduct Pentecostal meetings in Eluru, along with Jeevaratnam. After he preached in various places, Samuel left Andhra Pradesh (1932), and Murugeshan came later and worked with Mann Singh, Gurupadam, and Jeevaratnam. Some have suggested that Murugeshan visited the state of Andhra Pradesh to preach in Mann Singh's church and at the Pentecostal meetings Gurupadam conducted even before Samuel came there.[15] Mann Singh often received Pentecostal preachers from Tamilnadu and sent them to Gurupadam for lodging and hospitality and also to preach at his conventions. Whenever preachers visited Gurupadam, he sent them to Mann Singh's church as speakers, since they had become close friends.

Mann Singh was born in Vellore in Tamilnadu and served in the military during the First World War. His wife, Veda Navamani, studied in a Christian medical school in Vellore and graduated with a LMP (Licensed Medical Practitioner) degree. Mann Singh met her in a prayer meeting and they soon married (1924). Navamani practiced medicine in Gudiattram for a while after they married. She later moved to Andhra Pradesh to work in the Canadian Baptist Mission hospital in Vuyyuru (1925). Two influential people in Machilipatnam, Kasthuri Sitapathi Rao and Pattabhi Ramayya, convinced the Canadian Baptist Mission to bring Navamani to Machilipatnam to work in the Municipal Hospital. The couple then attended the CSI church.

Egbert, a Tamil Pentecostal preacher, came to Machilipatnam at the same time Jeevaratnam was preaching the Pentecostal message in Andhra Pradesh. Egbert worked with DeAlwis of the Ceylon Pentecostal Church, but he left the denomination because he disagreed with their doctrine of celibacy. When Egbert came to Machilipatnam, Govada Chandrahasan, a CSI believer, directed him to Mann Singh's house, since he was also from Tamilnadu. Mann Singh and his wife came to know the Pentecostal faith through him and were soon baptized in water by Egbert. Navamani had suffered from asthma since childhood. When Egbert prayed for her, she was healed (1930), but the asthma returned later. He advised Mann Singh to write to Smith Wigglesworth. Mann Singh wrote to England and received a prayer cloth from Wigglesworth, which he placed on his wife's chest and then he prayed. She never again suffered from asthma, according to Mann Singh's daughter, Merugu Annal Chandra Bai.

When Vedanayagam Samuel Azariah, bishop of the CSI church, learned that Mann Singh and his wife had been baptized by Egbert—a Pentecostal preacher—he threatened to excommunicate them. Mann Singh resigned his membership and left the CSI church. Before long, he started a Pentecostal church at Malakapatnam in Machilipatnam (1932). After his death, his wife looked after the church. Currently, his great-grandson, Peter Vijaya Pradeep, is the pastor of the church.

Therefore, it was Jeevaratnam, Gurupadam, Egbert, Mann Singh, and Murugeshan who pioneered Pentecostalism in Andhra Pradesh before P.M. Samuel arrived there. The first Pentecostal church was started in Gudivada by Jeevaratnam, and he also started other Pentecostal churches in Andhra. Mann Singh started a Pentecostal church in Machilipatnam, and Murugeshan started churches in Eluru, Vijayawada, Gudivada, and Machilipatnam.

Growth of the IPC and Key Contributors to its Growth

The IPC began to grow by the efforts of Samuel. Dalit pastors Pachigalla Lazarus Paramjyothi (P.L. Paramjyothi), Kallepu Rajarathnam David (K.R. David), Adidala Sundaram Paul (A.S. Paul), Korati George Paul (K.G. Paul), Kanumala Peturu Devasahayam (K.P. Devasahayam), Geddam Rathnam Purushotham (G.R. Purushotham), Komanapalli Sudarsanam Joseph (K.S. Joseph), Chatla Sudarsanam (Ch. Sudarsanam), Bathina Samuel Lukeson (B.S. Lukeson), Taragam Sathyavedam Sasthry (T.S. Sasthry), and others, contributed to the growth of the IPC in addition to Samuel. The Dalit pastors' selfless and sacrificial living, unwavering faith in and reliance on God for daily needs, and endurance of local opposition from both Hindus and mainline churches were all factors that contributed strongly to the growth of the IPC. Countless Dalits put everything they had on the line, while many even risked their lives to spread the Pentecostal faith and expand the IPC's work. A brief account of the efforts and contributions of a select few Dalit IPC pastors will serve as illustrations of their hard work and devotion.

Work of the IPC in the Eluru Area. Arava Manoharam's wife, Alisamma, fell seriously ill (1932) and consulted many doctors for healing, but without success. Local healing evangelist Jeevaratnam came to Eluru from Gudivada along with Samuel and prayed for her healing. She was miraculously cured and recovered not long afterward. Jeevaratnam also conducted healing meetings in Eluru at that time where he preached the Pentecostal message. Samuel, R. Coal, and Sadhu Paul stayed in Eluru for two more weeks, where Samuel preached on the baptism of the Holy Spirit. After his brief stay in Andhra Pradesh (1932), Samuel went back to Kerala.

Murugeshan, a Tamil Pentecostal preacher, came to Andhra Pradesh (1933) and preached the Pentecostal message of repentance, new birth, water baptism, and the baptism of the Holy Spirit with speaking in other tongues. He traveled to various places (Vijayawada, Machilipatnam, Gudivada, and Eluru) where he started small house churches, calling them "Apostolic Faith Bands" (groups) before Samuel planted the IPC churches in Andhra Pradesh.[16] These bands worked with Samuel and later were merged into the IPC after Murugeshan left the State. When Murugeshan came to Eluru, many Dalits, including Manoharam and his wife, Kancherla Rushamma (wife of Kancherla Reuben John or K.R. John), Pasala Prakasam and his wife, Saramma, Battu Kanakadri, Dondapati Andrews and Alugulu Yosepu (Joseph) responded to Murugeshan's message and became his followers. This became the first Pentecostal church in Eluru.[17]

When Samuel came to Eluru for the second time (1935), and saw the small band of believers led by Murugeshan, conflict arose between them. Both claimed to be the founder of the Pentecostal church in Eluru, but Samuel managed to prevail due to his authoritarian leadership style. Murugeshan did not desire to divide the infant church, so he entrusted his followers to Samuel and returned to Madras.

Thomson Mathew wrote that a Pentecostal congregation was already in Eluru when Samuel came there again (1935) as a result of the work of Murugeshan.[18] The origin of the first Pentecostal church in Eluru should be attributed to the efforts of Murugeshan. However, the genesis of Pentecostalism in Andhra Pradesh must be credited to Jeevaratnam. He was the earliest pioneer of Pentecostal work in the State, rather than Samuel. It was Samuel's zeal for evangelism and church planting that expanded the Pentecostal work throughout Andhra Pradesh.

The small congregation Samuel took over from Murugeshan began to conduct Sunday services in a rented house under the banner of the Indian Pentecostal Church. Chacko was appointed pastor of this Eluru IPC church (1936). Then K.E. Abraham went on a missionary trip to Sweden and received contributions for the church (1937). Upon his return, he and Samuel purchased the rented house where the services were being conducted.[19]

Chacko left for Hyderabad to look after the IPC work there (1940). He was succeeded first by C.P. Thomas, then C.A. Matthews (from Kerala), and then Potti Rajarathnam, a Dalit (1943 to 1950). Rajarathnam moved to Bhimavaram to pioneer an IPC church (1950). The same year Lukeson (also a Dalit, and the one who had been instrumental in registering the IPC with the state of Andhra Pradesh) was appointed pastor of the growing Eluru congregation. Lukeson's parents, Joseph and Sathyavani, belonged to the Lutheran Church. He graduated from high school in Rajahmundry and completed a Bachelor of Arts degree in Eluru. Before Lukeson joined the IPC, he worked as sub-registrar in various places, including Bhimavaram, Narsapuram, and Eluru. After he received a call to ministry, he resigned from his job and later became pastor of the IPC church in Eluru (1950).[20] When he became the pastor, Lukeson supported his fellow pastors with rice and money. He owned seven acres of land in Vatluru near Eluru and he would use the produce from his land to help the IPC pastors. Lukeson would give ten kilograms of rice along with five rupees per month to all the IPC pastors working under him in the Eluru area. Samuel also received financial assistance from Lukeson whenever he visited Eluru. When he went abroad for the first time, Lukeson financed his trip.[21]

Under Lukeson's leadership, the elders of the church passed a resolution to construct a permanent church building. One Sunday, Lukeson challenged believers with the importance of building a church through his inspired message on "Noah: His Sacrifice on Building the Ark" from Genesis 6:22. Believers then pledged money for construction. Pasala Saramma contributed five rupees and Kancherla Rushamma contributed ten. Kancherla Vivekavathi Johnamma sold her gold ornaments worth thousands of rupees and donated the money for the project. K.R. John also contributed 2000 rupees and P. Deevenamma gave 135 rupees, while Kuntam Rajamma (wife of Kuntam Sathyadas) gave eighty-five. As a result, the IPC church at Eluru under Dalit Pastor Lukeson's leadership was completed (1956) with the financial support of the local congregation and some Hindus for the glory of God.[22] After many years of faithful service to the IPC, Lukeson left because of conflict with church elders. He moved to Tadepalligudem (1960)[23] and later joined the newly-formed WME (1961). Before he left the IPC church at Eluru, Lukeson dropped a clay pot on the floor during the Eluru general convention and prophesied that the IPC work would be broken into pieces like the pot.[24]

Then, Taragam Sathyavedam Sasthry became an interim pastor. However, the local church elders learned that he had forged an alliance with John Douglas, Sr., which forced him to leave his pastorate. This conflict caused the split in the Eluru IPC church. Many who were loyal to Sasthry followed him and formed a new congregation under the WME.

After Sasthry joined the WME, Devasahayam, a Dalit from the Mala caste, became pastor of the IPC. The IPC experienced both numerical and spiritual growth under his leadership. His contribution to the Andhra IPC was invaluable. Devasahayam was born (May 15, 1934) in the village of Bhogapuram, West Godavari District, Andhra Pradesh. His parents, Kanumala Peturu and Lijamma, belonged to the Salvation Army denomination. Devasahayam was stricken with chickenpox as a teenager and lay on his deathbed (1949), where he saw a vision of the cross (like Sadhu Sunder Singh had) at three in the morning (April 20). He was instantly healed and became a Christian the same day. He was baptized in water at the IPC General Convention in Vijayawada (1950).[25]

After obtaining ministerial training at Zion Bible School (1950 to 1953) under Samuel, Paramjyothi, Chacko, David, Thottil K. Thomas (T.K. Thomas), A.S. Paul, and Jannu Joshua (J. Joshua), Devasahayam was sent by Lukeson to work in a village (1953) near Tadepalligudem. Two years later, Lukeson sent him to Nidadavole (1955) to pioneer the IPC work. Devasahayam and his wife Sanjeevamma traveled to many villages, including Korumamidi, Timmarajupalem, Jagannadhapuram, Purushothapalli, Veluvennu, Kannur, and Nandamuru, preaching the Pentecostal faith tirelessly. They received little support from others except Kati Das (brother in-law of Devasahayam), Marlapudi Samuel and his family who helped immensely in their efforts to spread the Gospel in these villages. Devasahayam and Sanjeevamma endured many hardships, including humiliation, ridicule, beatings, and financial problems for the sake of the gospel and to promote the Pentecostal faith in Nidadavole and surrounding villages. Many days they went without food and lived in a small hut, sleeping on the floor without a mat.

When Sasthry left the IPC church at Eluru, the elders of the church, Kuntam Sathyadas, Kancherla Moody, Podilaku Mark, and Maru Kondayya, went to Nidadavole and convinced Devasahayam to come to Eluru.[26] He moved there (1963) and remained senior pastor until his death. He suffered opposition and many financial difficulties in the ministry in Eluru also. For example, Devasahayam and Chikkala Lazarus went to the village of Kovvali to conduct a gospel meeting in Gandhi Nagar (1970). After the meeting, Hindus tried to kill them by poisoning their food. Lazarus died on his way to Eluru, but Devasahayam survived following the prayers of many believers.[27]

Recognizing Devasahayam's leadership skills and passion for lost souls, Samuel appointed him General Secretary of the IPC in Andhra Pradesh (1975), a position he held until he was elected Vice-President by the IPC Andhra State Council (1993). He served in that capacity until 1996. Then he was unanimously elected national Vice-President in Kumbanadu (September 1996). He was known as a great leader, pastor, speaker, and teacher. Devasahayam taught various subjects, including "Survey of the Bible," "Church History," and "The Book of Acts" at Zion Bible School (1975 to 1996). He trained hundreds of students and sent scores of graduates of the college to pioneer new churches in Eluru and other areas. He also published a book in Telugu, *Sangha Charithra* (History of the Church, 1985). Devasahayam was one of the most sought-after speakers for the IPC annual church

church conventions throughout Andhra Pradesh. He served forty-six years in various capacities in the IPC by the time he died (December 22, 1996).[28]

Work of the IPC in the Rajahmundry Area. The beginning of the work of the Andhra IPC in Rajahmundry was the direct result of the efforts of Lukeson, who wanted the Pentecostal faith to spread to other places. He and his brother, Baktan Samuel, arranged meetings in Rajahmundry (1932) with help from their teacher friend, Mungamuri Devadas. Devadas later founded another indigenous charismatic movement called "The Bible Mission." He was born (1875) to Dalits Mungamuri Jonah and Sathyavathamma in the village of Jegurapad (about ten miles east of Rajahmundry). He belonged to the Evangelical Lutheran Church and was very much influenced by Sundar Singh. Devadas became a celibate (sadhu) like Singh, remaining so until death. He was proficient in English and was an excellent translator, interpreting for Singh when he visited South India (1919). He taught in the Lutheran mission school and later in the seminary in Rajahmundry. While teaching there, Devadas attracted several young men to his revival meetings where he talked about visions and healing miracles.

At this time, Samuel happened to come to Rajahmundry to conduct a series of meetings on the baptism of the Holy Spirit (1932). He and Sadhu Paul preached in those meetings, which lasted several weeks. Many people confessed their sins and became Christians. In the first meeting, Lukeson and Paul received the baptism of the Holy Spirit with the initial evidence of speaking in other tongues.[29] Devadas helped to conduct these meetings, where he publicly acknowledged "that he was experiencing all these even from much earlier times."[30] He claimed to have experienced the baptism of the Holy Spirit decades before Samuel came to Andhra Pradesh. He had not revealed it because he feared expulsion from teaching and the Lutheran denomination. He mentioned his experience in a sermon delivered at an ordination service (1945): "I have received and am experiencing the full revelation and the complete presence of our Lord already since August 21, 1901, but did not reveal it to anyone."[31] Devadas then began to propagate his views more openly and boldly about dreams, visions, divine healing, and the baptism of the Holy Spirit after he attended the meetings of Samuel. As people became interested in Devadas' teachings, the Lutheran establishment expressed concerns about them and asked him to resign from his job in the Lutheran Church after several arguments and warnings. He resigned (February 1938) and then left the denomination when he was not permitted to participate in the Communion service (April 24, 1938) after having worked as a traveling evangelist for them for forty-six years. Before he resigned, Devadas claimed that God showed him a vision (January 31, 1938) in which the Lord wrote "The Bible Mission" in golden Telugu letters in the air in his room and asked him to resign from the Lutheran Mission.[32] He hesitated to resign because he was trying to bring revival in the Lutheran Church and did not want to found a new denomination. He was finally forced to resign a few months after the vision.

After Devadas left the Lutheran Church, he became an independent minister, teaching, preaching, and gathering followers. He established "The Bible Mission" (May 15, 1938) as God had shown him in the vision. He recalled a vision that a Western Pentecostal preacher once shared in an Eluru meeting. The preacher saw that God was going to raise up a "prophet like Moses" very soon in India. He said Devadas was chosen to spread "the Bible Mission."[33] It was registered at the District Registrar's office in Rajahmundry as the "India Bible Mission" under the Societies Act of 1860 (December 7, 1938), about three years after the IPC was registered at Eluru. Therefore, the Bible Mission is another indigenous Pentecostal and charismatic movement started by a Dalit from Andhra Pradesh. Devadas and Samuel labored together in the beginning. When Devadas founded his own denomination, Samuel cut ties with him, perhaps because he did not like the idea of a Dalit starting another indigenous Pentecostal denomination. He may have viewed the establishment of The Bible Mission as a threat to the IPC.

When American Lutheran missionary Ms. Targin was working at Dowleswaram, she heard of the Spirit's work among the Lutheran Churches in Rajahmundry and asked Samuel to conduct a revival meeting at her house (1932). Several women were touched in that meeting by the power of the Holy Spirit. Similar meetings were arranged in Dowleswaram for a week under Devadas' supervision. Soon the Lutheran churches, not only in Dowleswaram, but also in Samalkot, Nidadavole, Peddapuram, and Tadepalligudem, opened to the Pentecostal message and arranged meetings for Samuel. A number of people accepted the Pentecostal faith.

Lukeson and Tippalli Mrudhubhashini arranged a convention in Rajahmundry (1944) where Samuel, Chacko, Paramjyothi, David, and K.G. Paul preached, and hundreds were saved and received Spirit baptism. This was the beginning of the Andhra IPC Church at Rajahmundry. Lukeson led the infant church and Annamma Mammen, Rosamma, Kunjamma, Aleyamma, and Ludiamma from Kerala assisted in the growth of the church.[34] Later David was appointed pastor (1945). He was one of the most able and gifted Dalit leaders of the Andhra IPC, whose contributions were incalcuable.

David was born to Dalit parents Kallepu Ramaiah and Rajamanemma (March 25, 1917), in Tangutur, Nalgonda District of Andhra. He attended a mission boarding school in Janagama (1926) but was not interested in education. He left school and returned home, where he became a shepherd boy helping his father. He later returned to boarding school and continued his education (1934). After high school, he went to Hanumakonda and received training to become a doctor's assistant. Then he was hired as an inspector in the Warangal Municipal Corporation. Samuel went to Warangal with Paramjyothi (December 1938) to preach in gospel meetings hosted by Baptist churches. David heard the Pentecostal message for the first time there.[35]

On his way home from work, David stopped at the Warangal IPC church (January 14, 1939) which became the turning point in his life. A prayer meeting was going on and he had a powerful encounter with God, according to David. For eleven days he confessed his sins and wept before God, who spoke to him (January 25) saying, "My son, David! I have forgiven your sins. You will be my son from this day onward. Don't be afraid." Hearing these words brought him great joy and peace.[36]

David was baptized in water (February 17) and decided to become celibate and preach the gospel throughout India like Sunder Singh. After he was converted to Pentecostalism, he had a great change of heart. He returned the books he stole from the library when he was studying in the Baptist Mission School. Missionary Rutherford was so pleased with the change in David's life, he urged David to stay in the Baptist Church and do the work of the ministry. But David decided to work with the IPC instead.[37] His zeal for lost souls led him to spend time in street preaching and tract distribution with Paramjyothi after work each day. His family forced him to marry Leelamma, eldest daughter of Kothapalli Jonathan (March 15, 1940). David then resigned from his job and entered full-time ministry (January 18, 1941) and soon left for Vijayawada to work with Samuel. After a few months there, he was sent to Gandigunta (near Vuyyuru) to plant a church. There he went through hardships, financial difficulties, and opposition.

David later moved to the Eemani village in the Guntur District. Because of his tireless work, not only did the Pentecostal faith spread in the surrounding villages, but IPC churches were also established later in Sathenapalli, Dhonakonda, Vinukonda, Narsarao Pet, Tenali, Rapalle, Sajjavaripalem, and Pedapalem. Both David and his wife attended Zion Bible School after it was launched in Anthirvedipalem (1942). After he completed his training there, David returned to Eemani and continued his gospel work.

David moved from Eemani to Warangal to work with Thottil K. Thomas (T.K. Thomas) from Kerala (1943). He ministered there two years until he was sent to Rajahmundry (1945). He and his wife had no house to live in at the beginning, so they lived under the trees and on a school veranda. Many times, they spent days with no food. Mrudhubhashini, a medical doctor, used to provide them with rice and money. Based in Rajahmundry, David and his wife traveled to many surrounding villages to spread the Pentecostal truth, including: Katheru, Vootalanka, Konthamuru, Kolamuru, Gadala, Bommuru, Hakkumpet, Dowleswaram, Vemagiri, Rajavolu, Kondagunturu, Pasivedala, Chagallu, Sampadanagaram, Kovvuru, and Malakapalli. While pioneering these churches, they suffered immense poverty and hunger.[38] Despite the many difficulties, his ministry flourished and he established many congregations, including a church building in Pasivedala (1950), where the work had begun three years before (1947). He also built another church building in Rajahmundry (1953).

David was a great orator and a gifted writer. He was a frequent contributor to the "Gospel Illuminator" magazine and worked as an associate editor of the magazine (1947 to 1960). He was also editor-in-chief of the "Voice of World Missionary Evangelism" (1970 to 1977) and became editor of the

English magazine, "Ecclesia" (1975). He published many books in Telugu, including: *Chatusutra Suvartha* (The Fourfold Gospel, 1949) and *Yugamulu* (The Dispensations, 1951). He continued to publish various books (1956) including: *Parishudha Paulu* (Saint Paul), *Jeevajalamula Voota* (The Living Waters), *Jeeva Margamu* (The Way of Life), *Devuni Pilupu* (The Call of God), *Prasanga Manjari* (The Book of Sermons), *Prasnothari* (Questions and Answers), *Dhanya Jeevi* (The Blessed One), *Yooda Rajulu* (The Kings of Judah), and *Pandugalu* (The Feasts). He also published *Bibulu Sudhasaram* (The Message of the Bible, 1977), *Daarithappina Kumarudu* (The Prodigal Son, 1978) and *Pandreduguru Aposthalulu* (The Twelve Apostles, 1980).[39]

David was also a gifted Bible teacher who started teaching at Zion Bible School (1948) when it was shifted to Rajahmundry. He taught the "Book of Ephesians," "Survey of the Bible," and "Dispensations." He also traveled to the U.S., like Samuel and Paramjyothi, and preached in many churches. He started orphanages with help from John Douglas, Sr. David died at age seventy-seven, leaving behind many churches and thousands of followers. His sons currently continue the work he left.[40] When he left the IPC (1961), he kept the IPC church property with him. P.M. Samuel tried to get it back but did not succeed.

Work of the IPC in the Visakhapatnam Area. Pentecostalism came to Visakhapatnam when Samuel visited there on his preaching tour (1932). The Union Church Mission invited Samuel to preach in their convention. Many from various denominations and also non-Christians participated in meetings and heard the Pentecostal message. While in Warangal (1938), Samuel was in prayer and saw a vision. He saw Kakinada, Visakhapatnam, Rajahmundry, and Nellore written in golden letters in the sky. While he was pondering the vision's meaning, God impressed on him to start Pentecostal churches in those places. In correspondence with the vision, Gorla Isaac Nathan was later sent to Visakhapatnam to pioneer the IPC work.

Hence, the origin of the IPC church at Visakhapatnam must be attributed to Isaac Nathan, a Dalit pastor. He was originally from Mahaboobnagar. He worked as the IPC pastor in Malakapalli, West Godavari District, and moved down to the coastal region at Samuel's request (1957). Isaac Nathan went to Mrs. Rosario Dewis (an Anglo-Indian), a railway employee who was transferred to Visakhapatnam from Vijayawada. She directed him to the home of Botta Gabriel (a lab technician in King George Hospital) in the Dalit colony of Penta Veedhi. Gabriel and his wife, Karunamma, were attending the Baptist Church at that time, and conducting evening prayer meetings at their home. One evening while Gabriel was leading family devotions, Isaac Nathan came to their door. He was given a few minutes to speak in the meeting and he spoke on the baptism of the Holy Spirit. Then he prayed for the people gathered there and while he was praying, Gabriel's wife was filled with the Holy Spirit and began to speak in tongues. Gabriel and Karunamma opened their home later to Isaac Nathan for a few months and he began to conduct Sunday worship services in their home. This was the genesis of the first IPC church in Visakhapatnam.[41]

They met later in the house of Mrs. Dewis in the Kotaveedi area, Visakhapatnam. After meeting at several places in the city, they finally purchased a property in Gollalapalem near the Visakhapatnam Central Jail with contributions from local church believers.[42] Under the leadership of Isaac Nathan, the first IPC convention was held (March 1959) in which Samuel, Paramjyothi, Lukeson, David, and Thomas proclaimed the Pentecostal message. At its conclusion, forty-nine people were baptized in water, including Gabriel and Karunamma and Bantumilli Martin Luther.[43] B. Gabriel and B. Martin Luther later dedicated their lives for full-time ministry and became the IPC pastors at Vizainagaram and Chittivalasa at Isaac Nathan's request.

Isaac Nathan worked tirelessly spreading the Pentecostal faith in nearby areas until he left the IPC fellowship (1965). While pastoring at Gollalapalem, he also planted another church at Malkapuram. Later, Kakkhukuzhil Chacko Matthew (K.C. Matthew from Kerala) was appointed pastor at the IPC church at Visakhapatnam. Many Dalit pastors, including T. Yesudas, V. David Raju, B.S. Kruparakshana, K. Sanjeeva Rao, G. David, K. Priyanandam, G. Krupavaram, and J.A. David, worked in the Visakhapatnam area under his leadership. These Dalit pastors planted Pentecostal churches in many locations, including Anakapalli, Gajapathinagaram, Nellimarla, S. Kota, Gajuwaka, Marripalem, Mothugudem, Munjaru, Seleru, and others.

One prominent pastor in the Visakhapatnam area was Baddy S. Kruparakshana. He was born in Thatipaka near Razole (March 1959) to Dalit Christian parents, Baddy Rakshanandam and Krupamma, who belonged to the Canadian Baptism Mission. Kruparakshana accepted Christ while working as a government employee in the Zilla Parishad Office (August 14, 1947). He attended the IPC church in Machilipatnam.[44] He received the baptism of the Holy Spirit on his way home from his office and came home speaking in other tongues. Kruparakshana later resigned from his promising job and became involved in full-time ministry (1956). He married Vimalamma, a medical doctor (July 31, 1954) and they both dedicated their lives for the spread of the Pentecostal faith in Andhra.[45] Vimalamma also belonged to the Canadian Baptist Mission before she became a Pentecostal. After she became a Pentecostal, her father did not speak to her for three years.

Because of his passion for lost souls, Kruparakshana reached people in Narsipatnam, Seleru, Anakapalli, Nellimarla, and surrounding villages with the gospel. He was beaten many times for distributing Bibles and gospel tracts during Hindu festivals, but it did not deter him from preaching the gospel. During his long tenure as a pastor, he pastored IPC churches in Anakapalli, Malkapuram, and Visakhapatnam. He lived a very simple life and spent most of his money helping fellow IPC pastors and the poor in various congregations where he ministered. He also served as the Andhra IPC general secretary and as editor of *"Suvartha Prakashini"* (Gospel Illuminator), a monthly publication of the Andhra IPC. Kruparakshana was an able teacher who used his teaching expertise to train many young ministers at Zion Bible College for almost twenty-five years.[46]

Work of the IPC in the Vijayawada Area. The Pentecostal work began in Vijayawada (1937) when Samuel arrived there on a gospel tour with several believers from Eluru. He and co-workers Paramjyothi and Pedapudi Anandam conducted revival meetings several places in Vijayawada and hundreds were attracted to the Pentecostal message. A place was rented before long to conduct Sunday services in and this marked the beginning of the IPC work in Vijayawada. The church began to grow before long under Dalit pastor Pedapudi Anandam and his wife Deenamma. Anandam was born in Maheswarapuram near Gudivada. He and his wife accepted the Pentecostal faith through Murugeshan. Samuel later moved to Vijayawada permanently (1940) and left the work in Eluru under the care of P.T. Chacko. Not long after he moved there, Anandam was transferred to the IPC church at Machilipatnam. Samuel became pastor of the church that Anandam was serving.[47] When Anandam came to Machilipatnam, he lacked proper accommodations. Many times he and his wife had no food to eat and survived on whatever they received as an offering in the ministry. He also worked in various places, including Batlapenumarru, Gudivada, Vuyyuru, Pamarru, Palakol, Narsapuram, Dornakal, and Secunderabad.

Later K.R. David came to Vijayawada from Warangal (1941) to assist Samuel and take responsibility for the "Gospel Illuminator" magazine. They preached the Pentecostal faith in street meetings among Dalits throughout Vijayawada, including Wood Pet, Governor Pet, Israel Pet, Moghulraj Puram, Giripuram, Nizam Pet, and Bunder Pet. After six months, David was sent to Gandigunta near Vuyyur to start the IPC work.

In Vijayawada, Samuel and his family suffered a great deal, facing severe financial hardships and opposition from both Christians and non-Christians. Many times they went without food for days, living by faith and trusting God for their daily needs. While living in Islam pet in Vijayawada, they once went without food for three days. Samuel, his family, and his co-workers cried out to God to send them food. A Muslim lady suddenly came with a big bowl of fried rice with meat and spices (*biriyani*) and curries. A neighborhood wedding reception had many leftovers, so she decided to bring some for Samuel and his family. That day they ate until satisfied while glorifying God for answering their prayers. Samuel also lost his oldest son. His son became ill and Samuel could not afford to take him to the doctor, and he also did not believe in seeking medical help at that time. In spite of these hardships and setbacks, Samuel did not lose heart. He spearheaded a movement to spread the Pentecostal truth in Andhra Pradesh.

In the beginning of the IPC work in Vijayawada, there was only one church in Baptist Palem. After a few years, the second IPC church was started in Badava Pet. Other churches were slowly established in Singh Nagar (1968) and in Gunadala (1970). The work at Baptist Palem and other places in Vijayawada increased because of the selfless efforts of many Dalit pastors, including: P. Anandam, S.D. Barnabas, J. Joshua, John Joseph, K. Samuel, B.S. Krupanandam, M. Sunder Rao, Deekollu John Sunder Rao and Didla Rathnam (D. Rathnam).

Rathnam was one of the loyal Dalit pastors who worked at Baptist Palem. He served the IPC for fifty-two years. He was born in Yalamanchili village in the West Godavari District to Gangayya and Venkamma. After completing the ninth grade, he enlisted in the Indian Army where he worked as a motor technician.[48] He married a teacher named Kamalamma (1948). Rathnam came to know the Pentecostal faith through Kolagani Joshua in Vuyyuru (1949) and was baptized in water the same year. He attended Zion Bible School (1954) and started his ministry in Kanuru near Tanuku (1957). He planted churches in Eelabrolu and Prakashnagar and worked as a pastor in Jaggayya Pet, Kunderu, Vuyyuru, Vijayawada (Baptist Palem and Gunadala), and Guntur. During his long tenure as a pastor, he led hundreds of people to Christ and trained as many as forty people for full-time ministry. Other senior pastors in the Vijawada area are Desabathula Bhushanam, and Parangi Christopher, who contributed to the growth of the IPC in the past and they are still committed to spread the Pentecostal faith in this area.

Work of the IPC in the Antarvedipalem Area. Pentecostal work was started in Antarvedipalem by Dalit Potti Rajarathnam (1941). He migrated to Rangoon, the capital city of Burma (present-day Myanmar), where he attended a Pentecostal church established by Rathnam Manaseh, a Tamilian (1936). Rajarathnam had a gift of prophecy and he prophesied that Rangoon would be destroyed by bombs. Consequently, he and many others left Rangoon and returned to India. He and his family settled in Antarvedipalem where he started Pentecostal work (1941).[49] Rajarathnam used to invite Komanapalli Joseph Sudarsanam, who had already started a Pentecostal church in Narsapuram (1938) to spread the Pentecostal faith in the area. At his invitation, Samuel, Sudarsanam, and B.S. Lukeson came and conducted revival meetings (February 1942) in Antarvedipalem near the GDM church, with the help of Jillella Venkatarathnam. Many were converted to Pentecostalism. At the request of the village elders, the meetings were conducted for a second time (May 1942). At that time, Paramjyothi was working at Warangal and he came to Antarvedipalem to interpret for Samuel. After the meetings, Paramjyothi remained there to work with Rajarathnam. The church was started before long and Paramjyothi became its pastor (1942) along with Rajarathnam. Paramjyothi was a most outstanding and gifted Dalit leader in the Andhra IPC, the mainstay of the denomination for almost six decades.

Paramjyothi was born into a Dalit Christian family in Vuyyuru, Krishna District, Andhra Pradesh (March 2, 1921). His parents, Lazarus and Neelavathi, belonged to the Canadian Baptist Mission. His father was a teacher in the CBM School and simultaneously pastored a CBM church. When Sunder Singh came to Vijayawada on his preaching tour (1920),

Paramjyothi's mother attended his meetings. During the meetings, she asked God to grant her a male child so she could dedicate him for His service, and requested that the child should be used of God like Singh.[50]

Paramjyothi lost his father while he was still a boy. G. Kanthayya, a Brahmin convert, took responsibility for his education and sent him to a CBM school in Vuyyuru. One summer he went home to Maheswarapuram where he became a Christian (1933). He was baptized in the Holy Spirit (1934) while he was studying in the Canadian Baptist Mission boarding school in Vuyyuru even before he met Samuel.[51] Paramjyothi then began to preach in the streets and tell people about Christ. He attended McLaurin High School in Kakinada next, where Bible classes were mandatory for a year before enrollment. Then Paramjyothi took some theological and biblical courses for a year. While attending high school, he was inspired to become a minister (September 29, 1936), so he left school and entered full-time ministry at age fifteen (1937). He met Samuel for the first time in Eluru when he attended the dedication service of the IPC Church (1937). He was baptized in water by P.T. Chacko in Eluru (April 20, 1937).

Paramjyothi started his ministry in Hanuman Junction. He ministered later in Dondapadu and the surrounding villages of Pamarru, Ventrapragada, Manikonda, and Katuru. Many were healed and delivered from demon-possession and many others became Christians. He pastored an Indian Pentecostal church in Vuyyuru (August 1937 to February 1938). Paramjyothi was later sent to Vijayawada to work along with T.K. Thomas. He then moved to Warangal, where he faced constant opposition from non-Christians. He moved next to Antarvedipalem to pastor a church (1942). While serving there, he decided to become like Sundar Singh. He shaved his head and wore a saffron robe and preached in various villages and cities. His celibacy displeased his relatives, who found a bride for him. Paramjyothi finally surrendered his sadhu lifestyle and married Esther (March 13, 1944).

Esther was born (November 14, 1927) to Ganji Joseph from Tadepalligudem and Kanthamma from Vundrajavaram, both schoolteachers. They received the baptism in the Holy Spirit under the ministry of Mungamuri Devadas. Esther almost died from typhoid fever when very young. Her parents prayed earnestly and God healed her. She was baptized with the Holy Spirit and dedicated her life to full-time ministry at age eight.

Paramjyothi founded a magazine called *Suvartha Prakashini* (Gospel Illuminator) (1941) with financial help from his relatives and others (Appikatla Anandarao, K.R. John, Dr. Esther David, Dr. Mrudhubhashini, Mantada Mariyamma, Dr. T. Yesudas, B.S. Lukeson, and Dr. Vivekavathi Johnamma). Paramjyothi became co-editor of the magazine along with Samuel and David.[52] Through this magazine, Paramjyothi, Samuel, David, and other leaders made vigorous attempts to circulate Pentecostal views and to win over believers from mainline churches and non-believers to the IPC fold.

Paramjyothi co-founded Zion Bible School at Antarvedipalem (August 15, 1942). Classes were held there for three years (1942 to 1945) and then in various other locations, including Tadepalligudem, Rajahmundry, Eluru, Kakinada, Warangal, and Vijayawada (1946 to 1952). The school was then permanently established in Vijayawada (1960).[53] It played a key role in training IPC pastors and expanding the IPC work throughout Andhra.

After India obtained independence from the British (1947), the government started hostels for Dalit Hindus to provide them with a free education. Dalit Christians were denied admission. Paramjyothi started "Wings of Healing Children's Home" to help the Dalit Christians (June 1956). Hundreds of poor children and orphans grew up in that home and received a quality education. Many later became government officials, while others left for Gulf countries to pursue good paying jobs.[54]

Paramjyothi trained and helped hundreds of Telugu Dalit pastors, who advanced the work of the IPC in Andhra Pradesh and other parts of India. Many have passed away, but others still carry on the work in India in these areas: Gudimula, Rameswaram, Gondi, Antirvedi, Kesavadas Palem, Chintalamori, Kesanapalli, Ponnamanda, Nagaram, Medicherlapalem, Appanaramuni Lanka, Razole, Kadali, Tadipaka, Manepalli, Pasarlapudi, Badava, Enuguvari Lanka, Pujaripalem, Srikakulam, Palakol, Tadepalligudem, Velpuru, Bobbili, Visakkapatnam in Andhra, Pornia in Bihar, Haridwar in Uttar Pradesh, Ambernath in Maharashtra, and also other parts of the world (including Dubai, the United Arab Emirates in the Gulf countries).

Paramjyothi traveled in India extensively, to Jabalpur, Delhi, Bombay, Pune, Mysore, Bangalore, Madras, Trivandrum, Kumbanadu, Hubli, Bhuvaneswar, and other places. He also traveled abroad preaching the gospel in the United States, Holland, Sweden, Germany, Japan, Switzerland, England, Italy, Denmark, Norway, Singapore, and the Gulf countries.

Paramjyothi served the IPC for sixty years in various capacities: all-India IPC Vice-President (1984 to 1986), Acting President (1987 to 1988), and President again (1989 to 1996). He also served the body of Christ at large as an executive member of the Bible Society of India, President of the Ad-hoc Committee (All India Pentecostal Leaders Association), and President of the Full Gospel Leaders Fellowship of Andhra Pradesh. The Andhra Christian Council awarded him the title *"Andhra Kraistava Rathna"* (jewel among Andhra Christians) in recognition of his service to Christians in the state.

Work of the IPC in the Warangal Area. The IPC church in Warangal originated following a convention that the American Baptist Mission organized there (1938). A. Anandarao, a retired railway stationmaster, was a Dalit and close relative of Paramjyothi. He arranged meetings and invited Samuel to speak in them. Paramjyothi went as Samuel's translator and many embraced the Pentecostal faith during the revival meetings. They both preached in other Baptist churches also. One church had no pastor and the believers asked Paramjyothi to look after the church while Samuel had to go to Kerala to attend a business meeting. Samuel returned to Warangal a week later to continue his work but he met opposition from Baptist missionaries. Then Anandarao opened his house for services. This was the beginning of the Pentecostal church in Warangal.[55] The house quickly became too small for meetings and they had to erect a tent to accommodate more people.

Paramjyothi was left at Warangal to take charge of the church. He traveled by bicycle to other surrounding villages, including Janagama and Aleru, to preach the gospel. Even in the midst of severe opposition, he did not hesitate to preach among Muslims, atheists, and Hindus in Warangal. T.K. Thomas (from Kerala) moved there later with his family to pastor the church (1940). He worked in Vuyyuru and Vijayawada before he moved to Warangal. When he was based in Warangal, Thomas traveled to many villages promoting the Pentecostal faith and established approximately twenty churches in them, including the villages of Papayyapet, Dharmapuram, Dharmaram, Mandamari, Unikicharla, and Akkampet. Samuel purchased property for a church building (1940). Most of the members of the Warangal Pentecostal Church were Dalit cotton mill workers at the Azam Jahi Cotton Mills. Many contributed sacrificially, even to the extent of one month's salary, to purchase land and construct a permanent place of worship.[56] They erected the first and largest permanent building of the IPC under the leadership of Thomas.

Work of the IPC in the Hyderabad and Secunderabad Areas. The Mennonites and Wesleyan Missionaries organized revival meetings at Secunderabad (1932) in which Samuel preached. Thousands attended the meetings and embraced the Pentecostal message, including many government officials. Samuel held Bible studies with the help of Chacko. He then appointed Swamidas, a Dalit, as pastor when a small congregation was formed in a rented house. After a few years, Chacko took over the church following the untimely death of Swamidas.

Chacko (from Kerala) started his ministry there in Secunderabad in a rented house in the Regimental Bazar (1940). He held gospel meetings in various places in Secunderabad and conducted regular Bible studies and prayer meetings in a colony where Anglo-Indian widows lived. After a while, A.N. Matthew came from Kerala to assist Chacko in his pioneering work. Matthew started a Pentecostal church in Ramnagar. Later, Philip Abraham (from Kerala), who was working in Karnataka, moved to Hyderabad and started the IPC church in Hyderaguda.

Chacko invited Paramjyothi there regularly to preach in street meetings. While Paramjyothi preached in the streets, he was beaten many times by opponents of the gospel. Once he was dragged into the street and trampled by a mob. On another occasion he was locked up in a police station for preaching the gospel in Secunderabad. Several churches were established in various places in Secunderabad and surrounding villages, including: Atwelli, Gajwalli, Shameer Pet, Alwal, Siddi Pet, Toopran, Ghatkesar, Pamukunta, Gummadidala, and Masai Pet, due to Chacko's tireless efforts in spreading the gospel and his zeal for church planting. Through Abraham, the IPC work was spread to various places in the Hyderabad area, including: Macharla, Rentachinthala, Nellikallu, Markapuram, and Dachavaram.

Work of the IPC in the Kakinada Area. Samuel visited Kakinada at the invitation of John McLaurin (1932) and spoke in McLaurin High School about the baptism of the Holy Spirit. McLaurin and others responded positively to his message. However, the IPC work did not begin until Kundeti Gershon Paul came there to pioneer a church (1948). He was known as Chinna K.G. Paul. He was born in Uppalapadu (1924) to Dalit parents K.R. Moses and Rathnam. His father was a teacher in the Baptist school. K.G. Paul (Chinna) came to know the Pentecostal faith at a Pentecostal meeting at Bikkavole through Korati George Paul (Pedda K.G. Paul) (1947). He later resigned his job as rationing officer and dedicated his life to full-time ministry. K.G. Paul (Chinna) attended Zion Bible School at Vijayawada. Not long after his training, he started his work in Kakinada at the request of Samuel and built the IPC church in Kakinada (1953).[57] He worked as Kakinada area supervisor until he left the IPC (1959) and joined the Church of Christ (1960s). He objected to Samuel taking funds from John Douglas, Sr., which led to conflict between them.

After K.G. Paul (Chinna) left the IPC church in Kakinada, K.G. Paul (Pedda) became the pastor of the church. K.G. Paul (Pedda) was one of those who migrated from Rangoon during the Second World War, along with Rajaratnam and A.S. Paul. He worked as a teacher in Rangoon, where he received the baptism of the Holy Spirit. After he returned to India, Paul started Pentecostal work in Korumilli (1943) in East Godavari.[58] He planted another church later at Pamarru. While working in Pamarru, he worked as area pastor. Based in Pamarru, he worked in East Godavari to promote the Pentecostal faith, even in remote tribal areas, including Rampachodavaram. He moved to Kakinada (1959) under the direction of Samuel after K.G. Paul (Chinna) left the IPC. K.G. Paul (Pedda) was also a gifted writer and speaker who wrote many songs and books in Telugu, including the *Truth of the Pentecost* and the *Mystery of the Church of God*. He taught in Zion Bible School until he joined the WME (1960s).

Work of the IPC in the Mandapet Area. The IPC work in the Mandapet area was begun by A.S. Paul, a Dalit, who worked as a teacher in Burma. He became a Pentecostal believer through Pentecostal pastor Manaseh in Rangoon. He came to India during the Second World War. He worked as Grain Procuring Officer in Kakinada and resigned after he came to ministry. A.S. Paul met P.M. Samuel through Paramjyothi, and then decided to work with the IPC (1946). He, along with K.G. Paul (Pedda) and Mortha Philip, worked as a team to promote the Pentecostal faith throughout East Godavari, planting IPC churches. A.S. Paul had the gifts of healing and casting out of demons. When Samuel's oldest daughter, Glory, was demon-possessed, nobody was able to deliver her. Finally, A.S. Paul was able to cast the demons out of her through fasting and prayer and she was completely made whole

(1959). People from Srikakulam to Thada (the borders of Andhra Pradesh) would come to him for deliverance. Many were attracted to the Pentecostal faith throughout Andhra because of his deliverance ministry.[59]

Work of the IPC in the Rajanagaram Area. The work in Rajanagaram must be credited to Sudarsanam, who was born into a Dalit family in Vilasavilli village near Amalapuram. His parents, Chatla Narasanna and Nagamma, were Hindus when he was born, but later converted to Christianity and became members of the Godavari Delta Mission Church. Sudarsanam accepted Christ in Antarvedipalem Pentecostal meetings through Paramjyothi. While he was in the eighth grade in McLaurin High School in Kakinada, he received the call of God. Then he left his studies and entered full time ministry (1949).

One Sunday, Sudarasanam came to Rajanagaram and attended a service in a Lutheran Church. He was given a few minutes to share the Word of God. After he finished sharing, a convert from the Kamma caste named Sathyavathamma was astonished to see him in the congregation because she had just seen him in a dream the previous night. With her support, he started to pioneer the IPC work in Rajanagaram. Sathyavathamma sent Sudarsanam to Peda Rayavaram to share the Pentecostal faith with her relatives living there. He later established a church there also. Based in Rajanagaram, he promoted the Pentecostal faith in various villages, including Katralapalli, Sandredi, Kanavaram, Chagalnadu, and Vadisileru.

Sudarsanam planted twenty IPC churches in the Rajanagaram area. He rendered his services to the IPC as area pastor, state secretary, vice-president, and president. He taught at Zion Bible College to train pastors. He wrote four books: *The Book of Ruth*, *The Book of Esther*, *The History of the Kings of Israel and Judah*, and *God's Plan in Various Ages*. He also pastored in the IPC churches in Vizainagaram, Visakhapatnam, Korukonda, Secunderabad, Ibrahim Patnam (Vijayawada), and Warangal.[60]

Summary

After the IPC was formed (1932), it spread like wildfire to the four corners of Andhra Pradesh. It experienced rapid growth during its first two decades because of the untiring efforts of many Dalit pastors. The IPC began in Andhra by the invitation of Dalit Gurupadam to Samuel to come there. Samuel started the IPC work with the help of Jeevaratnam in Eluru. Many prominent Dalit leaders, including Paramjyothi and David, vigorously expanded the work, along with their fellow Dalit pastors. The most significant events that took place during this time were the establishment of Zion Bible School in Antarvedipalem and publication of the magazine *Suvartha Prakashini* by the efforts of Paramjothi. Dalits were thereby able to successfully promote the Pentecostal faith and establish churches throughout Andhra Pradesh.

Notes

1 P. J. Titus, "Pentecostal Indigenous Movements in Andhra," in Hedlund, *Christianity is Indian: The Emergence of an Indigenous Community*, 362.
2 Samuel, *Autobiography of Apostle P. M, Samuel*, 21.
3 Samuel, *Autobiography of Apostle P.M Samuel*, 21.
4 *Hand Book: The Indian Pentecostal Church of God*, 8.
5 *Hand Book: The Indian Pentecostal Church of God*, 9.
6 Samuel, *Autobiography of Apostle P.M. Samuel*, 14.
7 Mathew, "*A Study in the History of the Pentecostal Movement in South India*," 76.
8 *Hand Book: The Indian Pentecostal Church of God*, 38.
9 Noel Samuel Plathaneth (IPC President of Andhra Pradesh), e-mail message to the author, October 15, 2005.
10 Spurgeon Raju Pachigalla (President, Manna Ministries), interview with the author, January 3, 2006. Komanapalli Ernest (Founder, Manna Ministries), interview with the author, January 8, 2010. See also: Bergunder, *South Indian Pentecostal Movement in the Twentieth Century*, 273.
11 Samuel Pradhan Lam (grandson of Lam Jeevaratnam, Gudivada), interview with the author, January 26, 2011. Indira Vandanam Nanduri (daughter of T.P. Gurupadam), interview with the author, Guntur, January 20, 2011. See also: Ian Bain, *Before Kings: Life Story of Lam Jeevaratnam* (Toronto, n.d, 6).
12 Lester Sumrall, "Lam Jeevaratnam: A Messenger of Jesus" in *Pioneers of Faith*, 87. See also: "Unprecedented Scenes in Poona City, India: Mighty Signs and Wonders Follow the Preaching of the Gospel by Jeevaratnam," *The Pentecostal Evangel* (October, 20, 1934): 2. See also: Louise Boes, "Miracles Wrought Thru an Indian Sadhu: Evil Spirits Acknowledge the Supremacy of Jesus Christ" *The Latter Rain Evangel* (November 1934): 21.
13 Indira Vandanam Nanduri, interview with the author, Guntur, January 20, 2011. Samuel Pradhan Lam, interview with the author, Gudivada January 26, 2011. John Sudhir Dutt Thullimalli (grandson of T.P. Gurupadam), interview with the author, Machilipatnam, January 19, 2011. Swaroop Dutt Thullimalli (grandson of T.P. Gurupadam), interview with the author, Tanuku, January 17, 2011.
14 Indira Vandanam Nanduri, interview with the author, Guntur, January 20, 2011. John Sudhir Dutt Thullimalli, interview with the author, Machilipatnam, January 19, 2011. Swaroop Dutt Thullimalli, interview with the author, Tanuku, January 17, 2011. Samuel Pradhan Lam, interview with the author, Gudivada, January 26, 2011.
15 Annal Chandra Bai Merugu (daughter of Mann Singh), interview with the author, Machilipatnam, January 19, 2011. Indira Vandanam Nanduri, interview with the author, Guntur, January 20, 2011. John Sudhir Dutt Thullimalli, interview with the author, Machilipatnam, January 19, 2011. Swaroop Dutt Thullimalli, interview with the author, Tanuku, January 17, 2011.
16 Spurgeon Raju Pachigalla, interview with the author, Vijayawada, January 3, 2006. Ernest Komanapalli, interview with the author, Hyderabad, January 8, 2010. See also: Pachigalla Lazarus Paramjyothi, *The Life Story of Apostle Paramjyothayya* (Antarvedipalem: Paramjyothi Publications, 1996), 10.
17 Mark Podilaku, *Secretary's Report on Pentecostal Church Eluru, 1956* (Eluru: IPC Church, 1956), n.p.
18 Mathew, "A Study in the History of the Pentecostal Movement in South India," 70.

[19] Mark, *Secretary's Report on Pentecostal Church Eluru, 1956*, n.p.

[20] Samuel Rankin Pace Meriga (pastor of Independent Pentecostal Church and grandson of B.S. Lukeson), interview with the author, Chebrolu, January 14, 2011.

[21] Samuel Rankin Pace Meriga, interview with the author, Chebrolu, January 14, 2011.

[22] Mark, *Secretary's Report on Pentecostal Church Eluru, 1956*, n.p.

[23] Sanjeeva Rao Keethi (senior pastor of Indian Pentecostal Church), interview with the author, Chittivalasa, January 5, 2011. Prasad Kumar Marlapudi (elder of Indian Pentecostal Church), interview with the author, Eluru, January 22, 2011. Thomas Kumar Gorinkala (pastor of Indian Pentecostal Church), interview with the author, Warangal, December 31, 2010.

[24] Evangeline Grace Pedapudi (daughter of Kallepu Rajarathnam David), interview with the author, Machilipatnam, January 20, 2011. Sathyam Gubbala (former member of Indian Pentecostal Church), interview with the author, Machilipatnam, January 19, 2011. Prasad Kumar Marlapudi, interview with the author, Eluru, January 22, 2011.

[25] Das Kati (former member of Indian Pentecostal Church), interview with the author, Eluru, December 18, 2007. Thomas Kumar Gorinkala, interview with the author, Warangal, December 31, 2010. See also: "Divikegina Devasahayam Ayya Garu," *Suvartha Prakashini* (Gospel Illuminator) 57:1 (1997): 2

[26] Samuel Arun Das Kuntam (son of former elder of Indian Pentecostal Church), interview with the author, Eluru, January 29, 2011. Das Kati, interview with the author, Eluru, December 18, 2007. Prasad Kumar Marlapudi, interview with the author, Eluru, January 22, 2011.

[27] Daveedu Pitta (State secretary of Indian Pentecostal Church), interview with the author, Pedapadu, January 18, 2011. Mary Marlapudi (wife of former Indian Pentecostal Church pastor and daughter of Kanumala Peturu Devasahayam), interview with the author, Eluru, January 29, 2011. Sanjeeva Rao Keethi, interview with the author, Chittivalasa, January 5, 2011. See also: "Divikegina Devasahayam Ayya Garu," 2.

[28] "Divikegina Devasahayam Ayya Garu," 2.

[29] Samuel, *Autobiography of Apostle P.M. Samuel*, 24-25.

[30] K. Devasahayam, "The Bible Mission," *Religion and Society* 29:1, 55.

[31] B. Elisha, former president of the Bible Mission, "A Brief Biographical Note of Father Devadas," dated March 28, 1970. Cited in K. Devasahayam, 62.

[32] Devadas Mungamuri, "Woe Unto You," Bible Mission Booklet No. 14.

[33] Devadas Mungamuri, "Satyamsa Nirupana (The Proof of the Truth)," Bible Mission Booklet No. 28.

[34] Samuel, *Autobiography of Apostle P.M. Samuel*, 63-64.

[35] Rajarathnam David Kallepu. *Nenu Na Prabhuvu (Autobiography of Pastor K.R. David)*, Rajahmundry: Andhrasree Printers, 1981), 37-38.

[36] David. *Nenu Na Prabhuvu (Autobiography of Pastor K.R. David)*, 41.

[37] Evangeline Grace, interview with the author, Machilipatnam, January 20, 2011.

[38] Evangeline Grace, interview with the author, Machilipatnam, January 20, 2011. Samuel Pedapudi (son of former pastor of Indian Pentecostal Church), interview with the author, Machilipatnam, January 19, 2011. Daniel Kalyanapu (leader of Ecclesia Ministries), phone interview with the author, Virginia Beach, February 17, 2011.

[39] David, *Nenu Na Prabhuvu (Autobiography of Pastor K.R. David)*, as listed on the back of the cover page.

78   Dalit Pentecostalism

⁴⁰ Solomon Raj Pulidindi. *The New Wine-skins: The Story of the Indigenous Missions in Coastal Andhra Pradesh, India* (Delhi and Chennai: ISPCK/MIIS, 2003), 52.

⁴¹ Varaprasad Botta (pastor of Indian Pentecostal Church), interview with the author, Pendurthi, January 7, 2011. Diamond Hemalatha Bantumilli, (wife of B. Martin Luther, former pastor of Indian Pentecostal Church, BHPV), interview with the author, Visakhapatnam, January 7, 2011.

⁴² Yesunatha Das, "Pentecostal History of Visakhapatnam," *Souvenir of Pentecostal Fellowship of India: Seventh National Conference-2004* (Visakhapatnam, 2004), 12. Cited in Vegesana Vijaya Bhaskara Raju, "The Impact of Pentecostal Movement and Cross-Cultural Missionary Work in Andhra Pradesh: A Biography of Apostle K.C. Matthew" (M.Th. thesis, COTR College, 2005), 73.

⁴³ Varaprasad Botta, interview with the author, Pendurthi, January 7, 2011. Diamond Hemalatha Bantumilli, interview with the author, Visakhapatnam, January 7, 2011. See also: M. Vijaya Kumar, *Church History of Visakhapatnam.* Cited in Bhaskara Raju, "The Impact of Pentecostal Movement and Cross-Cultural Missionary Work in Andhra Pradesh," 74.

⁴⁴ Vimalamma Baddy (wife of B.S. Kruparakshana, former pastor of Indian Pentecostal Church), interview with the author, Visakhapatnam, January 6, 2011. Samuel Pedapudi, interview with the author, Machilipatnam, January 19, 2011.

⁴⁵ "Eternal Entrance of Pastor B.S. Kruparakshana," an obituary published for his memorial service held at the IPC Church, Visakhapatnam on September 11, 1996.

⁴⁶ "Eternal Entrance of Pastor B.S. Kruparakshana," n.p.

⁴⁷ Samuel Pedapudi, interview with the author, Machilipatnam, January 19, 2011.

⁴⁸ Mercy Samuel Didla (daughter in-law of D. Rathnam), interview with the author, Vijayawada, January 12, 2011.

⁴⁹ Paramjyothi, *The Life Story of Apostle Paramjyothayya*, 25-26.

⁵⁰ Paramjyothi, *The Life Story of Apostle Paramjyothayya*, 2.

⁵¹ Paramjyothi, *The Life Story of Apostle Paramjyothayya*, 4-8.

⁵² Paramjyothi, *The Life Story of Apostle Paramjyothayya*, 22-23.

⁵³ Paramjyothi, *The Life Story of Apostle Paramjyothayya*, 28-29.

⁵⁴ Paramjyothi, *The Life Story of Apostle Paramjyothayya*, 45-46.

⁵⁵ Paramjyothi, *The Life Story of Apostle Paramjyothayya*, 16-18.

⁵⁶ David, *Nenu Na Prabhuvu (Autobiography of Pastor K.R. David)*, 37-38.

⁵⁷ Gershon Paul Kundeti (former pastor of Indian Pentecostal Church), interview with the author, Kakinada, January 10, 2011. Adiyya David Jekkala (senior pastor of Indian Pentecostal Church), interview with the author, Visakhapatnam, January 6, 2011. See also: Samuel, *Autobiography of Apostle P. M. Samuel*, 67.

⁵⁸ Joythi Samuel Korati (pastor and daughter-in-law of K.G. Paul), interview with the author, Kakinada, January 10, 2011. John Shabdham Adidala (pastor and son of A.S. Paul), phone interview with the author, Virginia Beach, March 13, 2011. Adiyya David Jekkala, interview with the author, Visakhapatnam, January 6, 2011.

⁵⁹ John Shabdham Adidala, phone interview with the author, Virginia Beach, March 13, 2011. Adiyya David Jekkala, interview with the author, Visakhapatnam, January 6, 2011.

⁶⁰ Samuel Sudarsanam Chatla (pastor of Indian Pentecostal Church), interview with the author, Rajanagaram, January 19, 2010. Joshua Sudarsanam Chatla (pastor of Indian Pentecostal Church), interview with the author, Rajanagaram, January 19, 2010.

Chapter 5

Transition Years of the IPC in Andhra Pradesh (1960 to 1981)

Introduction

During the transition years, there were serious setbacks that led to schism in the IPC. The arrival of John E. Douglas, Sr. to Andhra presented many new challenges for the IPC as he attempted to introduce new and different ways of handling ministry. His initial intention was to help the IPC, not to start a new organization in Andhra. But eventual conflict with Plathaneth Matthew Samuel over financial and other matters paved the way for the formation of the rival World Missionary Evangelism organization in India. Similarly, the establishment of Manna Ministries posed a further setback to the IPC work.

Schism of the IPC and Major Players in the Schism

Douglas, Sr., Taragam Sathyavedam Sasthry, Kallepu Rajarathnam David, Bathina Samuel Lukeson, Pachigalla Lazarus Paramjyothi, Godi Samuel, Komanapalli Ernest, and Papabathini Philip were the most significant key players in the schism of the IPC during its turbulent transition years. All were from a Dalit background except Douglas, Sr. Douglas, Sr. and Sasthry played a direct role in the schism, while others, like G. Samuel, Paramjyothi and Ernest, played a more indirect role. In this section, the roles of these individuals who contributed directly to the schism in the IPC are discussed in detail.

John E. Douglas, Sr. and World Missionary Evangelism (WME)

The man whose arrival in India fostered the split in the IPC was Douglas, Sr., the founder of World Missionary Evangelism (WME). He was from the state of West Virginia in the U.S. After being a successful storeowner for two decades, he became dissatisfied and felt that he should do more with his life and reach out to others.

Douglas, Sr. came home from work one morning and asked his wife Edith to kneel in prayer with him. As they prayed, they had a vision of ministering to the world through Christian service. They sold everything and put their lives fully into God's hands. Not long afterward, he was invited to India (1957) where he went to the church of P. John Thomas in Kerala. While traveling and preaching throughout India, he discovered that many local Christians wanted to share the gospel but lacked training and resources. He recognized the advantage of using native preachers and workers in ministry, because they could reach more people than an American missionary. They already knew the languages, customs, and living conditions of their people. Consequently, he founded World Missionary Evangelism (WME) in Dallas, Texas, (1958) to advance his vision.

He later attended IPC conventions in Eluru conducted by P.M. Samuel (1959, 1960), where he met Paramjyothi and other co-workers of P.M. Samuel. Paramjyothi, Thomas Wyatt, and Douglas, Sr.'s son, John Douglas, Jr., were invited to Los Angeles, California, to preach in a convention. Douglas, Sr. learned of the meetings and Paramjyothi's attendance there, so he went to meet him and share his vision about ministry in India (1961). He also asked Paramjyothi to establish a childrens' home and disburse financial aid to needy pastors working in India. Paramjyothi was already operating an orphanage ("Wings of Healing") in Antarvedipalem with assistance from Wyatt by this time. Douglas, Sr. then proposed another location where he could establish and manage a childrens' home. He told Paramjyothi that he could remain with the IPC and receive help from Douglas, Sr. according to the constitution of the IPC. Paramjyothi accepted gladly and invited Douglas, Sr. to Antarvedipalem. Douglas, Sr. visited Paramjyothi there (1962), and he took him to Srikakulam also, where he introduced him to G. Samuel.

It was P.M. Samuel who invited Douglas, Sr. to speak in the Eluru convention. In the beginning, Douglas, Sr. helped the IPC pastors through P.M. Samuel. During the convention, he said that if he had a huge airplane, he would take all the IPC pastors and their congregations to visit America. He also shared a story of a duck and a hen. The hen brooded over the eggs of the duck. After they hatched, the baby ducks grew under the watchful eye of the hen. Then came the rainy season, and as the hen roamed on a mound for food, rain suddenly poured. It rained for days and the whole place flooded. The mound became an island surrounded by water. The hen thought the ducklings would stay with her since they did not know how to swim. At first they were afraid to get off the mound and get in the water. Once they did, they realized they could swim and were able to swim to the other side, leaving the hen behind on the mound.[1] The meaning of the story is that one day the ducklings (the IPC pastors) would leave the mother hen (P.M. Samuel). After that, P.M. Samuel feared that Douglas, Sr. would someday split the IPC.

Douglas, Sr. helped P.M. Samuel support Telugu pastors financially, but many of the IPC pastors did not believe P.M. Samuel used the funds as

Douglas, Sr. intended. Many IPC pastors later complained to Douglas, Sr. that they were not receiving funds he was giving to Samuel. As a result, Douglas, Sr. wanted to make the donations to the IPC organization, not to P.M. Samuel directly. He also wanted P.M. Samuel to give him an account of how the funds were disbursed, but P.M. Samuel did not agree to that condition. He insisted that Douglas, Sr. should send the money to him directly and he would spend the funds at his discretion. Douglas, Sr. then asked for the list of Telugu pastors so he could help them directly, but P.M. Samuel again did not like the idea. The reason may have been that P.M. Samuel did not want to give a foreigner intimate information about the IPC or control over the organization. He also may not have wanted Telugu Dalit pastors to benefit from Douglas, Sr.'s financial support. Douglas, Sr. finally terminated his funding through P.M. Samuel, choosing to contact and support the IPC pastors directly, knowing it displeased P.M. Samuel.[2] Later, when Douglas, Sr. started the WME, many IPC pastors joined his organization to take advantage of the opportunity to receive the financial help needed to sustain ministries and support families.

Michael Bergunder reports that pastors who received financial support remained members of the IPC at first. However, P.M. Samuel opposed the idea of Douglas, Sr. helping Telugu pastors because it would reduce his own influence in the IPC. Furthermore, it stood in contradiction to the faith teachings he had been propagating. The relationship between Douglas, Sr. and P.M. Samuel became strained when Douglas, Sr. insisted that the work he financially supported must go under his name.[3]

P.M. Samuel appeared to be maintaining a double standard. On the one hand, he was teaching Telugu pastors to lead a life of faith and discouraging them from taking any help from abroad or from any foreign missionaries. On the other hand, he, himself, went on foreign tours and accepted contributions from many Western countries, including Sweden, the United States, Germany, and Canada.

Douglas, Sr. was then perceived in a negative light by many in the IPC, but for many Telugu pastors, he was considered the answer to their prayers. His love for poor Dalit Telugu pastors was laudable. He helped immensely to alleviate the pastors' suffering, providing them with hostels, schools, and resources for their ministry not long after they came and joined the WME. He built them homes, gave them motorcycles and even automobiles to some senior pastors. He provided financial support for their children's education. Hundreds of Telugu orphan children were fed and educated in WME hostels and schools. Hundreds of Pentecostal churches were also established throughout Andhra Pradesh.[4] As a consequence, the IPC lost its status as the only Pentecostal denomination in Andhra Pradesh.

Godi Samuel

The next key player was G. Samuel, who was born (June 2, 1936) to Dalit parents Godi Daniel and Mariyamma in the village of Surasaniyanam, East

Godavari Distict of Andhra Pradesh. After completing elementary education in his village, his uncle took him to Narsapuram for further schooling. When he graduated from high school (1955), his plans for college had to be deferred one year due to lack of funds. In the interval he befriended a teacher named P. Stephen, a Christian who was filled with the Holy Spirit. This friendship paved the way for G. Samuel's salvation. He became a Christian, was baptized in water, and then attended an open-air prayer meeting where he was filled with the Holy Spirit and began to speak in other tongues.[5]

The following year, G. Samuel attended a junior college while Stephen resigned from his teaching job and left for Bombay to start a ministry. During his college days G. Samuel participated in Pentecostal conventions at Antharvedipalem hosted by Paramjyothi. Paramjyothi was very much impressed by young G. Samuel's zeal for the Lord, so he sent him to Doon Bible College in Dehra Dun, Uttar Pradesh, not long after he completed his intermediate program (associate degree).

After the completion of his theological education, G. Samuel left with Gutam Paul for Srikakulam to pioneer a church (August 15, 1960), as directed by Paramjyothi. Since they knew no one in that city, they went to a Telugu Baptist Church and took shelter on a porch for three days. Mornings were spent distributing tracts and evenings they returned late to sleep on the porch. G. Samuel finally found a mud hut to rent for five rupees per month.[6]

G. Samuel married Vijayaratnam, (May 24, 1961) second daughter of Sade Krupanandam. They lived in a single room mud hut with a bamboo roof and endured tremendous trials, hardships, and financial difficulties during this time. When they had rice, there was no firewood to cook it. When they had firewood, they had no rice. They faced such challenges without letting anyone know their needs or situation, depending instead on God for every need.

Two months into married life, after three days with no food, G. Samuel fainted from hunger. His wife could only cry. When the neighbors heard her, they rushed to the home, realized the situation, and provided food. The couple's situation did not change much after G. Samuel recovered. His wife wrote to her sister about the matter, but could find no money for postage. So G. Samuel mailed the letter to Visakhapatnam without postage.

After a while, G. Samuel sent a report of his ministry work to Paramjyothi and briefly mentioned his situation. When Paramjyothi learned of G. Samuel's condition, he began to support him with forty rupees per month out of funds he had been receiving from Douglas, Sr. Paramjyothi then started a childrens' home with five children in Srikakulam (October 1961) with financial help from Douglas, Sr., which became the starting point of the WME work in India.[7]

Since Paramjyothi had already been operating another orphanage ("Wings of Healing") with funds received from Thomas Wyatt in Antarvedipalem, he was forced to choose between receiving help from Douglas, Sr., or Wyatt. He therefore introduced Douglas, Sr., to G. Samuel, while he continued to work with Wyatt. G. Samuel soon undertook a leadership position with the WME (1962) and began the WME work officially with three ministers working under him, along with the childrens' home that Paramjyothi had started earlier in Srikakulam. The home grew from five to 500 children over time, and the ministry grew from three to 100 ministers working in 100 different areas. Five more WME childrens' homes were later started by G. Samuel in five separate locations. They were located in Vizainagaram, Ranastalam, and Mirthiguddivalsa in Andhra Pradesh, and Rayagadda and Parlakimidi in Orissa. Fifty children were cared for in each home. G. Samuel also started WME welfare projects for lepers in Srikakulam and Narsannapet until a permanent leper colony was built at Manguvarithota (1970s).

The WME work was extended to other states also. After Stephen led G. Samuel to become a Christian, he worked as a minister in Ambernath, Bombay. Then he came to Srikakulam to help G. Samuel in his pioneering ministry efforts to establish the WME work in India. G. Samuel sent Stephen back to Bombay with a mandate to start its work there. Before long, Jana Samuel (J. Samuel) was sent to Giddalur, T.K. Mahanty to K. Kotapadu in the Visakhapatnam area, and B. Johnson to Berhampur in Orissa. The work of the WME slowly spread to other places and it was not long before the World Missionary Evangelism organization was registered with the Government of India (1969). Reginald Courts was named chairman and G. Samuel became general secretary. In just a few years the WME became one of the largest Pentecostal denominations in India, establishing churches in almost every state of the country. G. Samuel was appointed chairman and national representative of the WME (October 1977), the position he held until his resignation many years later (1990).[8]

Before being promoted to general secretary, G. Samuel was the superintendent of the WME work in the Srikakulam District. His zeal for evangelism led him to undertake a tour of the district with a team of workers to reach every village with the gospel. He included women evangelists, who came to play a prominent role in evangelization of these villages. Foremost among them were Yerneni Estheramma and Tanamuri Marthamma. The result of these efforts was the establishment of more than sixty churches and 100 ministry centers in the district.[9]

G. Samuel was a prolific author who produced over twenty books. They include: *Prodigal Son, The Treasure of the Believer, No One is Nothing and Everyone is Something, Be Not Confounded, Psalm 119, What Does God Think of You?* *Model Men, Beware of Bad Women,* and *Bible Lessons and Sermons*. He served as an editor of the Telugu monthly Christian magazine "*Suvisesham*" (the Good News). He also composed more than seventy songs that have enriched the lives of Andhra Christians. He has maintained a Telugu radio program called "*Suviseshavani*" (the Voice of Good News), preaching on the FEBA (Far East Broadcasting Association) radio station since 1983.

Once the WME became established, the IPC suffered a severe setback. Douglas, Sr. contacted not only Paramjyothi, but also other co-workers of P.M. Samuel through letters and personal visits. Lukeson, Sasthry from Eluru, and J. Joshua from Warangal (who became a Christian under Paramjyothi's ministry) were also contacted. Almost all of the prominent IPC leaders in Andhra Pradesh later went over to the WME. Nearly 100 workers separated from the IPC in the Antarvedipalem area alone and joined the WME on the advice of Paramjyothi. In other places, many IPC pastors changed their signboards from the IPC to the WME overnight. They still remained on IPC church property. Lands and church buildings of the IPC were now occupied by former IPC pastors who had switched over to the WME.[10] Paramjyothi never joined the WME himself, remaining instead in the IPC until his death. However, he did introduce G. Samuel and other IPC pastors to the WME with the intention of helping the Telugu pastors financially.[11]

The WME was considered the largest Pentecostal denomination in Andhra Pradesh at that time, but it later weakened after the death of Douglas, Sr. His daughter, Yvonne Douglas, took over leadership of the WME, but she lacked a clear idea of ministry in India. After the passing of her father, funding for the work in India slowly declined. Internal struggles for power also began in the WME. The Dalit Madiga pastors thought the Dalit Mala pastors were getting more favors than they were, so they made complaints against G. Samuel to the WME leadership.

One of the main reasons for the decline of the WME was the conflict between G. Samuel of the Mala caste, and Komanapalli Issac, who was of the Madiga caste. G. Samuel visited the childrens' home in Narsapuram that was given to Isaac to determine how many children were actually there. He found twenty to twenty-five fewer children than what Isaac had reported to G. Samuel. G. Samuel said that he would only send funding based on the number of children staying in the home, not on the roster as reported. Issac felt humiliated by G. Samuel's sudden visit, which then strained the relationship between them.

In the meantime, Issac went to the U.S. and made complaints against G. Samuel to the WME. He convinced the leadership to remove G. Samuel as national supervisor and the WME leadership in the U.S. arbitrarily appointed Issac as the new chief of the WME in India without investigating the allegations. When G. Samuel learned of Issac's appointment, he refused to resign from his post. This angered the leadership in the U.S., so they stopped supporting G. Samuel and the pastors who were working under him. This precipitated the decline of the WME in India. Later, Issac passed away suddenly and the WME headquarters appointed someone from outside of Andhra as national supervisor. Issac's wife did not endorse the appointment, since she wanted to take over the reins of the organization herself. The conflict eventually ended up in legal battles.[12]

Taragam Sathyavedam Sasthry

Another key player in the schism of the IPC was Taragam Sathyavedam Sasthry (T.S. Sasthry). He was born and raised in a Dalit family in Mahaboobnagar. He worked in the Azam Jahi Cotton Mills in Warangal and accepted the Pentecostal faith there. After his conversion, he resigned from his job and worked as a pastor of the IPC church at Mahaboobnagar. When Sasthry first went there to pioneer the church, nobody was willing to rent him a house. He had three children at that time and they all had to stay on the verandas and porches of peoples' houses. Sasthry and his children went without food many days. One day it was pouring rain, and he had no place to stay, so he and his family stood at the edge of a house the whole night. Finally a home was found to rent, where he also started conducting services. This was the beginning of the IPC work in Mahaboobnagar. He had a conflict later with some of the believers in the church. Tension between Sasthry and the believers eventually forced him to leave the church. Then, at the request of P.M. Samuel, he went to Eluru to look after the IPC church there (1960).[13] He also pioneered the IPC work in Jedcherla and Theegalapalli while he was working in Mahaboobnagar.

Sasthry obtained Douglas, Sr.'s mailing address when he translated for him in Guntur. He wrote to Douglas, Sr. later, who sent him a hundred dollars for each of three consecutive months. The first month, he took the check to P.M. Samuel to let him know that he received the check from Douglas, Sr. P.M. Samuel was not pleased that he was receiving funds directly from Douglas. Sr. He argued that individuals should not receive funds from abroad and that all the funds should be sent to the IPC state headquarters. The headquarters would distribute the funds at its discretion. Sasthry received another check the second month and this time he took it to Paramjyothi to get his advice. Paramjyothi advised him to write to Douglas, Sr. and tell him that about fifty pastors who were working under him needed financial help. Douglas, Sr. requested the pastors' profiles and after he received them, he began to support all fifty pastors.[14] Not long after, Sasthry left the IPC (1961). He was the first one to leave the organization. He then began recruiting others for the WME, including S. Isaiah (from Tenali), Stephen Yesudas (from Guntur), and Kallepu Rajarathnam David (K.R. David from Rajahmundry). David did not want to join the WME in the beginning, but at Sasthry's insistence, he finally left the IPC.

Sasthry was a gifted speaker, teacher, writer, and interpreter. He was able to communicate in five different Indian languages. He taught at Zion Bible College until he left the IPC. Sasthry wrote ten books, including commentaries on *The Book of John, Ezekiel, Zechariah, Revelation,* and *the Acts*. He was pastor of the IPC church in Eluru (1960 to 1961). After Sasthry joined the WME (1961), he started a school, a childrens' home and a Bible school in Eluru with funds received from Douglas, Sr. He also published a monthly magazine called *"Suvartha Pracharam"* (the Gospel Proclamation).[15]

Komanapalli Ernest and Manna Ministries

Ernest successfully established a Pentecostal organization known as Manna Ministries in Andhra Pradesh (in the late1960s), but its formation was one of the major setbacks to the IPC. Ernest came from a Dalit Pentecostal family, the second son of K. Joseph Sudarsanam and Miriam. His father was a businessman dealing in lace who traveled on business to Mussoorie in Uttar Pradesh, North India, where he befriended Carl and Rosemary Linden, a Swedish-American family. The Lindens came to North India as missionaries of the Open Bible Standard Church from the U.S. Through their ministry, Sudarsanam came to know the Pentecostal faith (July 13, 1939) in Landour and before long received the baptism of the Holy Spirit. He then started a Pentecostal church in Narsapuram and later worked with P.M. Samuel. He and P.M. Samuel had conflict, so he left the IPC and joined the WME.[16]

Ernest became a Christian at age thirteen (1949). After graduation from high school (1956), he enrolled in Southern Asia Bible Institute, an Assemblies of God Bible School in Bangalore.[17] When he completed his theological studies (1960), he embarked on an itinerant ministry in Andhra. While in Madras (1961), he decided to attend the World Pentecostal Conference to be held in Jerusalem. His father had to mortgage his house to pay the airfare. Not long after the conference, Ernest went to England and spent a month with Roy and Myrtle Smith. Then he traveled to Switzerland, Germany, France, Belgium, and Holland, preaching in various churches (July 1961 to January 1962).[18]

While attending the Pentecostal conference, Ernest met Dr. Leonard Heroo, president of Zion Bible Institute in Providence, Rhode Island. He then contacted Heroo from Germany and was admitted to Zion (1962). After one semester, he enrolled in nearby Barrington College and earned a B.A. degree, and later obtained his M.Ed. degree from the University of Rhode Island. While studying at Barrington College, he had to return to India to see his mother, who was ill. He married Rachel, oldest daughter of Paramjyothi, during that time. Ernest was hired at a school for the mentally handicapped after he completed his M.Ed. degree (1966). He decided to use a portion of the first paycheck he received to help support pastors in Andhra Pradesh. This was the seed that began Manna Ministries.[19] Two years later, he started a childrens' home in his hometown (1968).

Ernest resigned his job as Director of Education at the school in Rhode Island and returned to India (1971) to continue the work started earlier. He successfully established a number of churches throughout Andhra Pradesh (1971 to 1974) with the help of his father-in-law, Paramjyothi. In order to help the work of his son-in-law, Paramjyothi introduced the IPC pastors to Ernest. Then many pastors left the IPC and joined Manna Ministries on the advice of Paramjyothi. The IPC pastors were getting only 100 rupees (about 2 dollars and fifty cents) per month at that time, but Manna Ministries was able to pay them from 400 to 500 rupees (about 10 dollars) per month.[20]

John Giminez, pastor of the Rock Church in Virginia Beach, Virginia, helped Ernest purchase property in Hyderabad (1977). Then Ernest moved to Hyderabad himself to expand the ministry in Andhra and other parts of India. The church that he built in Hyderabad was not called "Manna," but was separately registered as the "Rock Church." Ernest founded and ran three major associations: Miriam Children's Home (1969), Manna Full Gospel Ministries (1974) and Rock Church Ministries (1979). They are still in operation in 2010. A large portion of Manna Ministries' work was devoted to social work. An estimated forty-five orphanages, one center for lepers, ten schools, two junior colleges, and a fifty-bed hospital are operated by the organization.[21] Ernest gradually freed himself from administrative work and his brother-in-law, Pachigalla Spurgeon Raju (P. Spurgeon Raju), became president of Manna Ministries.

In 2010, Manna Ministries had 1500 churches in Andhra, making it the leading Pentecostal group there, surpassing even the IPC. Even though Manna Ministries was responsible for division in the IPC indirectly, it provided the Telugu pastors with the resources they needed for ministry, including the construction of permanent buildings for churches, monthly salaries, and vehicles for the pastors.[22]

Papabathini Philip

After the death of P.M. Samuel, Papabathini Pullayya (or Philip), a Dalit, wanted to be president of the IPC, but he was not chosen. Philip enjoyed P.M. Samuel's favor because he was loyal and his personal assistant. He was born in Gopinenipalem to Yesurathnam and Jogamma (1930). After losing his parents at age seventeen, he joined the Indian Army and participated in the war between Pakistan and India. After the war, he returned to Andhra and obtained employment in the police department and later studied a pharmacy course. His wife, Lilly Pushpamma, belonged to the CSI Church but came to the Pentecostal faith and then attended the IPC Church in Vijayawada. Philip was addicted to alcohol and both of his lungs were damaged. Doctors said he would die within four months. He went to Madras and checked into a hotel, planning to kill himself by taking poison. While he was reaching for the bottle, it fell on the floor. Suddenly, a great light came into his room and he heard a voice asking him to come to ministry. Philip then saw a vision of Jesus dying on the cross. He saw a drop of blood which came and fell on his body and he committed his life to Jesus Christ that day (1966). That same year, he attended Zion Bible College in Gunadala. After his training, Philip traveled with P.M. Samuel to translate for him.[23]

Several interviewees opined that before P.M. Samuel's death, Philip had him sign a blank paper with an IPC letterhead. He then took the signed paper and typed a letter stating that P.M. Samuel had appointed him to be the next president. After P.M. Samuel's death (1981), Philip sent the letter to the sponsors of P.M. Samuel and declared himself president of the IPC. The sponsors informed Plathaneth Abraham Samuel (P. Abraham Samuel, P.M.

Samuel's son) in Andhra that they would extend their support to Philip as the next leader. Abraham Samuel and Paramjyothi immediately went to the U.S. to explain the situation to the IPC sponsors, who showed them the letter sent by Philip. Paramjyothi and Abraham Samuel convinced many of the sponsors that Philip was not the new leader of the IPC. However, some still supported his candidacy. Then Abraham Samuel and Paramjyothi expelled Philip from the IPC. With the help of several sponsors, including John Upperman, Philip started his own organization called "The Indian Pentecostal Community Church" (1981).[24] This denomination claimed to have 500 churches throughout India under the leadership of his son, Papabathini Prabhudas, by 2010.

The splits put a tremendous strain on the leadership of the IPC. Overnight, P.M. Samuel lost many loyal soldiers and friends when they transferred their allegiance to the WME. He also lost the IPC properties that were under their control. Manna Ministries further eroded the work of the IPC. As a rival organization, Manna Ministries started Manna Churches in every village and town where the IPC worked and attracted a number of IPC pastors and believers to its fold. These splits weakened the work of the IPC at first, but over time it began to grow again. Those who remained in the IPC reaffirmed their allegiance to P.M. Samuel and vigorously worked for the growth of the organization. A new generation of pastors was trained and continued the work of the IPC in Andhra after the departure of most of the senior pastors. One positive result that came from these splits was the multiplication of Pentecostal chuches in Andhra.

Summary

Dalits played a key role not only in the formation and the growth of the IPC, but also in its division. G. Samuel, Sasthry, Paramjyothi, Philip, and Ernest were some key players who contributed to its schism either directly or indirectly. The major events that took place during this period were the division of the IPC and the death of P.M. Samuel. The establishment of both the WME and Manna Ministries were major blows to the IPC. Both organizations attracted many of the IPC pastors as well as believers to their fold. As a result, the IPC lost many gifted senior pastors and became weak for a while. However, over time it regained its momentum and growth resumed. Moreover, after the demise of P.M. Samuel, Philip, a Dalit, made attempts to take over the reins of the IPC but did not succeed. The IPC survived this turbulent period, but it was no longer the dominant Pentecostal organization in Andhra when this period ended.

Notes

[1] John Matthews Allil (former pastor of Indian Pentecostal Church), interview with the author, Vijayawada, January 12, 2011. Thomas Kumar Gorinkala, interview

with the author, Warangal, December 31, 2010. Adiyya David Jekkala, interview with the author, Visakhapatnam, January 6, 2011.

[2] Raja Rao (pseudonym), interview with the author, January 21, 2011. Evangeline Grace Pedapudi, interview with the author, Machilipatnam, January 20, 2011. Ernest Komanapalli, interview with the author, Hyderabad, January 8, 2010. Due to cultural sensitivities, pseudonyms have been used to protect the identity of some informants or interviewees in this and following chapters. Locations where their interviews were conducted have also been kept anonymous for the same reason. Thus confidentiality has been maintained.

[3] Bergunder, *The South Indian Pentecostal Movement in the Twentieth Century*, 96.

[4] Spurgeon Raju Pachigalla, interview with the author, Vijayawada, January 3, 2006. Ernest Komanapalli, interview with the author, Hyderabad, January 8, 2010. Evangeline Grace Pedapudi, interview with the author, Machilipatnam, January 20, 2011.

[5] Silver Jubilee Souvenir: World Missionary Evangelism-Silver Jubilee Convention-Srikakulam (India), 1964-1989, 23-24.

[6] Silver Jubilee Souvenir: World Missionary Evangelism, 25.

[7] Silver Jubilee Souvenir: World Missionary Evangelism, 26.

[8] Silver Jubilee Souvenir: World Missionary Evangelism, 31.

[9] Silver Jubilee Souvenir: World Missionary Evangelism, 31.

[10] Hedlund, Christianity is Indian: The Emergence of an Indigenous Community, 377.

[11] John Matthews Allil, interview with the author, Vijayawada, January 12, 2011.

[12] Mariya Das (pseudonym), interview with the author, January 12, 2011.

[13] Yesudas (pseudonym), interview with the author, January 3, 2011.

[14] Mariya Das, interview with the author, January 12, 2011.

[15] Ebinezer Sasthry Taragam (pastor and grandson of Taragam Sathyavedam Sasthry), interview with the author, Eluru, January 14, 2010.

[16] Ernest Komanapalli, interview with the author, Hyderabad, January 8, 2010.

[17] Kim Firlan, *Compassionate Love: A Story of Ernest and Rachel Komanapalli* (Hyderabad: Manna Ministries, 1999), 13-14.

[18] Firlan, *Compassionate Love*, 41.

[19] Firlan, *Compassionate Love*, 77.

[20] Yesudas, interview with the author, January 3, 2011. Mariya Das, interview with the author, January 12, 2011. Sambabu (pseudonym), interview with the author, January 5, 2011.

[21] Bergunder, *The South Indian Pentecostal Movement in the Twentieth Century*, 101.

[22] David Raju (pseudonym), interview with the author, January 26, 2011.

[23] Prabhudas Papabathini (leader of Indian Pentecostal Community Church), phone interview with the author, Virginia Beach, February 17, 2011.

[24] Jaya Raju (pseudonym), interview with the author, January 25, 2011. Mariya Das, interview with the author, January 12, 2011. Yesudas, interview with the author, January 3, 2011.

Chapter 6

Later History of the IPC in Andhra Pradesh (1982 to 2010)

Introduction

In this time period, the IPC has witnessed various transitions in leadership and has also survived various crises. This section deals with several key individuals, including Plathaneth Abraham Samuel, Geddam Rathnam Purushotham (G.R. Purushotham), Deekollu John Sunder Rao (D. John Sunder Rao), and Plathaneth Noel Samuel, who filled the leadership void created by the sudden demise of Plathaneth Matthew Samuel. In addition, for the last two decades the IPC has had to face internal fighting, power struggles, and court cases which have damaged its reputation in society.

Significant Contributions of Second Generation Leaders

During the last three decades, Abraham Samuel, Purushotham, John Sunder Rao, and Noel Samuel have each played a crucial role in the history of the IPC. In this section, their contributions to the organization will be discussed.

Not long after the death of P.M. Samuel, his second son, Abraham Samuel, took over the reins of the IPC. He was not a charismatic leader like his father, but was still able to keep the organization intact. In order to keep his position secure, Abraham Samuel garnered the support of Paramjyothi and other senior leaders in the IPC (G.R. Purushotham, Kanumala Peturu Devasahayam, and Chatla Sudarsanam).[1]

Abraham Samuel completed high school at a mission boarding school in Bhimavaram and then attended the Government Teachers' Training College in Rajahmundry (1946). In spite of his Christian upbringing, the influence of his Hindu friends led him astray. He attended a conference in Nagpur in North India where he accepted Christ and was baptized in water. It was not long before Abraham Samuel committed his life to full-time ministry. He studied at Elim Bible Institute in Lima, New York (1951 to 1954) and continued at St. Louis College for one and a half years, obtaining a B.D. degree. After completing his theological education, he returned to India and married Joy (second daughter of P.T. Chacko) in Vijayawada (May 3, 1956). Not long after his marriage, he returned with her to the U.S. and she earned an M.A. degree from Indiana University. They then returned to India and he was soon involved in full-time ministry helping his father. Abraham Samuel established a children's home and a school in Vijayawada (1961), which still exists in 2010. He was later appointed an area pastor of the Guntur and Krishna areas. He became the president of the IPC in Andhra and also National Vice-President of the IPC (1972).[2]

Abraham Samuel was then appointed registrar and later principal of Zion Bible College, Vijayawada (1976 to 1991). Paramjyothi reappointed Abraham Samuel as the president of the Andhra IPC not long after his father's death (1981) and he held that position until his own death (1993). A year after Abraham Samuel took over as president for the second time; the IPC celebrated its Golden Jubilee (1982), a great milestone in its history. During that time he was editor-in-chief of the monthly magazine, "Banner of Truth" (1980s).

Abraham Samuel took his first preaching trip to the U.S. in 1956 and made several more trips there later. He also made subsequent trips to other Western countries, including Holland, Germany, and Canada. He was invited to the Sixteenth World Pentecostal Conference in Oslo, Norway (1992) where he spoke on "Holiness and Harvest."[3] He died of a heart attack on his return trip from Holland to India (November 16, 1993), after having served the IPC for thirty-seven years.

Another outstanding leader during this period is G.R. Purushotham, who contributed to the IPC immensely until his departure (1999). He was born into a Dalit Christian family in Jedcherla. His parents belonged to the Mennonite Mission Fellowship. He came to the Pentecostal faith (1949) after hearing a sermon by Philip Abraham. Purushotham attended Zion Bible School (1950). Ivan Q. Spencer from Lima, New York, came to Eluru to preach in the IPC General Convention (1950), and prophesied over Purushotham that God had chosen him for the ministry. Then P.M. Samuel, Pachigalla Lazarus Paramjyothi, Kallepu Rajarathnam David, and Taragam Sathyavedam Sasthry ordained him into full-time ministry during the convention.

At the beginning of his ministry, Purushotham worked with T.K. Thomas in Warangal. He pastored an IPC church in Mahaboobnagar for ten years and also started the IPC church in Jedcherla (1960s). He was appointed State Vice-President of the IPC by P.M. Samuel (1975). After the death of Abraham Samuel (1993), Purushotham became president of the IPC and served in that capacity until his departure from the IPC (1999). He is a gifted speaker and teacher. He taught for many years at Zion Bible College

(1968 to 1995), training hundreds of students and sending scores of graduates of the college to pioneer new churches, not only in the Mahaboobnagar area, but also in other places. He wrote articles and sermons for the "Gospel Illuminator" magazine for almost fifty years. He was one of the most sought-after speakers for the IPC annual church conventions throughout Andhra.

Purushotham was beaten numerous times by both Hindus and Christians because he preached the Pentecostal message. On his way home after preaching in a meeting (1970), a strong man came and began to punch him in the face. The man told him not to preach the Pentecostal message again and left. Purushotham fell down, bleeding from his mouth and nose, but he did not stop preaching the Pentecostal gospel. He conducted the annual convention in Jedcheral that year and seventeen people accepted the Pentecostal faith.

Purushotham suffered severe financial difficulties while spreading the Pentecostal faith in Andhra. When he was pastoring in Jedcherla (1963), he and his family had no food for three days. His children went to school and fainted there. The headmaster thought they were having seizures, but the fact was they had not eaten for three days. At times, Purushotham would get *conjee* (starch that is filtered after rice is boiled in water) from neighbors' homes to feed his children. Once his youngest daughter, Jamima, asked why they had to drink *conjee* every day and not eat rice and curry. He told her that God would provide food for them the next day. That night, he and his wife prayed for food and the following day a crow landed in front of their house with a five rupee note in its beak. Purushotham told his wife to get rice from a neighbor to throw so the bird would come near them, but she did not want to ask their neighbor. She insisted that if it was sent by God, they would get the five rupees. The crow finally dropped the note and flew away. With that money they bought rice, tomatoes, and green chilies and enjoyed a nice meal on that day.[4]

John Sunder Rao was another notable leader during this period. He was born (1945) into a Dalit Hindu family in Movva, Krishna District. His parents, Ramaswamy (Peter) and Venkamma (Mary Rathnam), became members of the Canadian Baptist Mission after John Sunder Rao was healed of a severe illness as an infant (1946). They later became Pentecostals and joined the IPC. John Sunder Rao came to the Pentecostal faith while studying at Noble College, Machilipatnam. After completing his B.S. degree (1965), he worked as a teacher for a few years in Zilla Parishad High School in Pedamangalaram. He resigned to enter full-time ministry and then attended Zion Bible College, Vijayawada (1967). After that he worked in the office of the "Gospel Illuminator." He also became a personal assistant to P.M. Samuel. Sunder Rao simultaneously looked after three churches at that time. He was sent to Andaman and the Nicobar Islands by P.M. Samuel to pioneer an IPC church (1975). At the beginning of his ministry there, John Sunder Rao suffered many hardships, including hunger and financial difficulties. One time, his wife Suvarna was not able to breastfeed their three-month old son since she had not eaten for three days. He had no money to buy milk for the child. The child was crying and about to die from starvation. They finally had to give him *conjee* to survive. After serving seven years, he built a church and parsonage in Andaman. John Sunder Rao later returned to Andhra Pradesh to look after the IPC church at Gunadala (1982). Then he moved to Hyderabad (1988) to become the pastor of the IPC church there.

John Sunder Rao also held various executive positions in the IPC. He worked as Secretary of the Krishna area (1983 to 1985) and then became District Pastor of the Hyderabad area (1997). He still holds that position (2010). In 1997, he was elected national Vice-President of the IPC and worked in that capacity until 2006. John Sunder Rao was appointed State President of the IPC by Noel Samuel (2008) and still holds that office (2010). He taught in Zion Bible College (1983 to 1993) and has served as editor of the "Gospel Illuminator" magazine since 1994.

Purushotham and John Sunder Rao, along with K.P. Devasahayam and Ch. Sudarsanam, helped to fill the leadership vacuum after the deaths of P.M. Samuel and Abraham Samuel. Not long after that, Purushotham, the highly gifted senior leader, left the IPC and the crisis intensified. John Sunder Rao was then appointed president and tried to fill the gap left in the IPC. However, the IPC pastors interviewed do not consider him to be a capable leader. In spite of the fact that he is the IPC president currently, he makes no decisions without Noel Samuel's approval. Many of the pastors do not regard him as being aggressive enough, but very meek and soft-spoken instead. They allege that he avoids any confrontation with Noel Samuel at any cost. The pastors also believe that he functions as president for the name's sake, but that Noel Samuel actually directs the IPC.[5]

Noel Samuel is another notable leader in the IPC during the 1990s and early 2000s. He is the son of Abraham Samuel and Joy, and the grandson of P.M. Samuel. He grew up on the IPC campus in Vijayawada. During his youth, he associated with the wrong crowd and turned his back on God. Then he had a tragic motorcycle accident (1978) and was hospitalized for two months. Many in the IPC prayed for him and he soon recovered completely. After this trial, he dedicated his life to full-time ministry. Noel obtained an undergraduate degree from Dallas Christian College in Texas and a M.A. degree from Regent University in Virginia. He then returned to India (1990) to work with the IPC. With the recommendation of Paramjyothi, Noel Samuel became principal of Zion Bible College, Vijayawada (1991). A year after he took over the leadership of the college, it celebrated its Golden Jubilee (1992), which was another great milestone in the history of the IPC. He came into the spotlight after the sudden demise of his father (1993). He was appointed State Secretary of the IPC (1993), and served in that position until 2005.[6]

Those loyal to Noel Samuel describe him as an able administrator and a capable leader. They believe that he alone has the capacity and talent to lead the IPC. During his time of leadership, he started cell groups in the IPC churches and also conducted training seminars on cell groups. He arranged marriage and family seminars for pastors and their wives. Noel Samuel also concentrated on Sunday school and youth programs, which had been neglected earlier. With the help of Compassion International, he is able to provide food and clothing to hundreds of children and employment for more than 200 people through Child Development Centers that he established. Under his leadership, the number of IPC churches has grown to more than 600 churches throughout Andhra.[7] There are also some who view him as a dynastic leader who inherited churches, position, and wealth from his father and grandfather. They therefore feel that he lacks the vision and commitment to develop the work of the IPC in Andhra.[8]

Significant Events and Major Issues

This section provides details about major issues and events that have occurred in the IPC's recent history, as narrated by its constituents. The interviewees collectively portray the condition of the IPC in a very negative light. In the recent past, the IPC suffered many setbacks, including legal battles, desertion of leaders, and local church conflicts due to caste bias. In the following section, the state of the IPC between 1990 and 2010 will be discussed in detail.

Desertion of Leaders Due to Power Struggle

Before Paramjyothi passed away, he called his son, Samuel Finney, and Noel Samuel to the house of another son, Spurgeon Raju, in Vijayawada. There he advised both men to work together in unity and love. His advice fell on deaf ears and after his death (1996), Noel and Finney parted ways.[9] That same year, a cyclone hit Andhra Pradesh, damaging houses and crops throughout the state. Noel collected funds from abroad for relief efforts and promised Finney that he would provide funds to help pastors and churches affected by the cyclone in the Antarvedipalem area. Finney and the pastors from his area made repeated requests for the promised financial help, but received no funds from him.[10] Since Noel Samuel did not respond, Finney decided to leave the IPC and to work on his own. He then founded the "Indian Pentecostal Church Mission." More than 125 IPC churches left the IPC and went with him.[11]

Noel Samuel (grandson of P.M. Samuel) wanted to become the president of the IPC following the death of his father, Abraham Samuel (son of P.M. Samuel). Purushotham objected to this and the reason for his objection was that Noel Samuel had just returned from the U.S. after completing his studies and had no previous ministerial experience. Moreover, Purushotham believed that there were other senior Telugu pastors (including himself), who were more qualified for the job. Then Paramjyothi decided to appoint Noel Samuel as secretary, Purushotham as president, K.P. Devasahayam as vice president, K.J. Purushotham as joint secretary, and A. Ruben as treasurer. This created a rift between Noel Samuel and Purushotham. They often differed on various decisions since a large age gap existed between them. Purushotham would not only challenge Noel Samuel's administrative and financial decisions, but would also make him accountable for his choices. The common perception of the interviewees is that Noel Samuel felt Purushotham's continued presence in the IPC threatened his leadership. He convinced Kakamala Thomas Samuel (K.T. Samuel) and other council members to turn against Purushotham by insinuating that he was diverting IPC funds to his own work. As a result, Purushotham was forced to leave the IPC. He and others believed that Noel paid some members on the IPC council to vote him out as president (1999). Other council members who also voted him out may have done so reluctantly for fear of losing their churches and their livelihood if they did not.[12]

Another reason for Purushotham's departure from the IPC was that Mark Emerson of Canada wanted to provide him with 70,000 dollars to expand the work in Mahaboobnagar. Noel Samuel did not want Emerson to grant that amount directly to Purushotham, but to the IPC headquarters for distribution. It is possible that he did not want a Telugu pastor to benefit from Emerson's help. This dispute about finances forced Purushotham to leave the IPC after almost fifty years of serving the denomination faithfully.[13] When he departed, about seventy IPC churches followed him. He then formed a new independent work with those who left with him.[14]

Legal Battles

Court cases against the IPC seldom occurred in earlier periods, but in recent years, the organization has had to face many legal battles. Two crucial ones in the last few decades brought the organization into disrepute. This section narrates the issues and events that led to these legal battles.

Mortha Philip (M. Philip) migrated back to India from Rangoon during the Second World War, along with K.G. Paul and A.S. Paul. He came to the Pentecostal faith through Manaseh, a Ceylon Pentecostal pastor in Burma. Philip joined the IPC and began to work with P.M. Samuel in the Injaram area (1950). He taught disadvantaged blind children on his porch (1968). A school for the blind developed from this effort and accommodations were built with government assistance. When Abraham Samuel became IPC president (1972), he began to receive funds from abroad for this school that Philip launched. Abraham Samuel received enough funds for the operation of the school every month, but Philip would actually receive only a portion for the school. Philip would often use the income he received from ministry or proceeds from the sale of coconuts from his land to take care of the children, since the money he received from Abraham Samuel was not sufficient. Philip never dared to question Abraham Samuel as to how much he was receiving for the school.

When Noel Samuel assumed leadership of the IPC after his father's death, he wanted to remove the school from Philip's control and move it to Vijayawada (1995). Philip pleaded with him to leave the school under his control until his death, but Noel Samuel would not agree to his request. Philip's daughter, Mellimi Esther Rani, confronted Noel Samuel and tried to prevent him from taking over the school. According to Deva Kumari (pseudonym), Noel Samuel paid some people (including Philip's son, Sugandha Rathnam) to come and threaten the teachers and blind children. He promised Rathnam that he would pay 60,000 rupees to go against his father and sister and help him secure the school from them. With his help, Noel Samuel's representatives came in the middle of the night and forcefully took most of the children and teachers to Vijayawada. Before they left, they located the important documents pertaining to the school, including the registration, and tore all of them into pieces.

Samarpana Rao and Deenamma (pseudonyms) were two of the students forcefully taken to Vijayawada. They reported that they were promised monthly financial support by the supporters of Noel Samuel if they would move to Vijayawada, so they reluctantly went there. For the first few months, the blind children were fed and treated well in Vijayawada, but later they were verbally and physically abused by the cook. Meanwhile, Esther Rani moved to Rajahmundry with the rest of the blind children for security reasons. She decided to fight the battle legally. A domestic worker in Philip's house found a photocopy of the school registration in a trash pile. Esther took it to the registrar's office and obtained a replacement for the original document that was destroyed. Noel Samuel was unable to produce relevant documents to convince the court that the school belonged to him or to the IPC. Esther Rani won the court case and the school was returned to her.[15]

Another legal battle Noel Samuel faced was from fellow Malayali K.T. Samuel. After Purushotham left, Noel Samuel appointed Ch. Sudarsanam as President, K.T. Samuel as Vice President, and Giddla Bhagavan Das as Secretary to lead the organization. Noel Samuel chose K.T. Samuel because he was a Malayali, hoping he would be an asset to him, but he soon became a problem instead. Noel Samuel also appointed his son, Samuel Thomas, as dean of Zion Bible College and gave him many administrative responsibilities. A conflict arose between them when Thomas felt he had been accused of stealing after Noel inquired about a missing check.[16]

After the conflict, K.T. Samuel and his son confronted Noel about the two parallel councils he had formed, and the relationship between them was strained further.[17] During the period when Thomas had a cordial relationship with Noel Samuel, he noticed that he had formed two parallel state councils. One was to represent Andhra to Kumbanadu. Even though it was the official council, it had no power, but was formed for the sake of the name. The second was Noel Samuel's own handpicked committee. This committee acted like an official council and made unilateral decisions. It was appointed to represent another separate organization which his father, Abraham Samuel, had founded (1980s) to receive foreign funds. However, Thomas remained quiet about the issue at that time.

When K.T. Samuel was pastor of the IPC church in Gunadala, he collected funds from the congregants to remodel the church (2002) and the funds were used for renovations. One day Noel Samuel came and announced in the church that he was going to demolish it and rebuild an auditorium as a multi-purpose structure. He was able to obtain permission to build it with the help of Koneru Ranga Rao, a local influential political leader. However, K.T. Samuel and the congregation did not agree with his decision. Noel Samuel then asked K.T. Samuel and the congregation to find another place to conduct the services and proceeded to dismantle the building. K.T. Samuel and the elders then asked Noel Samuel for a place to meet on the IPC compound. He allowed them to conduct services in front of the demolished church building temporarily, but was unwilling to provide electricity or any room to store the musical instruments and sound system. Every week, the equipment had to be moved back and forth to K.T. Samuel's house. K.T. Samuel later shifted the services to his house due to the inconvenience. When the congregation requested a place in Zion High School, Noel Samuel refused to give them any. Because of the space problem, they decided to conduct Sunday services in a Roman Catholic compound nearby.

When Noel Samuel learned of this move, he provoked caste feelings and the IPC church in Gunadala split into two groups. The believers from the high caste background sided with Noel Samuel, and the Dalits followed K.T. Samuel and met in his home. Noel Samuel and his group met at Zion High School for Sunday worship services (2004). It is reported that Noel Samuel's family often claimed that they were Syrians and equal to Brahmins ever since the days of P.M. Samuel. They looked down on the IPC pastors and believers who were from a Dalit background.

Noel Samuel told K.T. Samuel and the congregation that the building they were meeting in was not actually the IPC church, but was the chapel that belonged to the Zion Bible College. He further contended that his grandfather, P.M. Samuel, had purchased the property and it really belonged to him, not the IPC. Because of Noel's claims, K.T. Samuel and his group went to court to settle the matter legally. Meanwhile, Noel Samuel removed K.T. Samuel from his position as Vice-President of the IPC (2005). While the lawsuit was still pending, K.T. Samuel died and Noel Samuel turned the situation to his favor. He reportedly bribed lawyers with *lakhs* of rupees (one *lakh* of rupees equals approximately 2,500 US dollars) to win the case. He may have paid the lawyers and judges between thirty and forty *lakhs*.[18] Part of this payment may have been their legal fees, and only the remainder a bribe. Since corruption and bribes are rampant in Indian society, nothing gets done unless some kind of bribe is paid. However, the amount appears to be somewhat exaggerated. This may also be no more than a rumor.

Other Conflicts within Local churches

In recent years, the IPC has been plagued by conflict within its local churches, including those in Eluru, Vijayawada, and Visakhapatnam. A sampling of these situations described by interviewees will be addressed in the following section.

After the death of K.P. Devasahayam (1996), his son-in-law, Marlapudi Peturu, (Peter), who was the assistant pastor, took over the church. After Peturu's sudden demise (2000), his wife, Mary, wanted to be the pastor of the church. However, Kancherla Hardy Moody's family controlled the affairs of the IPC church and did not want her to be pastor because of their caste bias. Peturu was from the Madiga caste, but his wife belonged to the Mala caste. The Kancherla family wanted someone from their own Madiga caste to be pastor of the church. They appointed Ch. Immanuel as the pastor, but the Kencherla family was dissatisfied with his preaching style.[19] Before long, Kunchala Sekhar Daniel became pastor of the IPC Church at Eluru. In the beginning, he had a good relationship with the Kancherla family, but conflict arose suddenly between them. IPC pastors did not have monthly salaries. Since the inception of the IPC, the pastors lived off the offerings and tithes of the church. Noel Samuel was the leader of the IPC at that time. He enforced the presbyterian form of church government in the IPC churches, where the elders control the affairs of the church and have a salary system, just like churches in the United States. Since many relatives of the Kancherla family live abroad, they supported the salary system Noel Samuel introduced. Daniel responded negatively to this new salary system. As a result, the relationship between him and the Kancherla family was strained. Moreover, caste bias added fuel to the conflict because Daniel was not from the Madiga community. The conflict escalated (December 2003) after a Sunday service and the Kancherla family padlocked the church and evicted Daniel and his family right before Christmas.[20] This caused the split in the IPC church, and some of the Dalits and most of non-Dalits left the church. They started another IPC church in Eluru under Daniel's leadership. Those who were predominantly from the Madiga caste remained in the Eluru IPC Church. Later, the Kancherla family appointed G.J. Raj Kumar from the Madiga caste as pastor. The conflict between the Malas and the Madigas not only exists in the Eluru church, but also in many other IPC churches. It remains the most threatening issue for the growth of the IPC at the present time.

Another conflict arose between Pastor Didla Rathnam and the elders of the IPC Church at Baptist Palem in Vijayawada (2008). The elders wanted to spend the funds of the church for church functions, but Rathnam wanted to use the funds to help the poor and needy in the church. The elders made false accusations against Rathnam and asked Noel Samuel to remove him from his pastorate. Noel Samuel sided with the elders and appointed a new pastor, Ravi Babu, without giving Rathnam a chance to explain his side of the story. As a result, the church split in two. One group followed Rathnam and conducted Sunday services downstairs, while the other group met upstairs under the leadership of Ravi Babu. Noel Samuel exerted pressure on Rathnam to vacate the parsonage downstairs. Rathnam refused to vacate the house since he had nowhere else to go. Noel Samuel encouraged the group meeting upstairs to take Rathnam to the police station to force him to leave the pastorate and parsonage. He was taken to the police station on three occasions because of these church problems. Rathnam approached the state IPC council to look into his situation and do justice for him. However, the state IPC council was controlled by Noel Samuel and he therefore received little help from the council. Noel Samuel tried to convince Rathnam to leave by offering him ten thousand rupees per month for one year if he stepped down from the pastorate and vacated the parsonage. Rathnam insisted that he was not wrong and he would not step down.[21] According to one of his relatives, the emotional trauma due to these church problems contributed to his death.

After the death of the senior pastors, most wives and children do not want to leave the church or the parsonage. They want to look after the church. When the IPC council asks them to vacate the place, they are unwilling to move. They want to fight legally in the courts instead, because families of deceased pastors are left with no income, no place to go, and no resources for survival. There is no system in place in the IPC to deal with such situations to help them financially. When senior pastors are transferred to a new place due to conflict in a local church, they are usually unwilling to relocate. They either go to court or leave the IPC. As a consequence, the IPC churches are being split. This has become a common occurrence in the IPC (1990 to 2010).

The generational gap between Noel Samuel and the senior leaders is also a source of conflict. When Noel Samuel was educated in the U.S., he was influenced by church governance and administration models and policies (salaries, transfers, membership fees, vacations for pastors) from the West. He tried to implement some of these ideas in the IPC churches in Andhra. The senior pastors disagreed with most of these changes, bringing sharp conflict with him. Since Noel Samuel is young and educated, he was able to relate and connect with the younger and educated pastors better than with the older ones. The senior pastors felt that he had isolated them. It is their common opinion that Noel Samuel, being a young and inexperienced pastor and administrator, should seek out and heed their advice. They, therefore, are not willing to follow his lead. Noel Samuel seems to feel that the senior pastors and administrators are from the old school and their ideas will not work for this generation, since times have changed. This issue has remained a source of tension between them.

Summary

During this time period, Dalit leaders Purushotham and John Sunder Rao provided leadership to the IPC, along with Abraham Samuel (P.M. Samuel's son), and Noel Samuel (Abraham Samuel's son and P.M. Samuel's grandson). The Golden Jubilee celebrations of the formation of the IPC and the founding of Zion Bible College were the two major milestones in the history of the IPC that occurred during this period. The sudden death of Abraham Samuel and the departure of Purushotham from the IPC created a leadership crisis in the organization. This has been a period of internal fighting, local church splits, and court cases, which, in combination, have tarnished the image of the IPC. However, under the leadership of Noel Samuel, the IPC is still progressing, despite the internal problems.

Notes

[1] Kanumala Peturu Devasahayam Kanumala and Chatla Sudarsanam also provided leadership to the IPC during this time period. Their role in the IPC was discussed in Chapter 4. Devasahayam served the IPC in Andhra as secretary (1975 to 1993). After the demise of Abraham Samuel, he was appointed vice-president (1993 to 1996). In the 1960s, Sudarsanam was elected as IPC vice president and later as secretary. After the death of Devasahayam, he was again appointed vice president (1996 to 1999). He became president of the IPC (1999 to 2005) because of Geddam Rathnam Purushotham's departure from the organization.

[2] Samuel, *Autobiography of Apostle P.M. Samuel*, 44.

[3] Joy A. Samuel Plathaneth, *Counting My Blessings!* (Vijayawada: Zion Printing Press, 1999), 72.

[4] Rathnam Purushotham Geddam (former state president of Indian Pentecostal Church), interview with the author, Jadcherla, December 30, 2010.

[5] Raja Rao (pseudonym), interview with the author, January 21, 2011. Johnson (pseudonym), interview with the author, January 19, 2010. Jacobson (pseudonym), interview with the author, January 19, 2010.

[6] Noel Samuel, (former state secretary of Indian Pentecostal Church), interview with the author, Vijayawada, January 4, 2010.

[7] Daveedu Pitta (state secretary of Indian Pentecostal Church), interview with the author, Pedapadu, January 18, 2011. Bhagavan Das Giddla (Ongole area pastor of Indian Pentecostal Churches), interview with the author, Ongole, January 2, 2011. Eliya Charugudi (pastor of Indian Pentecostal Church), interview with the author, Gannavaram, January 20, 2011.

[8] Ananda Rao (pseudonym), interview with the author, January 3, 2011. James (pseudonym), interview with the author, January 6, 2011. Deva Raju (pseudonym), interview with the author, January 17, 2011. Mariya Das, interview with the author, January 12, 2011. Yesudas, interview with the author, January 3, 2011. Aseervadam (pseudonym), interview with the author, January 6, 2011. Raja Rao, interview with the author, January 21, 2011.

[9] Samuel Finney Pachigalla (leader of Indian Pentecostal Church Ministries and former pastor of Indian Pentecostal Church), interview with the author, Anthirvedipalem, January 14, 2011.

[10] Mariya Das, interview with the author, January 12, 2011.

[11] Noel Samuel, E-mail received by the author, October 15, 2005.

[12] Yesudas, interview with the author, January 3, 2011. Rathnam Purushotham Geddam, interview with the author, Jadcherla, December 30, 2010. Raja Rao, interview with the author, January 21, 2011. Santhosh Kumar (pseudonym) interview with the author, January 17, 2011.

[13] Moses Kumar (pseudonym), interview with the author, January 2, 2011.

[14] Noel Samuel, E-mail received by the author, October 15, 2005.

[15] Deva Kumari (pseudonym), interview with the author, January 11, 2011. Samarpana Rao (pseudonym), interview with the author, January 11, 2011.

[16] Prem Kumar (pseudonym), interview with the author, January 20, 2011.

[17] Deva Raju, interview with the author, January 17, 2011. Santhosh Kumar, interview with the author, January 17, 2011. Aseervadam, interview with the author, January 6, 2011.

[18] Yesurathnam (pseudonym), interview with the author, January 17, 2011. Raja Rao, interview with the author, January 21, 2011. Deva Raju, interview with the author, January 17, 2011. Santhosh Kumar, interview with the author, January 17, 2011. Aseervadam, interview with the author, January 6, 2011.

[19] Rachel (pseudonym), interview with the author, January 29, 2011. Rathna Raju (pseudonym), interview with the author, January 22, 2011. David Raju, interview with the author, January 26, 2011.

[20] David Raju, interview with the author, January 26, 2011. Deva Raju, interview with the author, January 17, 2011. Santhosh Kumar, interview with the author, January 17, 2011. Rathna Raju, interview with the author, January 22, 2011.

[21] Deva Raju, interview with the author, January 17, 2011. Rathna Raju, interview with the author, January 17, 2011. Raja Rao, interview with the author, January 21, 2011. Lydia (pseudonym), interview with the author, January 12, 2011.

Chapter 7

Conclusion

Introduction

This chapter seeks to assess the viability of the IPC by analyzing key factors that influenced the movement's growth and the significant factors that led to its division in order to grasp the full imact it had on Indian society. After looking at the available printed material and interviewing scores of key denominational leaders, pastors, and adherents, the author has evaluated the movement in terms of the following categories: spiritual empowerment, personal wholeness, high commitment, numerical growth, training or development, resilience, unity, leadership style, inclusiveness, financial condition of workers, and social impact.

The Viability of the IPC

Spiritual Empowerment

According to the members of the IPC, the mainline churches in Andhra neither understood nor taught the scriptural teaching on the baptism of the Holy Spirit. However, since its inception, the IPC movement has emphasized the importance of the person and the work of the Holy Spirit in the Christian believer's life.[1] This movement taught and believed, like many classical Pentecostals, that the baptism of the Holy Spirit is the subsequent experience to regeneration, and that the initial evidence of baptism of the Holy Spirit is speaking in tongues. The concept of the baptism of the Holy Spirit was first referred to biblically in the book of Acts, when the Holy Spirit descended upon the first Christians in Jerusalem on the Day of Pentecost.

The IPC movement taught, and still teaches, that those baptized in the Holy Spirit can also receive other supernatural gifts that existed in primitive

Christianity, such as the ability to prophesy, to interpret unknown tongues, and to heal the sick. IPC adherents strongly believe that these supernatural gifts spiritually empowered the Dalit Pentecostals to spread the Pentecostal faith throughout Andhra. Taragam Sathyavedam Sasthry did not have much education but was able to communicate in six different languages, including English. He attributed this gift to the power of the Holy Spirit.[2] K. Sanjeeva Rao could barely read and write before he became a Pentecostal. He claims that after he received a call to full-time ministry in a vision, he was able to read the Bible by the power of the Holy Spirit. Sanjeeva Rao also received spiritual empowerment to start a Pentecostal work in the Chintalapudi area.[3] Godi Samuel points out that, in spite of the fact that the first and second generations of IPC pastors were not highly educated, they were bold and courageous when they preached. They could convince almost anyone about the necessity of the baptism of the Holy Spirit through their preaching. It was the demonstration of the power of the Holy Spirit, including the baptism of the Holy Spirit, speaking in tongues, visions, prophecies, and healings, which primarily caused the IPC churches to grow.[4]

Personal Wholeness

IPC adherents claim that many in Andhra were attracted to the Pentecostal message because it offered hope of personal wholeness through exorcisms and physical healings. Demon-possessed people and the sick were often delivered and healed when IPC pastors prayed for them.[5] Pastor Jekkala Adiyya David told about his oldest sister Paidamma's deliverance from demon-possession. After she had been possessed for many months, her father took her to several medical doctors and witch doctors, but no one could cure her from demon-possession. Then K. Israel from Thurangam came to preach in Sankavaram where they lived. He told them about Adidala Sundaram Paul, an IPC pastor in Mandapet, who dealt with exorcisms. He advised her father to take her there to Pastor A.S. Paul. When he did, Paul prayed for her and cast the demon out of her. A week after they returned from Mandapet, Paidamma and her husband converted to Pentecostalism and received water baptism.[6]

IPC adherents also claimed that physical healings greatly contributed to the spread of the IPC. According to B. Vimalamma, B.S. Kruparakshana went to the Seleru area (1960) where he found a man dying from tetanus. He told the man that Jesus could heal him if he believed. Kruparakshana prayed for him, and then left for another village. Kruparakshana's wife, Vimalamma (a medical doctor), was skeptical about the validity of the man's healing. The next year they returned to the same area. Vimalamma still doubted and was curious to know what happened to the man dying from tetanus. She asked the villagers, who told her that the man was alive and had gone to the market to sell tamarind. His family and many in his village had accepted the Pentecostal faith because of that healing. Vimalamma stated that many Hindus were attracted to the IPC because of healings and because they realized there was something different and special about the Pentecostal message.[7]

Dasi Franklin told of a healing which took place in his ministry in Alamanda. Nekkala Ramayamma came to him with breast cancer. Her husband, Nekkala Devudu, sent her to her parents' home since she was about to die. Doctors told her they would have to remove both breasts, but even if they did, she would not survive. Franklin anointed her with oil and prayed for her to be healed. After two months, she completely recovered. In gratitude, the couple donated land to build an IPC church (2009).

High Commitment

IPC pastors suffered a great deal while trying to promote the Pentecostal faith in Andhra. They lived by faith in God for their daily needs, without asking anyone else for anything. Many lived in huts, some had only one set of clothes, and many could hardly feed themselves or their children, much less afford to educate them.[8]

Kundeti Gershon Paul (Chinna K.G. Paul) said that when he came to Kakinada to pioneer the IPC work, he had only one pair of pants and one shirt. He could not find a house for rent. During the day he would visit various villages to evangelize and at night he would sleep under a banyan tree. Paul used his shirt as a bedsheet at night. The following day he would wear the same shirt and do the work of the ministry.[9]

Similarly, Jonnagaddi Das resigned from his job and went into full-time ministry. He went to Kothagudem to plant an IPC church (1953) and he and his family stayed with L.T. Manikyam for a month. He later found an abandoned rice mill, and with the owner's permission, he moved into it with his family and also conducted services there on Sundays. One Christmas, Das and his family had had nothing to eat for three days. He felt very sorry that he was not able to feed his three children during the Christmas season. His third child was nine months old at that time. He and his wife, Mariyamma, began to weep in prayer for their situation. Not long after they finished crying and praying, they heard a knock on the door. They opened it and saw two ladies, Santhamma and Deenamma, standing at the door, each with a basket on her head. One brought food in her basket while the other had new clothes for all of them.[10]

Anumala Finney Samuel told his story as a son of an IPC pastor. When his father pastored a church in Kunderu, they lived in a thatched-roof hut. A devastating cyclone (1977) came through, causing many to lose their lives and many houses to be swept away. The hut they lived in fell on them, but miraculously, none of them was hurt. Then the family took shelter in a Roman Catholic Church and later under a tree. Finally, they rebuilt their hut and lived in it until they moved to Vuyyuru, where his father worked as an IPC pastor (1979). He said that they often had no food. There were four children at that time and they would share one egg once a month.¹¹ These are a few examples of how they suffered and God met their needs.

Some Dalit pastors even lost their children to starvation or from lack of healthcare. When Botta Gabriel went to work in Kothavalasa, he had no money to buy milk for his daughter Gloria. She finally died of starvation when she was three.¹² When Kallepu Rajarathnam David was working in Gandigunta as an IPC pastor, his oldest daughter, Grace, was stricken with chickenpox and pneumonia. He was not able to take her to a doctor in time, and she died while his family visited relatives in Warangal.¹³

These cases demonstrate how Dalit pastors in Andhra lived sacrificial lives to promote the Pentecostal faith. These pastors believed they were suffering for Christ. They took their faith in Him seriously and endured all types of suffering for the sake of the gospel. They did not give up in their ministry in the midst of various hardships, financial difficulties, or from lack of necessities. When people witnessed their sacrifice for the gospel, they would begin to believe in what the Pentecostals were preaching.

The reason they could tolerate their hardships is closely linked with their view of suffering. There is a sense in which IPC pastors seemed to glorify affliction. Facing various difficulties in the ministry was considered a virtue or sign of piety. They also believed that misery for the sake of Christ in this world would be rewarded in the world to come. IPC pastors believed that a person was not a true Christian believer unless he or she endured hardships for Christ or in the ministry. They were driven by the fact that Jesus died and suffered for them, and they ought to suffer in return for Christ.¹⁴

Numerical Growth

The IPC started with one church in Eluru with a handful of believers and grew to 300 churches by the time of the WME's formation.¹⁵ In 2010, the IPC had about 660 churches with approximately 90,000 baptized believers.¹⁶ This numerical growth is attributed to the passion of the early IPC pastors, whose goal was to win souls and plant churches. Kuntam Edward states that thirst for evangelism and freedom of worship are the unique aspects of the IPC. Its pastors had but one aim: to evangelize and plant churches in Andhra. That was the reason many IPC churches were established there.¹⁷ The IPC pastors were aggressive and courageous in their efforts to promote the Pentecostal faith, and the main reason for their zeal was that they believed that the Pentecostal message was the "full gospel" and was biblical. It was their view that the mainline churches had failed to preach the "full gospel" and had neglected the teaching on the baptism of the Holy Spirit in their orthodoxy and praxis.

Fervor for evangelism and church planting motivated the IPC pastors to travel many miles by foot or bicycle to various villages to conduct open-air gospel meetings. Some conducted street evangelism in both villages and cities. Others would climb on trees and rooftops to preach the gospel, using aluminum trumpets to attract an audience.[18] Their determined evangelistic efforts bore fruit and resulted in the establishment of the IPC churches and denomination.

Leadership Training

The growth of the IPC is attributed to both the leadership and the ministerial training it provided through Zion Bible School. Constituents of the IPC pointed out that the organization produced hundreds of dedicated and committed pastors in order to provide leadership for the IPC churches. After their training, they were placed as pastors in the IPC churches or were sent to new villages to pioneer the work of the IPC.[19] Many of its leaders were trained at Zion Bible College, including: Kallepu Rajarathnam David, Geddam Rathnam Purushotham, Kanumala Peturu Devasahayam, Chatla Sudarsanam, Adidala Sundaram Paul, Korati George Paul, Bathina Samuel Lukeson, Taragam Sathyavedam Sasthry, and Deekollu John Sunder Rao. They later became teachers themselves in the Bible school and prepared hundreds of young leaders for the ministry. "Zion Bible College from the beginning trained and prepared many workers biblically, who totally dedicated their lives for the Lord's service. They were taught to lean upon the Lord for their needs and endure the sufferings in proclaiming the Pentecostal message."[20] The young people who were trained at Zion went to new areas without any hesitation to plant IPC churches. The training of the ministers at the school played a pivotal role in the growth of the IPC in Andhra.[21]

Zion Bible School was started in Anthirvedipalem (August 15, 1942) in a school building owned by Kollabathula Jagannadham, who offered his school to conduct the Bible classes in. B. John Reddy, who migrated back to Rangoon, contributed 100 rupees for the operation of the school. Others donated rice, various groceries, and firewood for cooking. One hundred students from various places in Andhra came and attended classes for thirty-eight days in the first year. Classes were held from eight in the morning until eleven at night. Bible school was later conducted in various locations in Tadepalligudem (1947), Rajahmundry (1948), Vijayawada (1952, 1953, 1956, 1959), Eluru (1950, 1957), Kakinada (1956), Mandapet, and Warangal (1958). A permanent building was built for the school (1960) in Gunadala, Vijayawada, from donations received from Holland and Germany.[22] It became a full-fledged college the same year. However, after it celebrated its Golden Jubilee (1992), the impact of Zion Bible College became minimal due to decline in enrollment. Currently, many young people in the IPC prefer to study in an English-medium Bible college elsewhere in Andhra or outside the state.

Resilience

Members of the IPC exhibited resilience in the midst of stiff opposition, providing another reason for its growth. They suffered not just from intense poverty and hunger, but also from humiliation and beatings coming primarily from Hindus, Communists, and the mainline denominations. The IPC was perceived as a threat to mainline denominations because many from among their church members left and became Pentecostals. Hindus considered Christianity to be a Western religion. The Communists opposed the Pentecostal message because it was in direct contrast to their atheistic propaganda.

Opposition from Hindus. Hinduism is the predominant religion in Andhra and many Hindus oppose Pentecostalism. They consider conversion to Christ to be the greatest threat to Hindu society because Christianity preaches equality. The following examples illustrate ways Pentecostal pastors suffered at the hands of Hindus and how Hindus were later converted to Pentecostalism.

B.S. Lukeson went to Gokavaram village to evangelize. Suryanarayana, a Hindu villager from the Golla caste, grabbed the scarf around his neck and pulled him to the floor. Lukeson fell and injured his head and his clothes were full of blood. Then Suryanarayana (who was drunk at the time) told him not to preach about the Western God and not to come to that village. Meanwhile, the village head intervened and told Suryanarayana that he should not hurt people in that way and that if he did not like what Lukeson was preaching, he had a right to reject his message. Lukeson did not give up. He returned to the village and continued to share the gospel. Later, Suryanarayana and his children were converted to Christianity and became Pentecostals.[23]

Medisetti Srinivasa Rao tells about his grandmother, Medisetti Gannamma, a Hindu in the village of Sallapudu. She and her whole village opposed Christian teaching and allowed no preacher to enter their village. IPC pastor Mortha Philip went there to preach the gospel, and the villagers threatened to kill him if he came again. He paid no attention to their threats because he was willing to die if necessary to promote the Pentecostal faith. Gannamma lost her sight and her family thought she would never see again. Philip told her to give Jesus a chance and He would restore her sight. She finally consented to his suggestion. After Philip prayed, she could see again. She soon became a Pentecostal but was excommunicated from the village. Then, those who opposed her began to experience problems in their lives. Gannamma and Philip would go and pray for them, and when they saw the power of Christianity, they slowly accepted the Pentecostal faith.[24] Today Medisetti Srinivasa Rao, the grandson of Gannamma, is an IPC pastor in Kolanki village.

Pandit Uma Maheswar propagated that Christianity was not the true religion, contending that it was a Western religion. He encouraged Hindus to excommunicate Christians in Andhra (1960s) and he started atheist centers all over the state. He opened one center near a statue of Mahatma Gandhi in Nidadavole. Kanumala Peturu Devasahayam once preached about Jesus near the statue and the followers of Maheswar and several Hindus beat him and dragged him on the road. Kati Das (brother-in-law of Devasahayam) watched this helplessly and then reported it to people in the Dalit colony. When they rushed to the spot, the mob dragging Devasahayam fled the scene. Devasahayam was confined to bed two or three days, then went later to Nanadamuru village to preach the gospel.[25]

Similarly, Jannu Krupa Prabhakar narrates his story of escaping from Hindu militants known as the Rashtriya Swayamsevak Sangh (RSS). While working as an IPC pastor in Illanda in the Warangal area (1997), followers of the RSS abducted him. They blindfolded him and took him into an interior place. He was in their custody three days without knowing where he was. After questioning him, they threatened him, telling him not to continue to propagate the gospel in the Illanda area. He thought they were going to kill him. They finally released him on the condition that he would not preach about Jesus in that area.[26]

Opposition from Communists. IPC pastors received opposition not only from the Hindus, but also from the Communists. When Pentecostal meetings were conducted in Antarvedipalem (1942), the Communists informed Potti Rajarathnam that he should cancel his meetings because the Communists were also conducting a meeting there at three in the afternoon. Rajarathnam told them they would conclude their meeting by one in the afternoon and it would not interfere with the Communists' meeting. About 400 Communist party cadres came with their red flags and pulled down the tent, scattering the people who came to participate in the Pentecostal meeting. One young man tried to beat Plathaneth Matthew Samuel, but the people surrounded and protected him. Rajarathnam and the participants then re-erected the tent that same night and continued the meetings. When the meetings concluded, many embraced the Pentecostal faith.[27]

Paramjyothi was spit upon in Antarvedipalem while preaching, then beaten and dragged in the streets by the Communists. He also received death threats from them. In a convention where he was preaching, a Communist came from behind and jumped on the platform to kill him. In so doing, he lost his balance and fell on the dais instead. The same one who came to kill him was later converted to Pentecostalism. Some of these Communist radicals who opposed Paramjyothi, including Dondapati Manoharam and Dondapati Krupanandam, eventually became his followers (1950s). But the Communists continued to be a menace to Paramjyothi's ministry. On one occasion, a group of Communists burned the tents in which he was hosting annual Pentecostal meetings (1982), but, miraculously, no one was injured. Later the attendants put up new tents and continued the meetings.[28]

Adidala John Shabdham (son of Adidala Sundaram Paul) tells about the Communists setting their house on fire in Mandapet (1961) because of his father's aggressive efforts to promote the Pentecostal message. It was in the summer. Communists came in the middle of the night and set his house on fire, thinking Paul and his family were in it. His oldest son, Immanuel, and Pakala Samson, another pastor, were sleeping instead under a nearby mango tree that night. Paul and his wife had gone to conduct annual meetings in Tapeswaram village. By the time fire engines came from Rajahmundry, their thatched roof house had burned to the ground. However, their lives were spared.[29]

Opposition from Mainline Denominations. IPC adherents and pastors alike encountered opposition from mainline denominations. Inje Abraham states that when they accepted the Pentecostal faith, the Baptists turned against them. They were excommunicated and not invited for a marriage reception by the Baptists. Children of Pentecostal believers were not allowed to study in Baptist schools. Whenever the IPC meetings were being conducted, Baptists came and threw stones, disturbing the meetings.[30] According to Appikatla Jeevanandam, when the family of his grandfather, A. Anandarao, left the Baptist church in Warangal, the Baptist believers attacked them in the night. They grabbed the shirt collars of Anandarao's relatives, tore their shirts, and beat them.

Samuel Vijaya Chandar was a rowdy drunkard whose family belonged to the Baptist Church. He did not like Pastor Giddla Bhagavan Das preaching the Pentecostal message in Kabadipalem in Ongole and wanted to eliminate him. One day he accompanied him to a meeting in Kaliki village (1980s). On their way back, he wanted to kill him and throw his body into a nearby canal. However, whenever Vijaya Chandar wanted to take the knife out of his bag, someone would come from the opposite direction. He finally accepted the Pentecostal faith and was baptized by Bhagavan Das. He sent him to Maranatha Bible College in Madras. After completing his studies, Vijaya Chandar started working as an IPC pastor in Siddapuram.[31]

The mainline churches and the Hindus once plotted together to kill John Sabdham's father, Adidala Sundaram Paul. They sent a woman named Ganni Mariyamma one night to give his father a bowl of plain yogurt filled with poison. Paul had just fasted and prayed for three days and ended his fast that evening. The yogurt came just in time. He began to eat and suddenly his eyes became dizzy and his tongue began to shrink. The Holy Spirit revealed to him that the yogurt was poisoned but he continued to eat since he felt that God would protect him. The next day Mariyamma came to see if Paul was dead so she could report the news to the people who hired her to kill him. She came to his home with the pretense of collecting her bowl, and to her surprise, Paul greeted and confronted her. When she realized that he had found out what she had intended to do, she grabbed her pot and ran home. Mariyamma later became a Pentecostal believer and attended Paul's church. Her testimony led more than 100 people to the Pentecostal faith and all became members of Paul's church.[32]

Leadership Style

The predominant opinion of the interviewees was that P.M. Samuel's leadership style and administration were a source of great dissatisfaction among many Telugu leaders. They repeatedly said that he dominated the Telugu pastors with his authoritarian attitude and kept them under his control. According to Yesudas (pseudonym), a senior IPC pastor, Samuel did not like others to prosper, especially Telugu pastors. He wanted to keep everyone in his grip. He was content with a pastor as long as he was in his grip or obeyed him. Otherwise, he would put him out of the IPC.[33] When it came to finances, nobody knew the amount of funds coming from abroad and how much was spent by Samuel. No one dared to ask him or question him. He was not accountable to anyone in the IPC.[34] Similarly, many think that Noel Samuel consolidated his position as the sole leader of the IPC by eliminating everyone from the IPC whom he thought presented a challenge to his leadership. He was seen as a leader who did not like to take the advice of the senior pastors in the IPC. [35] As a result, a number of faithful pastors left the IPC and started their own work.

Inclusiveness

Numerous IPC adherents believe that P.M. Samuel discriminated against Telugu pastors. They feel that he neglected the Telugu pastors while giving preferential treatment to Keralites who worked with him. They further believe that the Malayali pastors were appointed to churches in big cities so that they could earn a nice income, but the Telugu pastors were placed in villages only. Samuel helped the fellow Malayali IPC pastors build nice permanent church buildings. When Telugu pastors came to him for help in putting a thatched roof on their church building, he always told them that he had no money to help them.[36] Samuel allowed the children of Kerala pastors, including Philip Abraham, P.T. Chacko, and T.K. Thomas, to go abroad. However, he did not like for the children of Telugu pastors to do the same. [37] Komanapalli Ernest stated that P.M. Samuel never liked for Telugu people to go abroad. He recalled that Samuel was shocked to see him in Germany (1961), and insisted he should not go to the U.S. At the same time, he forced his son Stephen, who was traveling with him, to study in America.

Financial Condition

All of the interviewees said that the IPC pastors were taught to live by faith and not to seek after foreign money. Telugu pastors struggled to make ends meet because of the over-emphasis on this teaching. They struggled financially continually. The IPC pastors did not have proper places of worship or proper food and clothing. They could hardly feed their children or afford their education.[38] P.M. Samuel helped pastors and their children financially, but not sufficiently to meet their monthly needs. Whenever Telugu pastors came to Samuel with a need, he told them to trust God and He would provide. The IPC pastors came to the conclusion that if they remained in the organization, they would not succeed and would have no future.[39] Therefore, the poor economic conditions of the pastors and limited financial assistance from Samuel drove them to leave the IPC and join the WME.[40]

Unity

The common opinion among the adherents of the IPC is that in the first few decades of the IPC's history, there was unity and oneness of heart among the IPC pastors. They all worked together as a team to spread the Pentecostal message and to plant the IPC churches throughout Andhra. There was mutual trust, mutual help, and mutual respect among the pastors as well as believers.[41] They set aside their differences and followed the directives of P.M. Samuel.[42] However, many left the IPC and joined the WME because of the lack of sufficient finances. In the present situation of the IPC, there is little unity, fellowship, or partnership among the pastors, and among the pastors and the administrative leadership in the IPC.[43] Since the independent spirit has now taken over, the present generation of Pentecostals prefers autonomy rather than the leadership of anyone else. If they have sources and resources available, they prefer to separate from the IPC and develop their own ministry. This independent spirit has become a major obstacle for unity within the IPC, as well as in other Pentecostal denominations in Andhra today.[44]

The IPC members also noted that there was less caste bias in the first and second generations of believers in the Mala and Madiga castes, who are predominant in the IPC. Believers from the Mala caste even married Madiga believers and the reverse. However, since 1990 the caste bias between the Malas and Madigas has come to the forefront. This bias has been the source of splits and internal fighting in the local IPC churches throughout Andhra. It is very regrettable that the IPC believers currently prefer a pastor from their own caste. This is a growing menace for unity in the IPC today.[45]

Social Impact

IPC pastors claim that they have preached and continue to preach against sin and emphasize a life of holiness and sanctification. They point out that the Pentecostal message has brought welcome change in many drunkards, thieves, murderers, adulterers, and idol worshippers. Lives were transformed because of the power and presence of the Holy Spirit in their lives.[46] Keethi Sanjeeva Rao tells how transformation took place in his family. His family members used to worship the idols Durga, Hanuman, Vinayaka, and Venkateswara. They continually drank and fought among themselves and with other people in their village of Timmarao Gudem. A murder even took place in his family because of hatred and strife among relatives. After they embraced the Pentecostal faith, the internal strife came to an end. His cousins were delivered from alcohol addiction. At present, twelve family members are in the ministry and five are working as IPC pastors.[47]

Kilari Vekata Rao (or Barnabas) was born into a Hindu family. He was a pharmacist in a jute mill in Chittivalasa who was addicted to drinking and illicit sex. He used to take bribes from patients and use them on liquor. Barnabas had an affair and would spend two or three days at a time with the woman, telling his wife excuses about his absence. When his wife, Sanyasamma (Santoshamma), found out about the affair, there was discord between them and he would beat her violently. One day he wanted to commit suicide by taking sleeping tablets, but his wife thwarted his plans. Barnabas was introduced to B. Martin Luther, an IPC pastor in Chittivalasa. He became a Christian after hearing Luther's preaching (October 23, 1966) and not long afterward, he received the baptism of the Holy Spirit and his life was radically transformed. He was able to quit the bad habits and addictions.[48] Barnabas now works as a pastor in Visakhapatnam. His son, K. Anand Paul, is a well-known evangelist in both India and the West.

IPC pastors went to many remote villages and worked among their own people, the Dalits. The Pentecostal message they preached not only brought spiritual and moral transformation in the common man's life, but also contributed to improvement of his living conditions. The first generation of IPC adherents, especially the pastors, had little or no education. However, many in the second and third generations of IPC members became educated, obtained good paying jobs, and improved their social status. They claim that this was possible by the power of the gospel and the Pentecostal message.[49]

Conclusions

The IPC has strengths and weaknesses like any organization. Its strengths have enabled the organization to grow into a Pentecostal megadenomination in Andhra Pradesh. At the same time, its weaknesses have brought severe setbacks to its viability.

First, the IPC has empowered Dalits spiritually because of its Pentecostal emphasis on the baptism of the Holy Spirit and speaking in tongues. Second, spiritual empowerment has enabled Dalit Pentecostals to be resilient in the midst of suffering and opposition from their own family members, Hindus, Communists, and fellow Christians from mainline churches. Third, many were attracted to Pentecostalism because of the physical wholeness it brought them through healings and deliverance from demonic powers. Fourth, one of the primary reasons for the growth of the organization is that Dalit pastors exhibited extraordinary commitment to spreading the Pentecostal faith and planting IPC churches throughout Andhra, despite their financial struggles. Fifth, Dalit ministers were taught in their leadership training to live by faith in every situation. The training they received at Zion

Bible College prepared them to go to remote locations and face the challenges of pioneering churches in new locations. The zeal of the IPC pastors for evangelism and church planting augmented the numerical growth of the IPC from one church to 660 churches. The Pentecostal gospel message not only brought moral and personal transformation in the Dalits, but also effected a change in the living conditions of many Dalits because of that transformation.

One reason for the departure of several long-time Dalit pastors from the IPC was the financial stress they constantly faced and the mistreatment they felt they received from the leadership. The IPC once had unity among the pastors and believers and the pastors and the leadership, but now the organization suffers internally from disunity caused mostly by caste bias.

The adherents of the IPC may have used glossolalia as a kind of discourse of resistance to the oppressive system of Hinduism, especially the caste system. This may have accelerated the growth of the IPC. Tongues can be seen as the language of the faith community (the Pentecostal community) which is marginalized by the powers-that-be (the high castes, such as the Kammas, the Reddys, the Brahmins, the Kapus, and the Rajus). For many Dalits, tongues could be considered personal therapy and empowerment. Linda Mumford has pointed out that tongues can function to soothe, to protect, and to facilitate coping. They can lead to a sense of derived agency, authority and self-worth.[50] Studies done by Margaret Poloma (1989) and William K. Kay (1999) show a clear link between charismatic activity, including tongues, and the growth of local congregations.[51]

IPC adherents pointed out that the first and second generation of IPC pastors and believers gave much prominence to the experience of the baptism of the Holy Spirit and speaking in tongues. IPC churches would conduct fasting and prayer meetings for people to receive the baptism of the Holy Spirit. New converts would tarry in their churches until they were filled with the Holy Spirit. Many were not only attracted to the teaching of the baptism of the Holy Spirit, but also experienced Spirit baptism. Therefore, IPC members attributed the growth of their denomination to the teaching of the baptism of the Holy Spirit with speaking in tongues.

However, the current generation, especially the young people, is not interested in receiving the baptism of the Holy Spirit and speaking in tongues to the same degree.[52] This might be due to advances in technology and science that have encouraged people to avoid superstition and fanaticism. There are many independent Pentecostal and charismatic organizations in Andhra today, including Hosanna Ministries, Maranatha Vedasamajam, and Manna Ministries, who are not rigid on their view of speaking in tongues. The third generation of IPC members probably desire to be identified with other Pentecostal/charismatic believers in Andhra.

Most Christians in India are Dalits who come from the lowest social status in Indian society, as noted earlier. They live in two different worlds, the first being the Hindu world of the larger community, with its social practices and cultural overtones, and the second being the "other world," that is, the Christian world they inherited through their faith in Christ. Many beliefs, attitudes, and views concerning spirits, demons, devils, and other mysterious things, like visions and dreams, are also found in Hinduism.[53]

Rural people in India believe that demons and spirits are everywhere. Some are benign and some sinister, some bring disaster and disease, and others just frisk about and co-exist with human beings. They believe that some demons even protect them from other demons and are responsible for the well-being of their villages. Therefore, Hindus usually offer prayers to evil spirits for protection, healing, and well-being. Sometimes they implore the evil spirits to use their power against their enemies and wicked men.

India has always been a place of people with a positive attitude toward mystery and wonder, and an eagerness for the miraculous, including healings.[54] Miracle healing in a country like India is a part of the people's religious experience, not only in Hinduism, but also in Christianity. Christians in Indian villages believe in prayer for healing and deliverance from evil spirits, but they did not experience this in the mainline churches. The simple reason was that the mission churches were not interested in this type of ministry. They avoided the practice of prayer for healing because of fear of superstitious beliefs and rituals, and the danger of magic and demon worship that the Indian people were familiar with. However, a form of prayer for healing and deliverance has been practiced in the name of Jesus in IPC churches since the IPC's inception. It was these exorcisms and healings which contributed immensely to the growth of the IPC.[55] Even today in India, the most effective method of evangelism is to heal the sick. In that sense, the IPC movement can be seen as "experienced religion" or "folk religion" or "popular religion." Popular religion, in a general sense, refers to all forms of spirituality as practiced by the masses or the poor social classes.[56]

Up until the 1980s, IPC adherents completely relied upon God for healing because of their unwavering faith in Him, refusing to take medicine or visit hospitals for treatment when they got sick. They considered taking medicine or seeing a doctor to be a sin because they thought that it encouraged reliance on doctors rather than God. However, there has been a drastic shift in the current view of healing. Following the demise of the first and second generations, the third generation of Pentecostals does not solely depend upon divine healing, but also depends upon medical healing,[57] which is an expected change. The reason for this change is that the IPC movement in Andhra is about seventy years old. After a generation, the original impetus in any movement may become diluted or even lost. Present-day Pentecostals are more educated than previous generations of Pentecostals, which has brought an increased human understanding of medicine, science and technology. In the past, people in India often had little or no access to proper health care or lacked finances to get treatment. Many in need of healing would come to the IPC pastors instead for prayer. However, many now have access to healthcare and can afford to see a doctor. There is, therefore, less emphasis on supernatural healing among the present Pentecostals as well as among non-Christians.

When P.M. Samuel came to Andhra, numerous mainline churches invited him to preach in their churches. They stopped inviting him later when they realized that many of their adherents were attracted to the Pentecostal message and were leaving their congregations to join IPC churches. It was not only Samuel, but also the other IPC pastors who targeted the believers in the mainline churches in the name of preaching the "full gospel." IPC pastors found it easier to convert believers in mainline churches to Pentecostalism than Hindus, because they already had an idea about salvation through Christ. One of the primary reasons IPC pastors faced opposition from mainline churches was because they were viewed as "sheep-stealers." On the other hand, the mainline churches would excommunicate them once the leadership learned that their congregants had received baptism by IPC pastors. Those people would therefore have no option but to leave their original congregations.

There are various types of leadership styles. According to leading western research psychologist Kurt Lewin, the three main styles are: authoritarian (autocratic), participative (democratic) and delegative (*laiseez-faire*). Autocratic leaders usually inform their followers about what needs to be done, when it should be done, and how it should be done. They make decisions independently and arbitrarily with little or no input from the group. Abuse of this leadership style is often viewed as bossy, dictatorial, and controlling.[58] Democratic leaders not only provide guidance to their followers, but also actively participate in the group and solicit input from other group members. Delegative leaders offer little or no guidance to the group they are leading and leave decision-making up to their followers. Most Indian leaders follow the first type of leadership style since India is a patriarchal society. Other western leadership styles, such as participative and delegative styles, would most likely not prove to be conducive to India.

When it comes to finances, the validity of the claims made by the interviewees could not be verified. Many argued that the IPC leadership failed to distribute funds to their pastors for the intended donation purposes. Since the author was denied access to the auditor reports or council minutes of the IPC, he is unable to prove their claims either right or wrong. However, P.M. Samuel himself admitted in his autobiography that he received funds from abroad. Nobody in the IPC seemed certain about exactly how much money was received from abroad and how much was spent by the leadership. This situation might have caused jealousy and frustration among the Telugu pastors. On the one hand, the claims of the misuse of funds might be mere allegations. On the other hand, it is possible that the leadership might have taken advantage of Telugu pastors since they submitted to their authority without reservation. Whatever the reason, this issue led to the schism in the IPC.

The predominant opinion of the interviewees was that Telugu pastors felt that they were mistreated, while their colleagues from Kerala received preferential treatment from the IPC leadership. The problem of preferential treatment is not new to the Church. It arose in the early Christian community as mentioned in the book of Acts (chapter six). The Hellenistic Jews complained about the Hebraic Jews, saying that their widows were not being treated fairly in the daily distribution of food. The problem created a division in the church on a cultural and linguistic basis. It was the result of a social disagreement in the early church. However, the crisis dissolved after the appointment of seven Hellenists, including Stephen, the first Christian martyr. Similarly, in the IPC it seemed that division occurred on a regional and linguistic basis. This eventually paved the way for the split in the IPC.

In caste-ridden Indian society, chauvinism exists not only between the upper and lower castes, but also between the Dalit castes themselves. Traditional rivalry exists between the Malas and Madigas in India. Former Census Commissioner of India, J. H. Hutton, reports that a very strong sentiment of factional rivalry exists between these two leading Dalit castes in Andhra, which has led to frequent clashes, often with riots and violence.[59] The traditional antagonism and segregation persist even to this day, but to a lesser degree.

The Christian church in India has theologically been opposed to caste, but has compromised socially with the caste system. Almost all Christian churches in India allow its followers to practice caste. Caste has therefore transcended religion in the Indian context.[60] This is decidedly the case in Andhra Pradesh. The Baptist Church became known as the Madiga religion and the Lutheran church as the Mala religion. There has been internal rivalry, dissension and hostility between the Madiga Christians and the Mala Christians. Gurram Joshua, a Telugu Dalit Christian poet, bemoans the rivalry in his work, *Gabbilam (the Bat)*.

> It is a shame to speak of untouchability, Practiced by the untouchables Malas and Madigas, Neither Shiva nor several Krishnas nor many Christs Can unite these two castes, I dare say. Despite the prestigious B.A. and M.A. degrees, Their rivalries increase but not compromise; Of what use are religious teachings to them. For a hundred years, the substance of the Bible Has been ground into essence and drunk, But the quarrels of the depressed castes Have struck roots and grown a hundred fold.[61] (Stanza 128)

However, during the first period of the IPC's history, unity prevailed among the Malas and Madigas, and the caste barrier was broken because of the work of the Holy Spirit. But this unity lasted only a few decades. Over time, the IPC churches became as segregated as the rest of Christianity in Andhra. The same is true with Pentecostalism in the United States. The racial and social unity between the white and the black people which prevailed at Azusa did not last as long as William J. Seymour hoped, according to Allan Anderson and Walter Hollenweger.[62] Racial segregation still persists in American Pentecostal churches despite the "Miracle at Memphis," where white Pentecostal leader Donald Evans washed the feet of black Pentecostal leader Ithiel Clemmons in 1994.

The Pentecostal gospel message did not prove to be the source of economic uplift for all the Dalits. It did provide a social uplift for many, as observed by the author as well as by the interviewees. Three groups of Dalit Pentecostals in Andhra improved their social status. First, the people who left the IPC and started their own independent work were connected to an organization abroad which funded their work in India. Second, IPC believers who went abroad to pursue a higher education in the U.S., the U.K., Canada, and the Middle East generally obtained lucrative employment not long after their graduation, which drastically enhanced their social status in society. Third, IPC adherents who acquired a professional education in the engineering, computer, information technology, and medical fields secured jobs in those fields in India. They also have better living conditions than other IPC constituents.[63] However, the vast majority of IPC constituents, including pastors in Andhra, still live in poverty.[64]

As Amos Yong points out, even though Pentecostalism failed to give a social uplift to the majority of Dalits, it has empowered them spiritually, emotionally, and behaviorally. Pentecostalism thrived among the Dalits in the midst of widespread unemployment and abject poverty. He further states that they embraced it because the mainline churches failed to be as liberative as Dalits expected, while the egalitarian understanding of Spirit baptism promised them the liberation they sought. Pentecostalism also brought behavioral change and a higher standard of holiness among the Dalits. For example, there was a greater decrease in polygamy, adultery, and sorcery achieved among Dalits than in the mainline churches. Pentecostalism generated a sense of self-worth, of belonging, of superiority, and of solidarity among the Dalits, which enabled them in their ongoing efforts to develop a counter-caste discourse. The Spirit-filled celebrative worship provided a this-worldly uplift for the Dalits and cultivated an eschatological sense of hope. Pentecostal spirituality (that is, extended prayer meetings, zealous witnessing, and self-venting aggressive worship through songs and dance) brought Dalits out of depression, worthlessness, aimlessness in life, fear, and anxiety to a life of activity.[65] In other words, the Pentecostal brand of Christianity transformed the lives of the Dalits and their worldview. It gave them hope as well as dignity in caste-ridden Indian society.

Summary

The IPC as an organization has both strengths and weaknesses. The perception of most IPC adherents is that the denomination has spread to the four corners of Andhra because many people were attracted to the new teaching of the baptism of the Holy Spirit with the evidence of speaking in tongues. Pentecostalism grew among the Dalits because of its optimistic message, including divine healing and the supernatural in day-to-day life. Healings and exorcisms accelerated the growth of the IPC because its churches practiced prayer for healing. In addition, the sacrificial life lived by many Dalits, and their endurance and persistence in preaching the Pentecostal faith in villages and towns in the midst of financial hardships and opposition, helped the numerical growth of the IPC. As time passed, dissatisfaction spread among the Dalit pastors because of the autocratic leadership style and the mistreatment they believed that they received from the organization. It led to schisms in the IPC and also the desertion of a number of long-time loyal pastors. Moreover, caste bias between the Malas and the Madigas created unwanted church splits and disunity within the organization. Despite these weaknesses, the IPC has had a profoundly positive impact on Indian society, with many lives morally transformed and spiritually empowered. Even though Pentecostalism could not provide social uplift for all Dalits, it did give them new identity, dignity, and hope.

Notes

[1] John Sunder Rao Deekollu (state president of Indian Pentecostal Church), interview with the author, Hyderabad, December 30, 2010. Paul Papa Rao Rabbavarapu, interview with the author, Ongole, January 3, 2011. Bhushanam Desabathula, interview with the author, Gudivada, January 25, 2011.

[2] Ebinezer Sashtry Taragam, interview with the author, Eluru, January 14, 2010.

[3] Sanjeeva Rao Keethi, interview with the author, Chittivalasa, January 5, 2011.

[4] Samuel Godi (founder and leader of Good Shepherd Ministries; former chairman of World Missionary Evangelism), interview with the author, Srikakulam, January 5, 2011. John Lazarus Pachigalla (leader of Rock Church Ministries), interview with the author, Anthirvedipalem, January 14, 2011. Yacobu Kommu (senior pastor of Indian Pentecostal Church), interview with the author, Chirrikurapadu, January 2, 2011.

[5] Diamond Hemalatha Bantumilli, interview with the author, Visakhapatnam, January 7, 2011. Jyothi Samuel Korati, interview with the author, Kakinada, January 10, 2011. John Lazarus Pachigalla, interview with the author, Anthirvedipalem, January 14, 2011.

[6] Adiyya David Jekkala, interview with the author, Visakhapatnam, January 6, 2011.

[7] Vimalamma Baddy (former pastor's wife of Indian Pentecostal Church), interview with the author, Visakhapatnam, January 6, 2011.

[8] Bhushanam Desabathula, interview with the author, Gudivada, January 25, 2011.

[9] Gershon Paul Kundeti, interview with the author, Kakinada, January 10, 2011.

[10] Das Jonnagaddi, interview with the author, Kothagudem, January 3, 2011.

[11] Finney Samuel Anumala (pastor of Indian Pentecostal Church), interview with the author, Machilipatnam, January 20, 2011.

[12] Varaprasad Botta, interview with the author, Pendurthi, January 7, 2011.

[13] Evangeline Grace Pedapudi, interview with the author, Machilipatnam, January 20, 2011.

[14] Christopher Parangi, interview with the author, Vijayawada, January 21, 2011. Sanjeeva Rao Keethi, interview with the author, Chittivalasa, January 5, 2011.
[15] Sanjeeva Rao Keethi, interview with the author, Chittivalasa, January 5, 2011.
[16] Noel Samuel Plathaneth, E-mail received by the author, October 15, 2005.
[17] Edward William Kuntam (son of former elder of Indian Pentecostal Church), interview with the author, Anthirvedipalem, January 14, 2011.
[18] Samuel Arun Das Kuntam, interview with the author, Eluru, January 29, 2011. Evangeline Grace Pedapudi, interview with the author, Machilipatnam, January 20, 2011. Sanjeeva Rao Keethi, interview with the author, Chittivalasa, January 5, 2011.
[19] Rathnam Purushotham Geddam, interview with the author, Jadcherla, December 30, 2010. Gershon Paul Kundeti, interview with the author, Kakinada, January 10, 2011. Joseph Kalyanapu (former area pastor of Warangal area Indian Pentecostal Churches), interview with the author, Warangal, December 31, 2010.
[20] John Sunder Rao Deekollu, interview with the author, Hyderabad, December 30, 2010.
[21] Adiyya David Jekkala, interview with the author, Visakhapatnam, January 6, 2011. Joseph Kalyanapu, interview with the author, Warangal, December 31, 2010. Sanjeeva Rao Keethi, interview with the author, Chittivalasa, January 5, 2011. See also: *Souvenir: Golden Jubilee Celebrations-Zion Bible College, 1942-1992*, n.p.
[22] Paramjyothi, *The Life Story of Apostle Paramjyothayya*, 28-29. See also: *Souvenir: Golden Jubilee Celebrations-Zion Bible College, 1942-1992*. (Gunadala: Zion Bible College, 1992), n.p. See also: *Indian Pentecostal Church of God (A.P)-Golden Jubilee Souvenir, 1932-1982*, 56-57.
[23] Samuel Rankin Pace Meriga, interview with the author, Chebrolu, January 14, 2011.
[24] Srinivasa Rao Medisetti (pastor of Indian Pentecostal Church), interview with the author, Rajahmundry, January 11, 2011.
[25] Das Kati, interview with the author, Eluru, December 17, 2007.
[26] Krupa Prabhakar Jannu (pastor of Indian Pentecostal Church), interview with the author, Warangal, December 31, 2010.
[27] *Golden Jubilee Souvenir: Indian Pentecostal Church of God (Andhra), 1932-1982*, 1943.
[28] John Lazarus Pachigalla, interview with the author, Anthirvedipalem, January 14, 2011. Samuel Finney Pachigalla, interview with the author, Anthirvedipalem, January 14, 2011. Spurgeon Raju Pachigalla, interview with the author, Vijayawada, January 3, 2006 and January 17, 2011.
[29] John Shabdham Adidala, phone interview with the author, Virginia Beach, March 13, 2011. Bhushanam Desabathula, interview with the author, Gudivada, January 25, 2011.
[30] Abraham Inje (former elder of Indian Pentecostal Church), interview with the author, Warangal, December 31, 2011.
[31] Bhagavan Das Giddla, interview with the author, Ongole, January 2, 2011.
[32] John Shabdham, phone interview with the author, Virginia Beach, March 13, 2011.
[33] Yesudas, interview with the author, January 3, 2011.
[34] Aseervadam, interview with the author, January 6, 2011. Samuel Godi, interview with the author, Srikakulam, January 5, 2011. Samuel Pedapudi, interview with the author, Machilipatnam, January 19, 2011.
[35] Mariya Das, interview with the author, January 12, 2011. Yesudas, interview with the author, January 3, 2011. James, interview with the author, January 6, 2011.

Aseervadam, interview with the author, January 6, 2011. Deva Raju, interview with the author, January 17, 2011. Raja Rao, interview with the author, January 21, 2011. Ananda Rao, interview with the author, January 3, 2011.

[36] Yesudas, interview with the author, January 3, 2011. Spurgeon Raju Pachigalla, interview with the author, Vijayawada, January 17, 2011. Ananda Rao, interview with the author, January 3, 2011. John Shabdham Adidala, phone interview with the author, Virginia Beach, March 13, 2011. Evangeline Grace Pedapudi, interview with the author, Machilipatnam, January 20, 2011. Samuel Pedapudi, interview with the author, Machilipatnam, January 19, 2011.

[37] Yesupadam (pseudonym), interview with the author, January 29, 2011. David Raju, interview with the author, January 22, 2011. John Shabdham Adidala, phone interview with the author, Virginia Beach, March 13, 2011.

[38] Jaya Raju, interview with the author, January 25, 2011. Yesudas, interview with the author, January 3, 2011. Aseervadam, interview with the author, January 6, 2011.

[39] Devanandam (pseudonym), interview with the author, January 19, 2011. Yesudas, interview with the author, January 3, 2011. Aseervadam, interview with the author, January 6, 2011. Jaya Raju (pseudonym), interview with the author, January 25, 2011.

[40] Ananda Rao, interview with the author, January 3, 2011.

[41] Samuel Godi, interview with the author, Srikakulam, January 5, 2011. Varaprasad Botta, interview with the author, Pendurthi, January 7, 2011. Joseph Franklin Dasi (pastor of Indian Pentecostal Church at Alamanda), interview with the author, Visakhapatnam, January 8, 2011.

[42] Rathnam Purushotham Geddam, interview with the author, Jadcherla, December 30, 2010. Sanjeeva Rao Keethi, interview with the author, Chittivalasa, January 5, 2011. Bhushanam Desabathula, interview with the author, Gudivada, January 25, 2011.

[43] Joy Esther Rani Mellimi, interview with the author, Rajahmundry, January 11, 2011. Vimalamma Baddy, interview with the author, Visakhapatnam, January 6, 2011. Jyothi Raju (pseudonym), interview with the author, January 8, 2011. Spurgeon Raju Pachigalla, interview with the author, Vijayawada, January 14, 2011.

[44] Spurgeon Raju Pachigalla, interview with the author, Vijayawada, January 14, 2011.

[45] Raja Rao, interview with the author, January 21, 2011. Deva Raju (pseudonym), interview with the author, January 18, 2011. Ananda Rao, interview with the author, January 3, 2011.

[46] Jeevanandam Samuel Appikatla (former church elder of Indian Pentecostal Church), interview with the author, Warangal, December 31, 2011. Yacobu Kommu, interview with the author, Chirrikurapadu, January 2, 2011. Bhaskara Rao Kare, interview with the author, Vijayawada, January 17, 2011.

[47] Sanjeeva Rao Keethi, interview with the author, Chittivalasa, January 5, 2011.

[48] Barnabas Kilari, *My Life: Before Christ and After Christ* (Vijayawada: Spandana Christian Graphics), 5-19. Diamond Hemalatha Bantumilli, interview with the author, Visakhapatnam, January 7, 2011.

[49] Daniel Chittimuri, (founder and leader of Christian Faith Ministries), interview with the author, Visakhaptnam, January 5, 2011. Vimalamma Baddy, interview with the author, Visakhapatnam, January 6, 2011. John Sunder Rao Deekollu, interview with the author, Hyderabad, December 30, 2010.

[50] Linda Mumford, "An Expanded Psychological Understanding of Religious Glossolalia" (Ph.D. Diss., University of Boston, 1996). Cited in Mark J. Cartledge, *Speaking in Tongues: Multi-Disciplinary Perspectives* (Waynesboro: Paternoster Press, 2006), 107.

[51] M. M. Poloma, *The Assemblies of God at the Cross Roads* (Knoxville: University of Tennessee Press, 1989). W. K. Kay, "Pentecostalism: Charismata and Church Growth," in L.J. Francis, ed., *Sociology, Theology and Curriculum* (London: Cassell, 1999), 135-144.

[52] Vimalamma Baddy, interview with the author, Visakhapatnam, January 6, 2011. Prasad Kumar Marlapudi, interview with the author, Eluru, January 22, 2011. Varaprasad Botta, interview with the author, Pendurthi, January 7, 2011.

[53] Solomon Raj Pulidindi, *A Christian Folk Religion in India* (New York: Lang Publications, 1986), 55.

[54] Solomon Raj Pulidindi, *A Christian Folk Religion in India*, 5.

[55] Diamond Hemalatha Bantumilli, interview with the author, Visakhapatnam, January 7, 2011. Rathnam Purushotham Geddam, interview with the author, Jadcherla, December 30, 2010. Daniel Chittimuri, interview with the author, Visakhaptnam, January 5, 2011.

[56] Wilma Wells Davies, *The Embattled but Empowered Community: Comparing Understanding of Spiritual Power in Argentine Popular and Pentecostal Cosmologies*, (Leiden: Brill NV, 2010), 7.

[57] Jacob John Mattada (pastor of Indian Pentecostal Church), interview with the author, Khammam, December 31, 2010.

[58] Kendra Cherry, "Lewin's Leadership Styles," accessed June 25, 2010. Online: http://psychology.about.com/od/leadership/a/leadstyles.htm.

[59] J. H. Hutton, *Caste in India* (London: Oxford University Press, 1963), 11.

[60] Santishree Pandit D.N.B., "Dilemmas of Identity of Dalit Christians in India: A Case Study from Andhra Pradesh," *Dharma Deepika* 2 (December 1997): 43.

[61] Cited in Santishree, "Dilemmas of Identity of Dalit Christians in India," 46.

[62] Allan Anderson and Walter J. Hollenweger, *Pentecostals after a Century: Global Perspectives on a Movement in Transition* (England: Sheffield Academic Press, 1999, 41-43.

[63] John Sunder Rao Deekollu, interview with the author, Hyderabad, December 30, 2010. Paul Papa Rao Rabbavarapu, interview with the author, Ongole, January 3, 2011. Daniel Chittimuri, interview with the author, Visakhaptnam, January 5, 2011.

[64] John Sunder Rao Deekollu, interview with the author, Hyderabad, December 30, 2010. Finney Samuel Anumala, interview with the author, Machilipatnam, January 20, 2011. Samuel Thomas Kakamala, interview with the author, Gunadala, January 17, 2011.

[65] Reuben Gabriel, "Reflections on Indian Pentecostalism: Trends and Issues," *Dharma Deepika* 6:2 (2002): 67-76. Cited in Amos Yong, *The Spirit Poured Out on All Flesh*, 58.

Chapter 8

Epilogue

The Andhra portion of the history of the IPC has been neglected in the historiography of Indian Pentecostalism. The research indicates that it is due to deep-rooted culturally and socially motivated bias, because most of its constituents come from a Dalit background. Despite their low social and economic status, Dalits have made major contributions to the spread of Protestant Indian Christianity. When Protestant missionaries first arrived in India, Dalits played a crucial role in helping them to spread Christianity. Therefore, Dalits must be considered the true pioneers and founders of Protestant Christianity in India.[1] The same is true within the Indian Pentecostal movement. Since the very inception of the movement, Dalits have made a lasting contribution to its formation and growth.

In the second half of the 19th century and early 20th century, Proto-Pentecostal revivals in the states of Tamilnadu, Kerala, and Andhra Pradesh occurred primarily among the Dalits. The efforts of one particular Dalit, John Aroolappen, should not be minimized or ignored concerning the early revivals in Tirunvelli and Travancore, because these were the first recorded outpourings of the Holy Spirit which preceded all other Pentecostal revivals in India. Later, when Western Pentecostal missionary George Berg established a Pentecostal church in Thuvayoor, Kerala (early 1900s), most of its congregants were Dalits.[2] After the arrival of missionary Robert Cook to India, Dalit leaders Vellikara Matthai (Choti) and Poikayil Yohannan helped him spread the Pentecostal faith. Cook had a large Dalit following and approximately forty-three Dalit churches merged with the Church of God (Cleveland) when he joined the organization in the 1930s.

K.E. Abraham, a former Syrian Christian, received the baptism of the Holy Spirit (early 1920s) by the laying on of hands of C. Manaseh (former LMS pastor and a Dalit from the Nadar caste) and became a Pentecostal. Not only that, it was a Dalit, P. Ramankutty (Paul), who later ordained Abraham, one of the founders of the IPC. Paul was also instrumental in helping Plathaneth

Matthew Samuel (co-founder of the IPC) receive the baptism of the Holy Spirit in Lunav, Ceylon (late 1920s). He should be recognized as the founder of the first indigenous Pentecostal organization in India, contrary to the prevailing notion among IPC adherents. He had already established the Ceylon Pentecostal Mission at the time when Abraham became a Pentecostal. Both Samuel and Abraham worked with Paul and were impacted by his ministry, although they later parted ways.

Likewise, the IPC began in Andhra (early 1930s) because of Dalit Thullimalli Peter Gurupadam's invitation to Samuel to come there. Samuel went and stayed with Gurupadam, who took care of Samuel's needs in the early days of his ministry in Andhra. It was Lam Jeevaratnam, a Dalit from Gudivada, who first introduced the Pentecostal faith to Andhra Pradesh before Samuel arrived there, contrary to the popular opinion of the Andhra IPC constituents. Jeevaratnam took Samuel to Eluru to conduct Pentecostal meetings when Samuel arrived in Andhra and, as a result, Samuel started the IPC work in Eluru with his assistance. Later, Bathina Samuel Lukeson and Dondapati Andrews, both Dalits from Eluru, drafted the constitution and bylaws of the IPC and helped in the registration process (1935).[3] Moreover, the family of K.R. John in Eluru (from a Dalit background) often helped Samuel financially and met his needs in the early years of his ministry in Andhra. The family of another Dalit, Tippalli Mrudhubhashini from Vuyyuru, who settled in Rajahmundy, also assisted Samuel with financial support.

After the IPC was registered (1935), it experienced rapid growth in Andhra Pradesh during its first two decades due to the collective and untiring efforts of many Dalit pastors, K.G. Paul (Pedda), A.S. Paul, K.R. David, K.P. Devasahayam, G.R. Purushotham and Chatla Sudarsanam, etc. It did not grow from the efforts of just one man, Samuel (the founder of the IPC movement in Andhra), as traditionally believed in the IPC. Countless Telugu Dalit pastors put everything they had on the line, many even risking their very lives, to spread the Pentecostal faith and expand the IPC work throughout Andhra Pradesh. It was their unselfish lives of sacrifice, their unwavering faith in God, their reliance on Him for their daily needs, and their endurance of local opposition from both Hindus and mainline churches that caused the work of the IPC to grow.

IPC adherents claimed that the denomination spread like wildfire to the four corners of Andhra because many people were attracted to the novel teaching of the baptism of the Holy Spirit with the evidence of speaking in other tongues. The wider appeal of the holistic and optimistic Pentecostal message was another reason for the growth of the IPC among the Dalits. This message included divine healing, deliverance from demonic oppression, and the intervention of the supernatural in daily life.

Moreover, during this early period, Zion Bible School was established in Antarvedipalem, and the Telugu magazine, *Suvartha Prakashini*, was founded by the efforts of Pachigalla Lazarus Paramjyothi, a prominent Dalit pastor in the IPC. These two significant events had a lasting impact on the history of the IPC, and successfully contributed to the promotion of the Pentecostal faith and the establishment of IPC churches throughout the state of Andhra Pradesh.

Not only did Dalits contribute greatly to the formation and growth of the IPC, but they also played a role in its division. Godi Samuel, Taragam Sathyavedam Sasthry, Pachigalla Lazarus Paramjyothi, Papabathini Philip, and Komanapalli Ernest were key players who directly or indirectly contributed to the schism. Discontent over the style of leadership, the lack of accountability for funds, and the mistreatment of Telugu pastors were among the unresolved issues that led to the split in the IPC. Actual division occurred when the WME and Manna Ministries were established, because they attracted a number of IPC pastors as well as adherents to their fold. This was a major blow to the IPC. As a result, it lost many gifted and faithful pastors and became weak for a while. It also dropped to second in its ranking among the Pentecostal denominations in Andhra Pradesh.

In addition, the demise of P.M. Samuel created a temporary leadership vacuum for the IPC. During this interval, P. Philip, a Dalit, made an attempt to obtain full control over the IPC, but his effort was sabotaged by his fellow Dalit colleagues as well as the Malayali leadership. Taking the reins of the denomination completely from the dominance of the Malayalis still remains a dream for Dalit Telugu leaders. During this tumultuous period, the IPC managed to survive both external and internal threats, and was able to make a comeback within a short period of time.

From the early 1980s through 2010, the IPC was led by various Dalit leaders, including Geddam Rathnam Purushotham and Deekollu John Sunder Rao, along with Plathaneth Abraham Samuel and Noel Samuel. The Golden Jubilee of the formation of the IPC and the founding of Zion Bible College were the two major events celebrated during this period. However, the untimely and unexpected death of Abraham Samuel and the departure of Purushotham from the IPC combined to create a leadership crisis in the organization. This period also witnessed internal contention, a new independent spirit, and increased caste bias between the Malas and Madigas. These factors continue to threaten the survival and unity of the IPC.

The other stumbling blocks to the current growth of the IPC are lack of subjection to leadership, lack of financial accountability by the administration, and growing dissatisfaction over the performance of administrative functions by the present leadership. Nevertheless, in spite of these weaknesses, the impact of the IPC on Dalits has been profoundly positive. It has empowered them spiritually, emotionally, and behaviorally. The IPC failed to fulfill the dream of social and economic uplift for all the Dalits, but it did provide them with a means for newfound dignity and hope.

In the midst of all these challenges that the IPC has faced, and the various current problems being encountered as stated earlier, one might be prompted to ask if the organization has a promising future. The answer would have to be in the affirmative. Many members of the IPC have recognized that the organization has been facing internal fighting and schisms since the early 1960s, but they affirm that the IPC has always managed to survive the various setbacks it has encountered. The constituents argue that the organization came into being by the will of God, and was established by the power of God. Therefore, they believe God will also enable the work of the IPC to continue in the future, despite the problems and challenges it may face.[4]

Secularism and power politics have crept into all the Indian Pentecostal churches (including the IPC), as emphasized by Pulidindi Solomon Raj (Lutheran pastor, Indian scholar, and student of Walter Hollenweger). However, they have not done so as much as in the mainline churches. He further contends that since the gospel has no death, Pentecostal churches in India will continue to grow, along with all the other mainline churches. In Solomon Raj's opinion, Pentecostal churches experience more growth than denominational churches because of their emphasis on practical holiness, fasting, personal prayer, healings, and the like.[5] Moreover, the universal Church, including the IPC, belongs to Jesus Christ, who was its founder. He will therefore make sure of the continued existence of His Church until His return. He said, "...I will build my church; and the gates of hell shall not prevail against it" (Mt. 16:18 KJV).

This research leads to the conclusion that the Dalit contribution to Pentecostalism in South India cannot be minimized or dismissed. Not only did Pentecostalism thrive among Dalits, but they also were the pioneers of Indian Pentecostalism. Moreover, Dalits were also the founders of several indigenous Pentecostal organizations. As Amos Yong has aptly pointed out, "their pioneering charismatic ministries, sacrificial giving, establishment of schools and Bible colleges for Dalits and even the founding of Pentecostal denominations by Dalits exemplify their Christian commitment."[6] Even though marginalized and forgotten, Dalits empowered by the Holy Spirit have made a lasting contribution to Indian Pentecostalism, and, in the process, to the global renewal movement.

Notes

[1] McGavran, *The Founders of the Indian Church*, 77-79.
[2] Thomas, *Dalit Pentecostalism*, 158-164.
[3] Spurgeon Raju Pachigalla, interview with the author, Vijayawada, January 14, 2011.

⁴ John Sunder Rao Deekollu, interview with the author, Hyderabad, December 30, 2010. Thomas Kumar Gorinkala, interview with the author, Warangal, December 31, 2010. Bhagavan Das Giddla, interview with the author, Ongole, January 2, 2011.

⁵ Solomon Raj Pulidindi (scholar and Lutheran pastor), interview with the author, Vijayawada, January 20, 2011.

⁶ Amos Yong, *The Spirit Poured Out on All Flesh: Pentecostalism and the Possibility of Global Theology* (Grand Rapids: Baker Publishing Group, 2005), 58.

Appendix A:
A Chart of the History of Pentecostalism in India

USA	INDIA
1901 (Topeka Revival in Kansas) ↓	1860-1865 (Tirunelveli Revival), Tamilnadu, S. India Occurred among "Shanars" (Dalits) through John Aroolapen, a native CMS evangelist trained by Carl T. Rhenius
1906 (Azusa Street Revival in Los Angeles, CA) ↓	↓
1908 (George Berg arrival in Bangalore, South India) ↓	1873-1881 (Travancore Revival), Kerala, S. India Took place under Yusthus (Justus) Joseph who was saved under CMS missionary Joseph Peet
1913 (Robert Cook arrival in Bangalore, South India) ↓	↓
	1905-1907 (Mukti Revival at Kedgaon), Maharastra, N. India Occurred under Pandita Ramabai
1921 (Cook founded "Malankara Full Gospel Church") ↓	↓
	1905-1906 (Various Revivals), Andhra Pradesh, S. India:
1926-1930 (Merger of "South India Pentecostal Church" founded by K.E. Abraham and P.M. Samuel which resulted in the formation	1905 (Akividu Revival) under S.E. Morrow 1905 (Chettipet Revival) under E.S. Bowden of Godavari Delta Mission

of "Malankara Pentecostal Church." Cook and K.E. Abraham worked together)

↓

1930 ("Malankara Pentecostal Church was split into two again: South India Pentecostal Church and South India Full Gospel Church. Cook and K.E. Abraham parted ways)

1906 (Nellore Revival) under David Downe who came to India after he received a call during the 2nd Great Awakening

1906 (Ongole Revival) under James Baker of American Baptist Mission

1906 (Kurnool Revival) under William Stanton of American Baptist Mission

1906 (Kakinada Revival) in the Canadian Baptist Girls' High School

1906 (Bimilipatnam Revival) in the Canadian Baptist Churches

↓

1923 (Ceylon Pentecostal Mission was founded) by Ramankutty or Paul, a Dalit

↓

1924 (South India Pentecostal Church was founded by K.E. Abraham, P.M. Samuel and K.C. Cheriyan, who left Syrian Orthodox Church and joined Brethren movement. They later left Brethren movement to form South India Pentecostal Church)

↓

1926-1930 (Merger of South India Pentecostal Church founded by K.E. Abraham and P.M. Samuel and South India Full Gospel Church founded by Robert Cook, American Missionary. Malankara Pentecostal Church resulted through the merger)

Appendix A 131

↓

1930-1933 (K.E. Abraham joined the CPM, Pastor Paul, founder of Ceylon Pentecostal Church and K.E. Abraham worked together)

↓

1933 (Pastor Paul and K.E. Abraham parted ways)

↓

1934 (South India Pentecostal Church became the Indian Pentecostal Church—name change)

↓

1935 (The IPC was registered at Eluru with Government of India)

Bibliography

Primary Sources

Armstrong, Bob. *A Portrait of India's Visionary! The Thrilling Story of Dr. P.J. Titus.* Dallas: Christ for India, Inc., 1996.
Apostolic Faith, 1:3 (November 1906): 1.
Bain, Ian. *Before Kings: Life Story of Lam Jeevaratnam.* Toronto, n.d.
B. Elisha. Former president of The Bible Mission. "A Brief Biographical Note of Father Devadas." March 28, 1970.
Boes, Louise. "Miracles Wrought Thru an Indian Sadhu: Evil Spirits Acknowledge the Supremacy of Jesus Christ." *The Latter Rain Evangel* (November 1934): 21-22.
Burgess, John H. "South India—John and Bernice Burgess, 11-18-80."
Carner, Earl R. "Add This One Also." *The Alliance Weekly* 73:2 (1938): 23-25.
Chapman, Mary W. *Pentecostal Evangel* (December 16, 1916): 2.
Chatla, Sudarsanam. "A Short Autobiography." Unpublished document received by the author, January 19, 2010.
Cook, Robert F. *Half a Century of Divine Leading: 37 Years of Apostolic Achievements in South India.* Cleveland: Church of God Foreign Missions Dept., 1955.
Das, Yesunatha. "Pentecostal History of Visakhapatnam," *Souvenir of Pentecostal Fellowship of India: Seventh National Conference-2004.* Visakhapatnam, 2004.
Dibb, Ashton. "The Revival in North Tinnevelly." *Church Missionary Record* 5 (August 1860): 178.
Didla, Rathnam. "A Letter Addressed to the IPC State Council." February 9, 2009.
"Divikegina Devasayam Ayya Garu." *Suvartha Prakashini (Gospel Illuminator)* 57:1 (1997): 2.
Dyer, Helen S. *Pandita Ramabai.* New York: Fleming H. Revell Company, 1900.
"Eternal Entrance of Pastor B.S. Kruparakshna." An obituary published for his memorial service held at the IPC Church, Visakhapatnam on September 11, 1996.
Firlan, Kim. *Compassionate Love: A Story of Ernest and Rachel Komanapalli.* Hyderabad: Manna Ministries, 1999.
Geddam, Rathnam Purushotham. "The Brief History of the Indian Pentecostal Church of God." Unpublished document received by the author, February 28, 2010.
G.H. Lang. ed. *The History and Diaries of an Indian Christian.* London: Thynne, 1939.
Giddla, Bhagavan Das. "A Brief History of the IPC." Unpublished document received by the author, October 12, 2010.
Groves, Anthony Norris. *Memoir of Anthony Norris Groves, Complied Chiefly from His Journals and Letters.* London: James Nisbet, 1869.

Hand Book: The Indian Pentecostal Church of God. Kumbanadu: IPC General Council, 1999.
Human Rights Watch. *Broken People.* New York, 1999.
Hume, Robert Ernest. *The Thirteen Principal Upanishads.* London: Oxford University Press, 1921.
Indian Pentecostal Church of God (A.P)-Golden Jubilee Souvenir, 1932-1982. Gunadala: Zion Printing Press, 1982.
Jesus Never Fails: Golden Jubilee Celebrations, 1942-1992. Mysore: Jesus Never Fails Ministries, 1992.
_____. *Yesuchristhuvinte Eliya Dasan.* Kumbanadu: Pentecostal Young People's Association, 1965.
Kallepu, Rajarathnam David. *Nenu Na Prabhuvu (Autobiography of Pastor K.R. David).* Rajahmundry: Andhrasree Printers, 1981).
K. Devasahayam. "The Bible Mission." *Religion and Society* 29:1: 55.
K.E. Abraham, *A Humble Servant of Jesus Christ: Autobiography of Pastor K.E. Abraham.* Kumbanadu: K.E. Abraham Foundation, 1983.
Kilari, Anand Paul. *Left For Dead.* La Habra: The Lockman Foundation, 1997.
Kilari, Barnabas. *My Life: Before Christ and After Christ.* Vijayawada: Spandana Christian Graphics, 1996.
Marlapudi, Prasad Kumar. "Brief Biography of Kanumala Peturu Devasahayam." Unpublished document received by the author, January 20, 2011.
McDonald, W. and John E. Searles. *The Life of Rev. John S. Inskip, President of the National Association for the Promotion of Holiness.* Salem: Allegheny Publications, 1986.
Mungamuri, Devadas. "Satyamsa Nirupana (*The Proof of the Truth*)." Bible Mission Booklet No. 28.
_____. "Woe Unto You." Bible Mission Booklet No. 14.
Pachigalla, L. Paramjyothi. *Jyothayya Jeevitha Yathra (The Life Story of Apostle Paramjyothayya).* Antarvedipalem: Paramjyoti Publications, 1996.
Podilaku, Mark. *Secretary's Report on the Indian Pentecostal Church in Eluru, 1956.*
Poozhicalayil, T. Chacko. *Pastor P.T. Chacko: A Man of God.* Kumbanadu: Hebron Printing House, 1980.
Plathaneth, Joy Abraham Samuel. *Counting My Blessings!* Vijayawada: Zion Printing Press, 1999.
Plathaneth, Matthew Samuel. *Na Jeevitha Yathra: Autobiography of Apostle P.M. Samuel.* Vijayawada: Zion Printing House, 1980.
Plathaneth, Noel Samuel. "A Brief History of the IPC." E-mail message to the author, October 15, 2005.
Ramabai, Pandita. *A Testimony of Our Inexhaustible Treasure in Pandita Ramabai Through Her Own Words.* New Delhi: Oxford Press, 2000.
_____. *Mukti Prayer Bell* (September 1907): 11.
Sen, Makhan Lal. *Ramayana.* Calcutta: Oriental Publications, 1989.
Sengupta, Padmini. *Pandita Ramabai Saraswati: Her Life and Work.* Bombay: Asia Publishing Company.
Shah, Amritlal B. *Letters of Pandiata Ramabai.* Bombay: Maharashtra State Board for Literature and Culture, 1977.
Shamala, D. Barnabas. *God's Grace to Me.* Mysore: Jesus Never Fails Ministries, 1974.
Silver Jubilee Souvenir: Good News Festivals, 1971-1996. Vijayawada: Spandana Christian Graphics, 1996.
Silver Jubilee Souvenir: World Missionary Evangelism-Silver Jubilee Convention-Srikakulam (India), 1964-1989. Srikakulam, 1989.

Souvenir: Golden Jubilee Celebrations-Zion Bible College, 1942-1992. Gunadala: Zion Bible College, 1992.
Stanton, William A. *The Awakening of India: Forty Years Among the Telugus.* Portland: Falmouth Publishing House, 1950.
Sumrall, Lester. *Pioneers of Faith.* Sumrall Publishing, 1995.
"Unprecedented Scenes in Poona City, India: Mighty Signs and Wonders Follow the Preaching of the Gospel by L. Jeevaratnam." *The Pentecostal Evangel* (October, 20, 1934): 2-3.
"Untouchability through the drinking glass in TN." Accessed October 7, 2008. Online: http://www.rediff.com/cms/print.jsp?docpath=news/2008/oct/07tn.htm.
Varghese, Habel. *K.E. Abraham: An Apostle From Modern India.* Tiruvalla: Rhema Publishers International, 2000.

Secondary Sources

A.C. George. "Pentecostal Beginnings in Travancore, South India." *Asian Journal of Pentecostal Studies* 4:2 (July 2001): 215-237.
_____. "Pentecostal Beginnings in India." *Dharma Deepika* 6, no. 2 (July-December 2001): 41-45.
A.E. Medlycott. *India and The Apostle Thomas: An Inquiry, With a Critical Analysis of the Act A Thomae.* London: David Nutt, 1905.
Anderson, Allan. "The Origins of Pentecostalism and Its Global Spread in the Early Twentieth Century." Accessed 23 May 2006. Online: http://www.ocms.ac.uk/docs/Allan%20Anderson%20lectue20041005.pdf.
_____. *An Introduction to Pentecostalism.* Cambridge: Cambridge University Press, 2004.
_____. *Asian and Pentecostal: The Charismatic Face of Christianity in Asia.* Baguio City: Regnum Books International, 2005.
Anderson, Allan and Walter J. Hollenweger. *Pentecostals after a Century: Global Perspectives on a Movement in Transition.* England: Sheffield Academic Press.
Anderson, Rufus. *History of the Mission of the American Board of Commissioners for Foreign Missions in India.* Boston: Congregational Publishing Society, 1874.
Barrett, David & Todd Johnson. "Annual Statistical Table on Global Missions: 1999." *International Bulletin of Missionary Research* 23 (January, 1999): 24-25.
Bergunder, Michael. *The South Indian Pentecostal Movement in the Twentieth Century.* Grand Rapids: Wm. B. Eerdmans Publishing Company, 2008.
B. Sobhanan, ed. *A History of the Christian Mission in South India.* Thiruvananthapuram: Kerala Historical Society.
Burgess, Stanley M. ed. *The New International Dictionary of Pentecostal and Charismatic Movements.* Grand Rapids: Zondervan, 2002.
_____. "Pentecostalism in India: An Overview." *Asian Journal of Pentecostal Studies* 4:1 (January, 2001): 85-98.
B.V. Subbamma. *New Patterns for Discipling Hindus.* Pasadena: William Carey Library, 1970.
Cartledge, Mark J. *Speaking in Tongues: Multi-Disciplinary Perspectives.* Waynesboro: Paternoster Press, 2006.
Cherry, Kendra. "Lewin's Leadership Styles." Accessed June 25, 2010. Online: http://psychology.about.com/od/leadership/a/leadstyles.htm.

C.P. Matthew and M.M. Thomas, *The Indian Churches of Saint Thomas*. Delhi: DJVP/ISPCK, 2006.

C.V. Cheriyan. *A History of Christianity in Kerala: From the Mission of St. Thomas to the Arrival of Vasco Da Gama, A.D. 52-1498*. Kottayam: the CMS Press, 1973.

Davies, Wilma Wells. *The Embattled but Empowered Community: Comparing Understanding of Spiritual Power in Argentine Popular and Pentecostal Cosmologies*. Leiden: Brill NV, 2010.

Dayton, Donald. *Theological Roots of Pentecostalism*. Metuchen: Scarecrow Press, 1987.

D.N.B. Santishree. "Dilemmas of Identity of Dalit Christians in India: A Case Study from Andhra Pradesh." *Dharma Deepika* 2 (December 1997): 39-48.

D'Souza, Herman. *In the Steps of St. Thomas*. Madras: The Associated Printers Limited, 1952.

Eddy, Sherwood. *Pathfinders of the World Missionary Crusade*. New York: Abingdon-Cokesbury Press, 1945.

Faupel, D. William. *The Everlasting Gospel: The Significance of Eschatology in the Development of Pentecostal Thought*. London: Sheffield Academic Press, 1996.

Frykenberg, Robert. *Christianity in India: From Beginning to the Present*. Oxford: Oxford University Press, 2008.

Gabriel, Reuben. "Reflections on Indian Pentecostalism: Trends and Issues." *Dharma Deepika* 6:2 (2002): 67-76.

Graham, Carol. *Azariah of Dornakal*. Delhi: ISPCK, 1972.

Hedlund, Roger. ed. *Christianity is Indian: The Emergence of an Indigenous Community*. Delhi: ISPCK, 2000.

_____. *Quest for Identity, India's Churches of Indigenous Origin: The Little Tradition in Indian Christianity*. Delhi: ISPCK, 2000.

_____. "The Witness of New Christian Movements in India." Paper for the IAMS Assembly in Malaysia, July 31-Aug. 2004. Online: http://www.mission studies.org/conference/1papers/fp/Roger_Hedlund_Full_paper.pdf.

_____. "Critique of Pentecostal Missions by a Friendly Evangelical." *Asian Journal of Pentecostal Studies* 8, no. 1 (2005): 67-94.

_____. "Nationalism and the Indian Pentecostal Church of God." *Indian Church History Review* 39, no. 2 (December 2005): 91-106.

_____. "Indian Instituted Churches: Indigenous Christianity Indian Style." *Missions Studies* 16, no. 1 (1999): 26-42.

Hutton, J.H. *Caste in India*. London: Oxford University Press, 1963.

Jadhav, Narendra. *Untouchables: My Family's Triumphant Journey Out of the Caste System in Modern India*. New York: Scribner, 2003.

Kakkhukuzhil, Sam Mathews. "An Assessment of the Dawn and Growth of the Indigenous Pentecostal Movement in the State of Andhra Pradesh." Master's thesis, SAICS, 1990.

K.B. Simon. *The Andhra Churches*. Bezwada: A.G. Press, 1942.

K.E. Rajpramukh. *Dalit Christians of Andhra: Under the Impact of Missionaries*. New Delhi: Serials Publications, 2008.

Khan, Benjamin. *Dalit Christian Movement and Christian Theology*. Indore: Sat Prachar Press, 1995.

Kothapalli, Joseph Raju. "A Survey on the Origin and Growth of Dornakal Diocese of the Church of South India with Respect to its Expansion in the District of Khammam." Masters thesis, COTR Seminary, 2001.

K. Srinivasulu. *Caste, Class and Social Articulation in Andhra Pradesh*. Hyderabad: Osmania University, 2002. Accessed May 21, 2010.

Online: http://www.odi.org.uk/resources/download/1998.pdf.
K.Y. Ratnam. *The Dalit Movement and Democratization in Andhra Pradesh*. Washington: East-West Center, 2008), 9-10. Accessed May 21, 2010.
Online: http://www.ciaonet.org/wps/ewc/0016466/f_0016466_14236.pdf.
Lichtman, Alan and Valerie French. *Historians and the Living Past*. Arlington Heights: AHM Publishing Company, 1978.
MacNicol, Nicol. *What Liberates a Woman? The Story of Pandita Ramabai, A Builder of Modern India*. New Delhi: Nivedit Good Books, 1996.
Masilamani, Azariah. *A Pastor's Search for Dalit Theology*. Delhi: ISPCK, 2000.
Massey, James. *Roots of Dalit History, Christianity, Theology and Spirituality*. Delhi: ISPCK, 1996.
Mathew, Thomson K. "A Study in the History of the Pentecostal Movement in South India." Master's thesis, Yale University Divinity School, 1975.
McGavran, Donald. *The Founders of the Indian Church*. Chennai: Church Growth Association of India, 1998.
McGee, Gary B. "Latter Rain Falling in the East: Early Twentieth-Century Pentecostalism in India and the Debate over Speaking in Tongues." *Church History* 68:3 (September 1999): 648-665.
_____. "Pentecostal Phenomena and Revivals in India: Implications for Indigenous Church Leadership." *International Bulletin of Missionary Research* 20 (July 1996): 112-114.
_____. *People of the Spirit: The Assemblies of God*. Springfield: Gospel Publishing House, 2004.
Mumford, Linda. "An Expanded Psychological Understanding of Religious Glossolalia." Ph.D. Diss., University of Boston, 1996.
M. Vijaya Kumar. "Church History of Visakhapatnam." Accessed May 2, 2011.
Online: http://ipcvizag.blogspot.com/2010/03/history_07.html.
Nirmal, Arvind, ed. *A Reader in Dalit Theology*. Madras: Gurukul Lutheran Theological College, 1990.
Oommen, George. "Growth of Pentecostalism in Central Kerala from 1921-47: A Paradigm for Pentecostal Growth of Churches in North India." *Indian Church History Review* 35:2 (December 2001): 132-133.
_____. "The Emerging Dalit Theology: A Historical Appraisal." *Indian Church History Review* 34:1 (June 2000): 19-37.
Orr, J. Edwin. *Evangelical Awakening in India in the Early Twentieth Century*. New Delhi: Christian Literature Institute, 1970.
Palla, Victor. *Origins, Growth and Development of Christianity in the Srikakulam District of Andhra Pradesh, India*. Unpublished document, n.d.
Pickett, J. Waskom. *Christian Mass Movements in India*. New York: Abingdon Press, 1993.
Poloma, M.M. *The Assemblies of God at the Cross Roads*. Knoxville: University of Tennessee Press, 1989.
Possehl, Gregory L. *Ancient Cities of the Indus*. New Delhi: Vikas, 1979.
Pothen, Abraham Thottumkal. "The India Pentecostal Church of God and Its Contribution to Church Growth." Master's thesis, Fuller Theological Seminary, 1988.
Pulidindi, Solomon Raj. *A Christian Folk Religion in India: A Study of the Small Church Movement in Andhra Pradesh, With Special Reference to the Bible Mission of Devadas*. New York: Lang Publications, 1986.
_____. *The New Wine-skins: The Story of the Indigenous Missions in Coastal Andhra Pradesh, India*. New Delhi: Cambridge Press, 2003.

Pulikottil, Paulson. "As East and West Met in God's Own Country: Encounter of Western Pentecostalism with Native Pentecostalism in Kerala." Accessed November 23, 2006. Online: http://www.pctii.org/cyberj/cyberj10/paulson.html.

Smith, Badley. *History of Christianity in India; with its Prospects: A Sketch*. Madras: SPCK Press, 1895.

Snyder, Howard A. "Holiness Heritage: The Case of Pandita Ramabai." *Wesleyan Theological Journal* 40 (Fall 2005): 31-51.

Synan, Vinson. *The Holiness Pentecostal Tradition*. Grand Rapids: Wm. B. Eerdmans Publishing Co., 1997.

Thackil, Chacko George,. "The Growth of the Pentecostal Churches in South India." Master's thesis, Fuller Theological Seminary, 1975.

T.S. Samuel Kutty. *The Place and Contributions of Dalits in Select Pentecostal Churches in India*. Delhi: ISPCK, 2000.

Varghese, Kunjappan C. "Reformation Brings Revival: A Historical Study of K.E. Abraham and His Contributions in the Founding of the Indian Pentecostal Church of God." Ph.D. diss., Trinity International University, 1999.

V. Devasahayam. *Doing Dalit Theology in Biblical Key*. Madras: Gurukul Lutheran Theological College, 1997.

Vegesana, Vijaya Bhaskara Raju. "The Impact of the Pentecostal Movement and Cross-Cultural Missionary Work in Andhra Pradesh: A Biography of Apostle K.C. Matthew." M.Th. thesis, COTR College, 2005.

V.V. Thomas. *Dalit Pentecostalism: Spirituality of the Empowered Poor*. Bangalore: Asian Trading Corporation, 2008.

Winter, Ralph. *Perspectives on the World Christian Movement*. Pasadena: William Carey Library, 1981.

Yong, Amos. *The Spirit Poured Out on All Flesh: Pentecostalism and the Possibility of Global Theology*. Grand Rapids: Baker Publishing Group, 2005.

Interviews

Addepalli, Suryanarayana. Former member of Zion Educational Society. Rajahmundry, January 11, 2011.

Adidala, John Sabdham. Son of A.S. Paul, phone interview. Virginia Beach, March 13, 2011.

Allil, John Matthews. Former pastor of Indian Pentecostal Church. Vijayawada, January 12, 2011.

Anumala, Finney Samuel. Pastor of Indian Pentecostal Church. Machilipatnam, January 20, 2011.

Appikatla, Jeevanandam Samuel. Former church elder of Indian Pentecostal Church. Warangal, December 31, 2011.

Baddy, Vimalamma. Wife of B.S. Kruparakshana, former pastor of Indian Pentecostal Church. Visakhapatnam, January 6, 2011.

Bantumilli, Diamond Hemalatha. Wife of B. Martin Luther, former pastor of Indian Pentecostal Church, BHPV. Visakhapatnam, January 7, 2011.

Botta, Varaprasad. Pastor of Indian Pentecostal Church. Pendurthi, January 7, 2011.

Charugudi, Eliya. Pastor of Indian Pentecostal Church. Gannavaram, January 20, 2011.

Chatla, Joshua Sudarsanam. Pastor of Indian Pentecostal Church. Rajanagaram. January 19, 2010.
Chatla, Samuel Sudarsanam. Pastor of Indian Pentecostal Church. Rajanagaram, January 19, 2010.
Cheedi, George. Local church secretary of Indian Pentecostal Church. Visakhapatnam, January 6, 2011.
Chittimuri, Daniel. Founder and leader of Christian Faith Ministries. Visakhapatnam, January 5, 2011.
Dasi, Joseph Franklin. Pastor of Indian Pentecostal Church. Visakhapatnam, January 8, 2011.
Deekollu, John Sunder Rao. State president of Indian Pentecostal Church. Hyderabad, December 30, 2010.
Desabathula, Bhushanam. Senior pastor of Indian Pentecostal Church. Gudivada, January 25, 2011.
Didla, Ratnam. Pastor of Indian Pentecostal Church. Vijayawada, December 19, 2006.
Didla, Mercy Samuel. Wife of former pastor of Indian Pentecostal Church. Vijayawada, January 12, 2011.
Geddam, Rathnam Purushotham. Former state president of Indian Pentecostal Church. Jadcherla, December 30, 2010.
Giddla, Bhagavan Das. Ongole area pastor of Indian Pentecostal Churches. Ongole, January 2, 2011.
Godi, Samuel. Leader of Good Shepherd Ministries and former chairman of World Missionary Evangelism. Srikakulam, January 5, 2011.
Gorinkala, Thomas Kumar. Pastor of Indian Pentecostal Church. Warangal, December 31, 2010.
Gubbala, Sathyam. Former member of Indian Pentecostal Church. Machilipatnam, January 19, 2011.
Inje, Abraham. Former elder of Indian Pentecostal Church. Warangal, December 31, 2011.
Jannu, Krupa Prabhakar. Pastor of Indian Pentecostal Church. Warangal, December 31, 2011.
Jekkala, Adiyya David. Senior pastor of Indian Pentecostal Church. Visakhapatnam, January 6, 2011.
Jonnagaddi, Das. Senior pastor of Indian Pentecostal Church. Kothagudem, January 3, 2011.
Kakamala, Samuel Thomas. Pastor of Indian Pentecostal Church at Vijayawada. Gunadala, January 17, 2011.
Kakkhukuzhil, Chako Matthew. Former pastor of Indian Pentecostal Church. Visakhapatnam, January 05, 2011.
Kalyanapu, Daniel. Leader of Ecclesia Ministries, phone interview. Virginia Beach, February 17, 2011.
Kalyanapu, Joseph. Former area pastor of Warangal area Indian Pentecostal Churches. Warangal, December 31, 2010.
Kare, Bhaskara Rao. Former state treasurer of Indian Pentecostal Church. Gunadala, January 17, 2011.
Kati, Das. Former member of Indian Pentecostal Church. Eluru, December 17, 2007.
Keethi, Sanjeeva Rao. Senior pastor of Indian Pentecostal Church. Chittivalasa, January 5, 2011.
Komanapalli, Ernest. Founder and leader of Manna Ministries. Hyderabad, January 8, 2010.

Komanapalli, Sudarsan Jyothi. Leader of Manna Ministries. Vijayawada, January 17, 2011.
Kommu, Yacobu. Senior pastor of Indian Pentecostal Church. Chirrikurapadu, January 2, 2011.
Korati, Joythi Samuel. Pastor and daughter-in-law of K.G. Paul. Kakinada, January 10, 2011.
Kunchala, Sekhar Daniel. Pastor of Indian Pentecostal Church. Eluru, January 26, 2011.
Kundeti, Gershon Paul. Former pastor of Indian Pentecostal Church. Kakinada, January 10, 2011.
Kuntam, Samuel Arun Das. Son of former elder of Indian Pentecostal Church. Eluru, January 29, 2011.
Kuntam, Edward William. Son of former elder of Indian Pentecostal Church. Antarvedipalem, January 14, 2011.
Lam, Samuel. Pradhan. Grandson of Lam Jeeva Rathnam. Gudivada, January 26, 2011.
Marlapudi, Prasad Kumar. Elder of Indian Pentecostal Church. Eluru, January 22, 2011.
Marlapudi, Mary. Wife of former pastor of Indian Pentecostal Church. Eluru, January 29, 2011.
Mattada, Jacob John. Kammam area pastor of Indian Pentecostal Churches. Khammam, December 31, 2010.
Mellimi, Joy Esther Rani. Daughter of former pastor of Indian Pentecostal Church. Rajahmundry, January 11, 2011.
Meriga, Samuel Rankin Pace. Pastor of Independent Pentecostal Church and grandson of B.S. Lukeson. Chebrolu, January 14, 2011.
Merugu, Annal Chandra Bai. Daughter of Mann Singh. Machilipatnam, January 19, 2011.
Nanduri, Indira Vandanam. Daughter of T.P. Gurupadam. Guntur, January 20, 2011.
Pachigalla, John Lazarus. Leader of Rock Church Ministries. Antarvedipalem, January 14, 2011.
Pachigalla, Samuel Finney. Leader of Indian Pentecostal Church Ministries and former pastor of Indian Pentecostal Church. Antarvedipalem, January 14, 2011.
Pachigalla, Spurgeon Raju. President of Manna Ministries. Vijayawada, January 3, 2006.
Papabathini, Prabhudas. Leader of Indian Pentecostal Community Church, phone interview. Virginia Beach, February 17, 2011.
Parangi, Christopher. Senior pastor of Indian Pentecostal Church. Vijayawada, January 21, 2011.
Parla, Rathna Jyothi. Former teacher of Zion Bible College. Vijayawada, January 17, 2011.
Pedapudi, Evangeline Grace. Daughter of Kallepu Rajarathnam David. Machilipatnam, January 20, 2011.
Pedapudi, Samuel. Son of former pastor of Indian Pentecostal Church. Machilipatnam, January 19, 2011.
Pitta, Daveedu. State secretary of Indian Pentecostal Church. Pedapadu, January 18, 2011.
Plathaneth, Noel Samuel. Former state secretary of Indian Pentecostal Church. Vijayawada, January 4, 2010.
Pulidindi, Solomon Raj. Lutheran pastor and scholar. Vijayawada, January 20, 2011.

Rabbavarapu, Paul Papa Rao. Leader of Indian Christian Ministries. Ongole, January 3, 2011.
Taragam, Ebinezer Sasthry. Pastor and grandson of Taragam Sathyavedam Sasthry. Eluru, January 14, 2010.
Thullimalli, John Sudhir Dutt. Grandson of T.P. Gurupadam. Machilipatnam, January 19, 2011.
Thullimalli, Swaroop Dutt. Grandson of T.P. Gurupadam. Tanuku, January 23, 2011.

Index

Abrams, Minnie, 27, 30
Achaia, 51
A.C. George, 25, 26, 27, 48, 135
A.C. Mathai, 44
Adidala, John Shabdham, 78 109, 120, 121, 138
Adidala, Sundaram Paul (A.S. Paul), 60, 63, 74, 78, 96, 104, 107, 109, 110, 124, 138
Adultery, 118
Adur, 35
A.E. Medlycott, 51, 135
Afghanistan, 43
Africa, 1, 7
Agrippa, 4
A.J. John, 37
Aki(vi)du, 30, 129
Akkampet, 73
A.K. Varghese, 40
Alamanda, 105, 121
Alamgirpur, 8
A.L. Basham, 20
Aleru, 73
Alexandria, 43
Aleyamma, 65
Alice Rathnam, 58
Alisamma, 61
Allil, John Matthews (A.J. Matthews), 88, 89, 138
Alugulu, Yosepu, 61
Alwal, 73
Amalapuram, 75
Ambernath, 72, 83
American Holiness evangelists, 48
American Baptist Church, 16, 32
American Baptist Mission, 15, 32, 72, 130
American Baptist Missionary Union, 14, 15, 16, 19
American Episcopal Church, 27
American Lutheran Church, 32
Anakapalli, 68
Ananda Pet, 58, 59

Anbu Mariammal, 34
Andaman and the Nicobar Islands, 93, 94
Anderson, Allan, 30, 49, 50, 117, 122, 135
Anderson, Rufus, 33, 49, 135
Andhra Awakening, 33
Andhra Baptist Church, 20
Andhra Christian College, 58
Andhra IPC, 3, 17, 53, 62, 64, 65, 68, 69, 70, 92, 124
Andhra Pradesh, 1, 2, 3, 4, 12, 13, 14, 15, 16, 17, 18, 20, 21, 30, 31, 32, 41, 44, 53, 54, 55, 56, 57, 58, 59, 60, 61, 62, 63, 64, 65, 69, 70, 72, 75, 76, 78, 79, 81, 82, 83, 84, 85, 86, 87, 89, 91, 94, 95, 113, 117, 122, 123, 125, 129, 136, 137, 138
Andrew, 51
Anglican Church, 32, 34, 40, 48
A.N. Matthew, 73
Antarvedipalem, 70, 71, 72, 75, 76, 80, 84, 95, 109, 124, 134, 140
Antirvedi, 72
Antirvedi, Das, 19
Anumala, Finney Samuel, 105, 119, 122, 138
Apostle Thomas, 42, 43, 51, 137
Apostolic Faith Bands, 61
Appanaramuni Lanka, 72
Appikatla, Anandarao (A. Anandarao), 71, 72, 110
Appikatla, Jeevanandam Samuel, 110, 121, 138
Arabian Sea, 23
Arava, Manoharam, 61
Arkansas, 36
Armstrong, Bob, 133
Aroolappen, John, 24, 25, 33, 47, 123, 129
A. Ruben, 17, 96
Aryans, 8, 9

Asarappa, 46
Asia, 1, 50, 135
Assemblies of God, 36, 37, 38, 39, 50, 86, 122, 137
Atmakuru, 16, 30
Atwelli, 73
Australia, 50, 56
Autocratic leaders, 116
Avanigadda, 20
Avarnas, 7
A.V. Timpany, 19
Azam Jahi Cotton Mills, 73, 85
Azusa Revival, 24, 30, 32, 35, 50, 117, 129

Badava, 72
Badava Pet, 69
Baddy, Rakshanandam and Krupamma, 68
Baddy, S. Kruparakshana (B.S. Kruparakshana), 68, 69, 78, 104, 133, 138
Baddy, Vimalamma, 68, 78, 104, 119, 121, 122, 138
Bain, Ian, 76, 133
Baker, Henry, 44
Baker, James, 31, 130
Baktan Samuel, 64
Bandaru, 55
Bangalore, 35, 36, 49, 72, 86, 129, 138
Bantumilli, Diamond Hemalatha, 78, 119, 121, 122, 138
Bantumilli, Martin Luther, 68, 78, 113, 138
Bapatla, 16
Baptism in the Holy Spirit, 4, 26, 71
Baptism of the Holy Spirit, 23, 25, 26, 27, 28, 29, 35, 40, 41, 42, 44, 45, 46, 47, 48, 49, 51, 54, 57, 58, 61, 64, 67, 68, 74, 86, 103, 104, 106, 113, 114, 118, 123, 124
Baptist Church, 16, 66, 67, 110, 117
Baptist Palem, 69, 70, 99
Baptists, 57, 110
Barrett, David, 4, 135

Barrett, Thomas, 35, 49
Barrington College, 86
Bathina, Samuel Lukeson (B.S. Lukeson), 56, 60, 62, 63, 64, 65, 68, 70, 71, 77, 79, 84, 107, 108, 124, 140
Batlapenumarru, 69
Battu, Kanakadri, 61
Bay of Bengal, 23
Beer, George, 44
Belgium, 86
B. Elisha, 77, 133
Berg, George, 35, 36, 42, 49, 123, 129
Bergunder, Michael, 38, 39, 50, 51, 76, 81, 89, 135
Berhampur, 83
Bethel Bible School, 37
Bhagatrov, 8
Bhimavaram, 62, 91
Bhimrao, Ramji Ambedkar, 7
Bhogapuram, 63
Bhuvaneswar, 72
Bible Mission, 64, 65, 77, 133, 134, 137
Bible Society of India, 72
Bihar, 44, 72
Bikkavole, 74
Bimilipatnam, 20, 30, 32, 130
Bishop Corrie, 16
B. John Reddy, 107
B. Johnson, 83
Bobbili, 20, 72
Boes, Louise, 76, 133
Boggs, 31
Bombay, 12, 19, 29, 37, 43, 48, 49, 72, 82, 83, 134
Bommuru, 66
Book of Acts, 26, 63, 103, 117
Botta, Gabriel (B. Gabriel), 67, 68, 106
Botta, Varaprasad, 78, 119, 121, 122, 138
Bouncil, 35, 36, 49
Bowden, William, 15, 30, 44, 129
Bowery Theater, 31
Brahmin priests, 42, 43
Brahmins, 12, 42, 98, 114
Brethren church, 40, 44, 45

Brethren movement, 40, 41, 44, 45, 49, 130
Bristol, 44
British Assemblies of God, 57
Brown, 31
B. Sobhanan, 50, 135
B.S. Krupanandam, 70
Buckingham Canal, 15
Buckingham Palace, 57
Bunder Pet, 69
Burgess, John H., 36, 37, 50, 133
Burgess, Stanley, 4, 48, 135
Burma, 34, 70, 74, 96
B.V. Subbamma, 21, 135

Calcutta, 12, 21, 134
C.A. Matthews, 62
Canada, 19, 47, 50, 56, 81, 92, 96, 118
Canadian Baptist Mission, 19, 20, 32, 57, 59, 68, 70, 71, 93
Cape Comorin, 23
Carner, Earl R., 133
Cartledge, Mark J., 122, 135
Caste system, 3, 7, 9, 10, 11, 12, 17, 20, 114, 117, 136
Cathedral Church of the Epiphany of Our Lord, 34
Caughey, James, 48
Cavpacas, 9
Ceylon, 34, 42, 45, 46, 54, 55, 124
Ceylon Pentecostal Church, 41, 42, 45, 46, 47, 51, 60, 131
Ceylon Pentecostal Mission, 23, 39, 41, 45, 46, 47, 124, 130
Ch. Immanuel, 99
Chagallu, 66
Chagalnadu, 75
Chandalas, 7, 9
Chandogya Upanishad, 9
Chapman, Mary, 36, 37, 38, 50, 133
Charismatics, 1, 4
Charugudi, Eliya, 101, 138
Chatla, Narasanna and Nagamma, 75
Chatla, Joshua Sudarsanam, 78, 139
Chatla, Samuel Sudarsanam, 78, 139

Chatla, Sudarsanam (Ch. Sudarsanam, 60, 75, 91, 94, 97, 101, 107, 124, 133
Chauvinism, 117
Chayal, 42
Cherry, Kendra, 122, 135
Chester, Susan 36, 37, 50
Chettipet Revival, 30, 129
Chettipet, 30
Chikkala, Lazarus, 63
Chile, 30
Chilean Pentecostalism, 30
Chintalamori, 72
Chintalapudi, 104
Chittimuri, Daniel, 121, 122, 139
Chittivalasa, 68, 77, 113, 119, 120, 121, 139
Christian Missionary Alliance, 28
Christian Perfection, 28
Christmas, 99, 105
Churas, 13
Church Missionary Society, 14, 16, 17, 18, 24, 48
Church of Christ, 74
Church of Constantinople, 43
Church of England, 18, 27
Church of God, 39, 123, 133
Church of God for Visible Salvation, 40
Church of South India, 49, 137
Clark, Margaret, 37
Classical Pentecostals, 1, 4, 26, 48, 103
Clay, John, 18
Clemmons, Ithiel, 118
Cleveland, 39, 123, 133
Clough, John E., 15, 16, 19
C. Manaseh, 41, 44, 123
Colombia, 50
Colombo, 41, 46
Colonial Pentecostalism, 23, 34, 40
Communists, 108, 109, 110, 113
Compassion International, 95
Conjee, 93, 94
Connoor, 49
Constitution of India, 11

Cook, Robert F., 34, 35, 36, 37, 38, 39, 40, 41, 42, 46, 47, 51, 123, 129, 130, 133
Courts, Reginald, 83
C.P. Matthew, 52, 135
Craig, 31
Cranganore, 42
C.V. Cheriyan, 51, 136
Cuddapah, 18
Cumbum, 16
Cumine, Charles (Robert), 35, 36

Dachavaram, 74
Dalit hristians, 3, 72, 122, 136
Dalit Hindus C, 72
Dalit pastors, 60, 68, 70, 72, 75, 81, 106, 113, 114, 119, 124
Dalit Pentecostalism, 2, 4, 8, 10, 12, 14, 16, 18, 20, 24, 26, 28, 30, 32, 34, 36, 38, 40, 42, 44, 46, 48, 49, 50, 52, 54, 56, 58, 60, 62, 64, 66, 68, 70, 72, 74, 76, 78, 80, 82, 84, 86, 88, 92, 94, 96, 98, 100, 102, 104, 106, 108, 110, 112, 114, 116, 118, 120, 122, 124, 126, 138
Dalit Pentecostals, 3, 104, 113, 118
Dalits, 3, 4, 5, 7, 9, 10, 11, 12, 13, 14, 15, 16, 17, 18, 20, 24, 30, 34, 36, 37, 38, 39, 40, 41, 46, 47, 50, 51, 53, 56, 60, 61, 64, 69, 75, 88, 98, 99, 113, 114, 118, 119, 123, 124, 125, 126, 129, 138
Dallas, 80, 133
Dallas Christian College, 94
Dandiganipudi, 58
Darby, John Nelson, 44, 48
Darling, John, 17, 18, 20
Das, Yesunatha, 78, 133
Dasaratha, 10
Dasi, Joseph Franklin, 105, 121, 139
Dasas or Dasyas, 9
David (known as "Tamil David"), 25
Davies, Wilma Wells, 122, 136
Downie, David, 31

Day, Samuel Stearns 15
Day of Pentecost, 103
Dayton, Donald, 49, 136
DeAlwis, Alwin R., 46, 47, 60
Deekollu, John Sunder Rao, 70, 91, 93, 94, 101, 107, 119, 120, 121, 122, 125, 127, 139
Deenamma, 69,
Dehra Dun, 82
Delegative leaders, 116
Delhi, 5, 12, 20, 21, 48, 49, 50, 52, 72, 78, 134, 135, 136, 137, 138
Democratic leaders, 116
Demonic oppression, 124
Demon-possession, 71, 104
Demons, 58, 74, 115
Denmark, 72
Depressed Classes, 8
Desabathula, Bhushanam, 70, 119, 120, 121, 139
Devils, 115
Dewis, Rosario, 67, 68
Dharmapuram, 73
Dharmaram, 73
Dhonakonda, 16, 66
Dibb, Ashton, 25, 48, 133
Didla, Mercy Samuel, 78, 139
Didla, Rathnam (D. Rathnam), 70, 99, 133, 139
Dionysius IV, 51
Ditt, 13, 20
D.N.B. Santishree, 122, 136
Dondapadu, 71
Dondapati, Andrews, 61, 124
Dondapati, Krupanandam, 109
Dondapati, Manoharam, 109
Doon Bible College, 82
Dornakal, 33, 34, 49, 69, 136
Dornakal Diocese, 34, 49, 137
Douglas, Jr., John, 80
Douglas, Sr., John, 62, 67, 74, 79, 80, 81, 82, 83, 84, 85
Douglas, Yvonne, 84
Dowleswaram, 65, 66
Dr. T. Yesudas, 71
Dravidians, 8, 9
Dreams, 24, 28, 33, 64, 115
Dronacharya, 10
D'Souza, Herman, 51, 136

Dubai, 72
Dublin, 44
Duff, Alexander 31
Durga, 112
Dyer, Helen S., 48, 49, 133

E.C. Stuart, 44
E.S. Bowden, 30, 129
Early church, 117
East Coast, 43
East Godavari, 74
Eastern Europe, 7
Eastern Full Gospel Mission, 57
Ecclesia, 67
Ecclesia Ministries, 77, 139
Eddy, Sherwood, 34, 49, 136
Edessa, 42, 43
Edinburgh Missionary
    Conference, 34
Edith, 80
Eelabrolu, 70
Eemani, 66
Ekalavya, 10
Elanthoor, 35
Elim Bible Institute, 92
Eluru, 15, 16, 41, 55, 56, 59, 60,
    61, 62, 63, 65, 69, 71, 72, 75,
    76, 77, 80, 84, 85, 89, 92, 99,
    106, 107, 119, 120, 122, 124,
    131, 134, 139, 140, 141
Emerson, Mark, 96
Engdiyur, 45
Engineering, 118
England, 16, 17, 18, 24, 27, 35,
    36, 44, 48, 57, 60, 72, 86,
    122, 135
Entire Sanctification, 29
Enuguvari Lanka, 72
Ephesus, 51
Epirus, 51
Esther, 71
Esther David, 71
Evans, Donald 118
Evil spirits, 58, 76, 115, 133
Exorcisms, 41, 104, 115, 119
Experienced religion, 115
Expressive worship, 3
Eyeranipuram, 49

Fanaticism, 114

Far East Broadcasting
    Association, 88
Faupel, D. William, 48, 49, 136
Fenn, David, 25
Finney, Charles, 48
Firlan, Kim, 89, 133
First World War, 36, 59
Folk religion, 115, 122, 137
Fox, Henry 16, 17
Fox, Silas, 44
France, 50, 86
Frykenberg, Robert, 136
F.W.N. Alexander, 15

Gabbilam, 117
Gabriel, Reuben, 122, 136
Gad, 42, 43
Gadala, 66
Gajapathinagaram, 68
Gajuwaka, 68
Gajwalli, 73
Gandigunta, 66, 69, 106
Gangayya and Venkamma, 70
Ganji, Joseph, 71
Ganni, Mariyamma, 110
G. David, 68
Geddam, Rathnam
    Purushotham (G.R. Purushotham),
    60, 91, 92, 93, 94, 95, 96, 97, 101,
    102, 107, 120, 121, 122, 124, 125,
    133, 139
Gee, Donald, 4
Germany, 72, 81, 86, 92, 107,
    111
Ghaggar, 8
Ghatkesar, 73
G. H. Lang, 48, 133
Giddalur, 83
Giddla, Bhagavandas, 97, 101,
    110, 120, 127, 133, 139
Giminez, John, 87
Giripuram, 69
G.J. Raj Kumar, 99
G. Kanthayya, 71
G. Krupavaram, 68
Gloria, 106
Glossographia, 24
Glossolalia, 24, 26, 28, 114, 122,
    137
Godavari Delta Mission, 19, 75, 129

Godi, Daniel and Mariyamma, 81
Godi, Samuel (G. Samuel), 79,
    80, 81, 82, 83, 84, 88, 104,
    119, 120, 121, 125, 139
Gokavaram, 108
Golla caste, 108
Gondi, 72
Gondophares, 42, 43
Gopinenipalem, 87
Gordon, 20
Gorinkala, Thomas Kumar, 77,
    88, 127, 139
Gorla, Isaac Nathan, 67, 68
Gospel Illuminator, 66, 69, 71,
    77, 93, 94, 133
Govada, Chandrahasan, 60
Government of India, 56, 83,
    131
Government of Travancore, 41
Governor Pet, 69
Graham, Carol, 49, 136
Great tradition, 5
Gregory Nazianzen, 43, 51
Groves, Anthony Norris, 24, 44,
    48, 133
G.P.V. Somaratna, 46
Gubbala, Sathyam, 77, 139
Gudiattram, 59
Gudimula, 72
Gudivada, 55, 57, 58, 60, 61, 69,
    76, 119, 120, 121, 124, 139,
    140
Gujarat, 27
Gummadidala, 73
Gunadala, 69, 70, 87, 94, 98,
    107, 120, 122, 134, 135, 139
Gundlakamma River, 16
Guntur, 32, 57, 58, 70, 76, 85,
    92, 140
Guntur District, 16, 66
Gupta, Paul V., 44
Gurram, Joshua, 117
Guru-dakshina, 10
Gurujala, 16

Hakkumpet, 66
Hampstead Bible School, 57
Hanumakonda, 65
Hanuman, 112
Hanuman Junction, 71

Harappa, 8, 20
Haridwar, 72
Harijan, 7
Healings, 33, 58, 104, 105, 113,
    115, 119, 126
Health care, 115
Hebraic Jews, 117
Hedlund, Roger, 5, 50, 52, 76,
    89, 136
Hellenistic Jews, 117
Heroo, Leonard, 86
Higgins, 18
High caste Hindus, 11, 17, 18
Hindus, 3, 9, 17, 21, 30, 60, 62,
    63, 73, 75, 93, 108, 109, 110,
    113, 115, 116, 124, 135
Hinduism, 10, 33, 46, 108, 114,
    115
Hindustan Bible Institute, 44
Hogavo, 8
Holiness, 92, 112, 118, 126
Holiness message, 48
Holiness Movement, 29
Holiness teaching, 48
Holland, 72, 86, 92, 107
Hollenweger, Walter, 117, 122,
    126, 135
Hoover, Willis, 30
Hosanna Ministries, 114
Hubli, 72
Human Rights Watch, 12, 21,
    134
Hume, Robert Ernest, 20, 134
Husen, Van, 15
Hyderabad, 21, 41, 62, 73, 74,
    76, 87, 89, 94, 119, 120, 121,
    122, 127, 133, 136, 139
Hyderaguda, 73

Ibrahim Patnam, 75
Illanda, 109
Immanuel, 110
India, 1, 2, 3, 5, 7, 8, 9, 11, 13,
    15, 20, 21, 23, 24, 25, 26, 27,
    28, 29, 30, 31, 32, 34, 35, 36,
    37, 38, 39, 40, 41, 42, 43, 44,
    45, 46, 47, 48, 49, 50, 51, 56,
    57, 58, 65, 66, 70, 72, 74, 76,
    78, 79, 80, 82, 83, 84, 86, 87,
    88, 89, 92, 94, 96, 113, 114,

115, 116, 122, 123, 124, 126, 129, 130, 133, 134, 135, 136, 137, 138
Indian Christianity, 1, 4, 5, 7, 9, 11, 13, 15, 17, 19, 20, 21, 26, 30, 123, 136
Indian Church history, 13
Indian Constitution, 7, 8
Indian government, 3, 12, 55
Indian Missionary Society of Tirunelveli, 33
Indian Ocean, 23
Indian Pentecostal Church of God, 1, 2, 5, 23, 37, 39, 41, 42, 45, 47, 50, 51, 54, 56, 61, 71, 76, 77, 78, 88, 101, 102, 119, 120, 121, 122, 126, 131, 133, 134, 136, 138, 139, 140
Indian Pentecostal Community Church, 88, 89, 140
Indian Pentecostal movement, 123
Indian Pentecostalism, 4, 23, 38, 47, 50, 52, 122, 123, 126, 136
Indian society, 3, 4, 7, 11, 20, 98, 103, 114, 117, 118, 119
Indiana University, 92
Indigenous Christianity, 1, 5, 136
Indigenous Pentecostal denominations, 41
Indigenous Pentecostal movement, 3, 53
Indigenous Pentecostalism, 23, 41, 45
Indus civilization, 8
Indus people, 8
Indus Valley, 8
Information technology, 118
Initial physical evidence, 28, 29
Inje, Abraham, 110, 120, 139
Inskip, John, 29, 49, 134
Interpretation of tongues, 24
IPC General Convention, 63, 92
Ireland, 44
Isabel, 58
Israel Pet, 69
Italy, 51, 72
Jabalpur, 72

Jacobite Syrian Church, 43, 45, 51, 52
Jadhav, Narendra, 20, 136
Jaffna, 34
Jagannadhapuram, 63
Jaggayya Pet, 70
Jana, Samuel, 83
Janagama, 65, 73
Jannu, Joshua (J. Joshua), 63, 70, 84
Jannu, Krupa Prabhakar, 109, 120, 139
Japan, 72
Jatis, 9
J.C. Gergson, 44
Jedcherla, 85, 92, 93
Jerusalem, 86, 103
Jewett, Lyman, 15
J.H. Hutton, 117, 122, 136
J.H. Ingram, 39
Jillella, Venkatarathnam, 70
John, 51
John Joseph, 70
Jekkala, Adiyya David (J.A. David), 68, 78, 89, 104, 119, 120, 139
Johnson, Todd, 4, 135
Jonnagaddi, Das, 105, 119, 139
Joseph and Sathyavani, 62
Justification, 29, 48
Justus (Yusthus), Joseph, 25, 129

Kabadipalem, 110
Kadali, 90
Kakamala, Thomas Samuel (K.T. Samuel), 96, 97, 98
Kakamala, Samuel Thomas, 97, 122, 139
Kakinada, 19, 20, 32, 67, 71, 72, 74, 75, 78, 105, 107, 119, 120, 130, 140
Kakkhukuzhil, Chacko Matthew (K.C. Matthew), 68, 78, 138
Kakkhukuzhil, Sam Matthews, 21, 136
Kalasapad, 18
Kalibangan, 8
Kaliki, 110
Kallepu, Rajarathnam David (K.R. David), 60, 69, 77, 78, 79,

85, 92, 106, 107, 124, 134, 140
Kallepu, Ramaiah and
 Rajamanemma, 65
Kalyan, 43
Kalyanapu, Daniel, 77, 139
Kalyanapu, Joseph, 120, 139
Kamalamma, 70
Kamma caste, 75
Kammas, 12, 114
Kammavoor, 11
Kanaka Rathnam, 57
Kanakiah, 15
Kanavaram, 75
Kancherla, Reuben John
 (K.R. John), 61, 62, 71, 124
Kancherla, Hardy Moody, 99
Kancherla, Moody, 63
Kancherla, Rushamma, 61, 62
Kancherla, Vivekavathi
 Johnamma, 62, 71
Kanegiri, 16
Kannur, 63
Kanthamma, 71
Kanumala, Peturu
 Devasahayam
 (K.P. Devasahayam), 60, 62, 63,
 77, 91, 94, 95, 99, 101, 107,
 109, 124, 134
Kanumala, Peturu and Lijamma, 63
Kanuru, 70
Kapus, 12, 114
Kare, Bhaskara Rao, 121, 139
Karma, 11
Karnataka, 36, 41, 55, 73
Kartar Singh, 58, 59
Karunamma, 67, 68
Kasthuri, Sitapathi Rao, 59
Kathanar, Joseph, 51
Katheru, 66
Kati, Das, 63, 77, 109, 120, 139
Katralapalli, 75
Katuru, 71
Kavali, 16
Kay, William K., 114, 122
K.B. Simon, 21, 136
K.C. Cheriyan, 37, 41, 44, 45, 47,
 54, 56, 130
K. Devasahayam, 77, 134
Kedgaon, 27, 129
Keekozhoor, 42, 54

Keethi, Sanjeeva Rao (K. Sanjeeva
 Rao), 68, 72, 104, 112,
 119, 120, 121, 139
Kenya, 50
K.E. Rajpramukh, 136
Kerala, 2, 14, 25, 30, 35, 36, 37,
 38, 39, 44, 45, 46, 48, 50, 51,
 54, 55, 56, 61, 62, 65, 66, 68,
 72, 73, 80, 111, 117, 123,
 129, 135, 137, 138
Keralites, 56, 111
Kesanapalli, 72
Kesavadas Palem, 72
Khan, Benjamin, 20, 136
Kidangnoor, 35
Kilari, Anand Paul (K. Anand
 Paul), 113, 134
Kilari, Vekata Rao (Barnabas),
 113, 121, 134
King George Hospital, 67
King George V, 57
K. Israel, 104
K.J. Purushotham, 96
K. Joseph Sudarsanam and
 Miriam, 60, 70, 86
Kokkamangalam, 42
Kolagani, Joshua, 70
Kolamuru, 66
Kolanki, 108
Kollabathula, Jagannadham,
 107
Kolleru Lanka, 19
Kolleru Mission, 19
Komanapalli, Ernest, 76, 79, 86,
 87, 88, 89, 111, 125, 133,
 134, 139
Komanapalli, Issac, 84
Komanapalli, Sudarsan Jyothi, 140
Kommu, Yacobu, 119, 121, 140
Kondagunturu, 66
Koneru, Ranga Rao, 98
Konthamuru, 66
Koodarapallil, Thommen, 25
Korati, George Paul
 (Pedda K.G. Paul), 60, 65, 74,
 78, 96, 107, 124, 140
Korati, Jyothi Samuel, 78, 119,
 140
Korukonda, 75
Korumamidi, 63

Korumilli, 74
Kotapadu, 83
Kothagudem, 105, 119, 139
Kothapalli, Joseph Raju, 49, 136
Kothapalli, Jonathan, 66
Kothavalasa, 106
Kottarkkara, 35
Kottayam, 43, 48, 51, 135
Kovvali, 63
Kovvuru, 66
K. Priyanandam, 68
Krishna, 10
Krishna District, 17, 18, 70, 93
K. Samuel, 70
Kshatriya, 9, 10
K. Srinivasulu, 21, 136
Kucera, Martha, 36, 37, 50
Kulathumoolackal, Eapen Abraham (K.E. Abraham), 2, 5, 34, 37, 38, 41, 45, 51, 52, 55, 56, 61, 123, 129, 130, 131, 134, 135, 138
Kulchal, 49
Kumbanadu, 40, 42, 46, 52, 56, 63, 72, 97, 133, 134
Kunchala, Sekhar Daniel, 99, 140
Kunderu, 70, 105
Kundeti, Gershon Paul (Chinna K.G. Paul), 74, 78, 105, 119, 120, 140
Kunjamma, 65
Kunjappi Upadesi, 43
Kuntam, Edward William, 106, 120, 140
Kuntam, Rajamma, 62
Kuntam, Samuel Arun Das, 77, 120, 140
Kuntam, Sathyadas, 62, 63
Kurnool, 16, 18, 32, 130
Kutty, Samuel, 38, 39, 40, 50, 51, 138
K.V. Simon, 44, 45
K.Y. Ratnam, 21, 137

Lady Ampthill High School, 58
LaFlamme, 31
Lambadis, 34
Lam, Jeevaratnam, 57, 58, 59, 60, 61, 75, 76, 124, 133, 135

Lam, Samuel Pradhan, 76, 140
Landour, 86
Latin America, 1
Lazarus and Neelavathi, 70
Leeds, 57
Leelamma, 66
Lewin, Kurt, 116
Lilly Pushpamma, 87
Lima, 92
Linden, Carl and Rosemary 86
Little tradition, 5, 136
L.J. Francis, 122
London, 20, 48, 51, 57, 122, 134, 136, 137, 138
London Missionary Society, 14, 18
Lothal, 8
L. Sam, 48
L.T. Manikyam, 105
Ludiamma, 65
Luke, 51
Lunav, 42, 46, 54, 124

Macharla, 94
Machilipatnam, 16, 17, 55, 58, 59, 60, 61, 68, 69, 76, 77, 78, 89, 93, 119, 120, 121, 122, 138, 139, 140, 141
Mackay, Ernest, 8
Madhya Pradesh, 27
Madiga caste, 15, 16, 17, 84, 99
Madigas, 12, 18, 99, 112, 117, 119, 125
Madras, 15, 19, 20, 21, 36, 41, 45, 51, 55, 57, 61, 72, 86, 87, 110, 136, 137, 138
Madras Province, 18
Madras State, 39
Madura, 33
Mahabharata, 10
Mahaboobnagar, 67, 85, 92, 93, 96
Maharashtra, 30, 37, 72
Mahatma Gandhi, 7, 109
Maheswarapuram, 69, 71
Mailady, 14
Mainline churches, 3, 60, 71, 103, 106, 110, 113, 115, 116, 118, 124, 126
Mainline denominations, 40,

108, 110
Mala caste, 62, 84, 99, 112
Malabar Coast, 42
Malakapalli, 66, 67
Malankara, 39, 42
Malankara Full Gospel Church, 37, 38, 129
Malankara Pentecostal Church, 38, 130
Malankara Poorna Suvishesha Sabha, 37
Malas, 12, 18, 99, 112, 117, 119, 125
Malayali leadership, 125
Malayali pastors, 111
Malaysia, 50, 136
Malkapuram, 68
Malpan, Abraham, 45, 51
Mammen, Annamma, 65
Mammen, Umman, 35
Mandamari, 73
Mandapet, 74, 104, 107, 109
Manepalli, 72
Manguvarithota, 83
Manhattan, 57
Manifestation(s) of the Holy Spirit, 23, 24, 26, 32, 33
Manikonda, 71
Mann Singh, 58, 59, 60, 76, 140
Manna Ministries, 76, 79, 86, 87, 88, 89, 114, 125, 133, 139, 140
Manoramabai (Mano), 27, 28, 29
Mantada, Mariyamma, 71
Manu Dharma Sastra, 9
Manu Smruti, 9, 10
Mar Dionysius V, 51
Mar Matthew Athanasius, 51
Mar Philoxenus of Thozhiyoor, 51
Mar Thoma church, 43, 44, 45, 51, 52
Mar Thomas Athanasius, 45, 51, 52
Mar Thoma Syrian church, 45, 54
Martin, Samuel, 13, 20
Maranatha Bible College, 110
Maranatha Vedasamajam, 114

Mariyamma, 105
Mark, 51
Markapuram, 16, 74
Marlapudi, Mary, 77, 99, 140
Marlapudi, Peturu (Peter), 99
Marlapudi, Prasad Kumar, 77, 122, 134, 140
Marlapudi, Samuel, 63
Marripalem, 68
Marshall, Sir John, 20
Maru Kondayya, 63
Mary, 54
Masai Pet, 73
Masilamani, Azariah, 5, 137
Massey, James, 14, 20, 21, 137
Mathew, Thomson K., 2, 5, 61, 137
Mattada, Jacob John, 122, 140
Mavelikara, 36, 37
McGavaran, Donald, 13, 21, 126, 137
McGee, Gary B., 24, 26, 30, 48, 49, 50, 137
McLaurin High School, 71, 74, 75
McLaurin, John, 19, 20, 74
Mead, Charles, 14
Medicherlapalem, 72
Medisetti, Gannamma, 108
Medisetti, Srinivasa Rao, 108, Medukonduru, 57
Mellimi, Joy Esther Rani, 97, 121, 140
Mennonite Mission Fellowship, 92
Meriga, Samuel Rankin Pace, 77, 120, 140
Merugu, Annal Chandra Bai, 60, 76, 140
Mesopotomia, 42
Methodist Church, 30
Mexico, 50
Middle East, 50, 118
Miracle at Memphis, 118
Miriam Children's Home, 87
Mirthiguddivalsa, 83
M.M. Thoams, 52, 135
Moghulraj Puram, 69
Mohenjo-daro, 8, 20
Mortha, Philip, 74, 96, 97, 108

Mothugudem, 68
Movva, 93
Mrs. Shilling, 15
Ms. Targin, 65
M. Sunder Rao, 70
Mukti Mission, 27, 30
Mukti Revival, 27, 28, 30, 129
Mukti Sadan, 27
Muller, George, 44
Mumford, Linda, 114, 122, 137
Mungamuri, Devadas, 64, 65, 71, 77, 133, 134, 137
Mungamuri, Jonah and Sathyavathamma, 64
Munjaru, 68
Murugeshan, 58, 59, 60, 61, 69
Mussoorie, 86
Muttampackal, Kochukunju, 44
Mutyalapad, 18
M. Vijaya Kumar, 78, 137
Mylapore, 43
Mysore, 41, 72, 134
Mysore State, 36

Nadar caste, 123
Nadars, 14
Nagaram, 72
Nalgonda District, 65
Nandamuru, 63
Nanduri, Indira Vandanam, 59, 76, 140
Nandyal, 18
Narsannapet, 83
Narsapuram, 19, 62, 69, 70, 82, 84, 86
Narsarao Pet, 16, 66
Narsipatnam, 68
National Association for the Promotion of Holiness, 29, 49, 134
National Christian Council of India, Burma and Ceylon, 34
Nattu, 13
Neelam, Sundaramma, 58
Nekkala Devudu, 105
Nekkala Ramayamma, 105
Nellikallu, 74
Nellimarla, 68
Nellore, 15, 16, 19, 30, 31, 32, 57, 67, 130

Neocharismatics, 1, 4
Nepal, 50
New York, 20, 21, 31, 48, 49, 57, 92, 122, 133, 134, 136, 137
Nidadavole, 63, 65, 109
Nilgiris, 39
Niranam, 42
Nirmal, Arvind, 20, 137
Nizam Pet, 69
Noble, Robert, 16, 17
Noble College, 17, 93
Noble High School, 58
Nonchar, 18
Non-Christians, 31, 32, 67, 69, 71, 116
Non-Dalits, 11, 99
North India, 41, 44, 50, 55, 86, 91, 137
North India Assemblies of God, 37
Norton, Albert 27
Norway, 30, 35, 72, 92

Ongole, 15, 16, 19, 30, 31, 32, 101, 110, 119, 120, 122, 127, 130, 139, 140
Ontario, 19, 47
Oommen, George, 20, 38, 39, 50, 137
Orissa, 83
Orr, J. Edwin, 21, 49, 137
Osborn, William Bramwell, 39
Oslo, 35, 92
Outpouring(s) of the Holy Spirit, 24, 26, 27, 28, 30, 123

Pachigall, John Lazarus, 119, 120, 140
Pachigalla, Lazarus Paramjyothi (P.L. Paramjyothi), 55, 60, 63, 65, 66, 67, 68, 69, 70, 71, 72, 73, 74, 75, 76, 78, 79, 80, 82, 83, 84, 85, 86, 88, 91, 92, 94, 95, 109, 120, 124, 125, 134
Pachigalla, Samuel Finney, 95, 102, 120, 140
Pachigalla, Spurgeon Raju, 76, 87, 89, 95, 120, 121, 126, 140

154 Index

Pagolu, Venkayya, 16, 17, 18, 20
Paidamma, 104
Pakala Samson, 110
Pakistan, 8, 87
Palakol, 15, 69, 72
Pali language, 43
Palla, Victor, 21, 137
Palur, 42
Palmer, Walter and Phoebe, 48
Pamarru, 69, 71, 74
Pamukunta, 73
Panchamas, 7
Pandalam, 44
Pandalam, Mattai, 39
Papabathini, Prabhudas, 88, 89, 140
Papabathini, Pullayya (or Philip), 79, 87, 88, 125
Papua New Guinea, 50
Papayyapet, 92
Paraneeyam, 49
Parangi, Christopher, 70, 120, 140
Parlakimidi, 83
Parla, Rathna Jyothi, 140
Parnal, John, 44
Parousia, 24, 25
Parur, 42
Paruttupara, Ummachan, 41
Pasala, Prakasam, 61
Pasala, Saramma, 61, 62
Pasarlapudi, 72
Pasivedala, 66
Pasupati, 8
Patriarch Elias, 51
Pattabhi, Ramayya, 59
P. Deevenamma, 70
Peda Rayavaram, 75
Pedamangalaram, 93
Pedapalem, 66
Pedapudi, Anandam (P. Anandam), 69, 70
Pedapuid, Evangeline Grace, 77, 89, 119, 120, 121, 140
Pedapudi, Samuel, 77, 78, 120, 121, 140
Peddapuram, 65
Peddukapavaram, 30

P.E. Mammen, 48
Pentecostal and charismatic Christianity, 1
Pentecostal and charismatic organizations, 114
Pentecostal believer(s), 74, 110
Pentecostal faith, 37, 58, 59, 60, 63, 64, 65, 66, 68, 69, 70, 72, 73, 74, 75, 85, 86, 87, 92, 93, 96, 104, 105, 106, 108, 109, 110, 113, 119, 123, 124, 125
Pentecostal historiography, 42
Pentecostal message, 34, 36, 41, 43, 53, 54, 55, 57, 60, 61, 65, 67, 68, 69, 73, 93, 104, 113, 116, 124
Pentecostal spirituality, 118
Pentecostal-charismatic movement(s), 1, 4, 65, 135
Pentecostalism, 7, 25, 27, 29, 30, 31, 33, 34, 35, 37, 38, 39, 40, 41, 43, 45, 47, 49, 51, 57, 60, 61, 66, 67, 70, 104, 108, 109, 113, 116, 117, 118, 119, 122, 126, 127, 129, 135, 136, 137, 138
Peter Vijaya Pradeep, 60
Philip Abraham, 73, 92, 111
Philip, Robert, 19
Pickett, J. Waskom, 21, 137
Pitta, Daveedu, 77, 101, 140
P. John Thomas, 80
P.J. Titus, 76, 133
Planthoppu, 49
Plathaneth, Abraham Samuel (P. Abraham Samuel), 87, 88, 91, 92, 94, 95, 96, 98, 101, 125
Plathaneth, Joy Abraham Samuel, 92, 94, 101, 134
Plathaneth, Matthew Samuel (P.M. Samuel), 41, 52, 53, 54, 56, 57, 60, 67, 74, 76, 77, 80, 81, 84, 85, 86, 87, 88, 91, 92, 93, 94, 95, 96, 98, 101, 111, 112, 116, 125, 129, 130, 134
Plathaneth, Noel Samuel, 76, 91, 94, 95, 96, 97, 98, 99, 100, 101, 102, 111, 120, 125,

134, 140
Plymouth Brethren, 24, 48
Podali, 16
Podilaku, Mark, 63, 76, 134
Poikayil, Yohannan, 34, 37, 38, 40, 41, 42, 47, 123
Poloma, Margaret, 114
Polygamy, 118
Ponnamanda, 72
Poona (Pune), 27, 29, 72, 76, 135
(P.T. Chacko), 55, 56, 61, 62, 63, 65, 69, 71, 73, 92, 111, 134
Popular religion, 115
Pornia, 90
Possehl, Gregory L., 20, 137
Post-holiness movement, 29
Pothen, Thottumkal Abraham, 2, 5, 50, 137
Potti, Rajarathnam, 62, 70, 109
Powell, William, 31
Power of the (Holy) Spirit, 31, 32, 45, 104
Prakashnagar, 70
P. Ramankutty (Paul), 41, 42, 45, 46, 47, 123, 130
Prathyaksha Raksha Daiva Sabha, 40
Prayer for healing, 3, 40, 115, 119
Pre-Aryan People, 8
Prophecies, 24, 25, 33, 104
Prophecy, 24, 25, 70
Prophetic office, 26
Prophetic utterances, 3
Protestant Christianity, 13, 53, 123
Protestant missionaries, 33, 34, 45, 123
Proto-Pentecostal phenomenon, 24, 26, 33
Proto-Pentecostalism, 23, 24
Providence, 86
P. Stephen, 82, 83
Pujaripalem, 72
Pulidindi, Solomon Raj, 78, 122, 126, 127, 137, 140
Pulikottil, Paulson, 39, 51, 52, 138
Punalur, 36, 37

Punjab, 13, 14
Punthala, 35
Purusha, 9
Purushothapalli, 63
P.V. John, 37

Queen Mary, 57
Quilor, 43

Rabbavarapu, Paul Papa Rao, 119, 122, 141
Rabel Jeeva, 59
Rachel, 86, 89, 133
Raghavapuram, 16, 17, 18
Rajahmundry, 19, 62, 64, 65, 66, 67, 72, 77, 85, 91, 97, 107, 110, 120, 121, 124, 134, 140
Rajanagaram, 75, 78, 139
Rajanya, 9
Rajavolu, 66
Rajus, 114
Rama, 10
Ramabai, Sarasvati Mary (Pandita Ramabai), 27, 28, 29, 30, 48, 49, 129, 133, 134, 137, 138
Ramabai Association, 27
Ramachandrapuram, 32
Ramaswamy (Peter) and Venkamma (Mary Rathnam), 93
Ramayana, 10, 21, 134
Ramayapatnam, 16, 19
Rameswaram, 72
Ramnagar, 73
Rampachodavaram, 74
Ranastalam, 83
Rangoon, 70, 74, 96, 107
Ranny, 54
Rapalle, 78
Rashtriya Swayamsevak Sangh (RSS), 109
Rathnam Manaseh, 70, 74, 96
Ravi Babu, 99, 100
Ravi, 8
Rayagadda, 83
Razole, 68, 72
R. Coal, 55, 61
Reddys, 12, 114

Regent University, 94
Regimental Bazar, 73
Rentachinthala, 74
Rhenius, Carl T. E., 24, 129
Rhode Island, 86
Rig-Veda, 9
Ringeltaube, William, 14, 20
Rock Church, 87
Rock Church Ministries, 87, 119, 140
Roman Catholic Church, 105
Roman Catholic compound, 98
Roman Catholicism, 1
Ropar, 8
Rosamma, 65
Rudravaram, 18
Rukmaniammalpuram, 11
Rutherford, 66

Sade, Krupanandam, 82
Sadhu Paul, 61, 64
Saint Thomas, 42, 43, 51, 52, 135, 136
Sajjavaripalem, 66
Sallapudu, 108
Salvation Army, 57, 63
Samalkot, 32, 76
Samavesham of Telugu Baptist Churches, 25
Sambavar caste, 20
Sambavar community, 20
Sambuka, 10
Sampadanagaram, 79
Samuel and Harriet, 60
Samuel Vijaya Chandar, 110
San Thome Cathedral, 43
Sanctification, 28, 29, 35, 48, 112
Sandredi, 75
Sanjeevamma, 63
Santhamma and Deenamma, 105
Sanyasamma, 113
Sathenapalli, 16, 66
Sathyanandam, 62
Satluj, 8
Scheduled Castes, 8, 12
Scheduled Tribes, 12
Science and technology, 115
S.D. Barnabas, 70, 134

Searles, John E., 49, 134
Second World War, 74, 96
Secunderabad, 69, 73, 75
Seleru, 68, 104
S.E. Morrow, 30, 129
Sengupta, Padmini, 49, 134
Sen, Makhan Lal, 21, 134
Seychelles, 50
Seymour, William J., 50, 117
S.F. Smith, 15
Shah, Amritlal B., 48, 49, 134
Shameer Pet, 73
Shanars, 14, 24, 129
Sharada Sadan, 27
Sharampur, 37
Sialkot, 13, 20
Sialkot District, 13
Siddapuram, 30, 110
Siddi Pet, 73
Signs in the heavens, 24
Sindhu Valley, 8
Singapore, 50, 72
Singh Nagar, 69
S. Isaiah, 85
Sister Geraldine, 28, 29
Siva, 8
Six Years Party, 25
Sixteenth World Pentecostal Conference, 92
S. Kota, 68
Smalley, William, 4
Smith, Amanda Berry 29
Smith, Badley, 21, 138
Smith, Roy and Myrtle, 86
Snyder, Howard A., 29, 48, 49, 138
Society for the Propagation of the Gospel in Foreign Parts, 14, 18
Sompeta, 32
Sorcery, 132
South Asia, 20
South India, 5, 8, 25, 26, 33, 34, 35, 36, 37, 48, 49, 50, 51, 52, 56, 64, 76, 126, 129, 133, 135, 136, 137
South India(n) Pentecostal Church of God, 37, 38, 39, 41, 45, 46, 51, 129, 130, 131
South Indian Pentecostal

Movement, 50, 76, 89, 135
Southern Asia Bible Institute, 86
Speaking in tongues, 3, 24, 28, 30, 35, 44, 45, 49, 58, 103, 104, 113, 114, 122, 135, 137
Spencer, 18
Spencer, Ivan Q., 92
Spiritual empowerment, 103, 104, 113
Spiritual gifts, 24
Srikakulam, 20, 21, 72, 75, 80, 82, 83, 89, 119, 120, 121, 134, 137, 139
St. Louis College, 92
Stanton, William Arthur, 32, 33, 49, 130, 135
Stephen, 111
Stephen Yesudas, 85
Sudras, 9, 11
Sugandha Rathnam, 97
Sumrall, Lester, 57, 76, 135
Sunder Singh, 58, 63, 66, 70
Superstition, 114
Suranadu, 36
Surasaniyanam, 81
Surkotada, 8
Suryanarayana, 108
Sutkagendor, 8
Suvarna, 93
Suvartha Pracharam, 85
Suvartha Prakashini, 68, 71, 75, 77, 124, 133
Suvisesham, 83
Suviseshavani, 83
Swamidas, 73
Sweden, 56, 61, 72, 81
Switzerland, 50, 72, 86
Syrian Christians, 27, 37, 38, 43, 44, 47
Syrian Orthodox Church, 44, 51, 130

Tadipaka, 72
Takht-i-Bahi, 43
Tallakondapud, 15
Tamilnadu, 11, 24, 30, 33, 36, 41, 43, 55, 56, 59, 60, 123, 129
Tanamuri, Marthamma, 83
Tangutur, 65

Tanjavur, 18
Tanjore, 14
Tanuku, 70, 76, 141
Tapasya, 10
Taragam, Ebinezer Sasthry, 89, 119, 141
Taragam, Sathyavedam Sasthry (T.S. Sasthry), 60, 62, 63, 79, 84, 85, 88, 89, 92, 104, 107, 125, 141
Taylor, William, 29
Telugu pastors, 80, 81, 84, 87, 95, 111, 116, 117, 125
Telugus, 15, 17, 49, 53, 56, 135
Tenali, 66, 85
Texas, 80, 94
Thackil, Chacko George, 2, 5, 138
Thalluri, Marayya (Thomas Gabriel, 19, 20
Thatipaka, 68
The Blacks, 50
The Gulf countries, 56, 72
The Indian Army, 70, 87
The Indus, 8, 20, 137
The IPC, 1, 2, 3, 4, 39, 41, 45, 47, 53, 54, 55, 56, 57, 59, 60, 61, 62, 63, 64, 65, 66, 67, 68, 69, 70, 71, 72, 73, 74, 75, 79, 80, 81, 83, 84, 85, 86, 87, 88, 89, 91, 92, 93, 94, 95, 96, 97, 98, 99, 100, 101, 103, 104, 105, 106, 107, 108, 110, 111, 112, 113, 114, 115, 116, 117, 118, 119, 123, 124, 125, 126, 131, 133, 134
The Pentecostal Mission, 50
The state of Tinnevelly, 24
The Vedas, 12
The Whites, 50
The WME, 62, 74, 81, 82, 83, 84, 85, 86, 88, 106, 112, 125
The work of the Holy Spirit, 23, 33, 35, 41, 43, 47, 103, 117
Theegalapalli, 85
Tadepalligudem, 62, 63, 71, 72, 107
Theosis, 27
Thevars, 11
Thoburn, John, 29

Thottil, K. Thomas (T.K. Thomas), 63, 66, 71, 73, 92
Thullimalli, John Sudhir Dutt, 76, 141
Thullimalli, Peter Gurupadam (T.P. Gurupadam), 55, 58, 59, 60, 75, 76, 124, 140, 141
Thullimalli, Swaroop Dutt, 76 141
Thuvayoor, 35, 36, 123
Timmarajuppalem, 63
Timmarao Gudem, 112
Tipalli, Mrudhubhashini, 65, 66, 71, 124
Tirunelveli, 24, 50
Tirunelveli district, 11, 33
Tirunelveli Revival, 25, 129
T.K. Mahanty, 83
Tobago, 50
Toopran, 73
Trances, 30, 31, 32, 33
Tranquebar Conference, 34
Travancore, 14, 20, 25, 26, 33, 36, 37, 39, 40, 41, 43, 46, 48, 49, 51, 55, 123, 129, 135
Trichur District, 46
Trinidad, 50
Trivandrum, 40, 44, 48, 72
Tuni, 20
T. Yesudas, 68

Udayagiri, 16
UK, 50
Ulster, 24
Uma Maheswar, 108, 109
Unikicharla, 73
Union Church Mission, 67
United Arab Emirates, 90
United Presbyterian Church of North America, 13
United States (USA), 7, 15, 24, 27, 36, 37, 50, 56, 57, 72, 81, 99, 117, 129
University of Rhode Island, 86
Unknown tongues, 24, 26, 28, 44, 104
Untouchability, 11, 12, 21, 38, 117, 135
Upanishads, 9, 20, 134
Uppalapadu, 74

Upper caste Hindus, 3, 13
Upperman, John, 88
Uttar Pradesh, 72, 82, 86

Vadisileru, 75
Vaisya, 9
Valmiki, 10
Valparaiso, 30
Varghese, Habel, 51, 135
Varghese, Kunjappan C., 2, 5, 43, 45, 52, 138
Varghese, V. Titus, 51
Varna, 9
Varna dharma, 10
Vatluru, 62
V. David Raju, 68
V. Devasahayam, 21, 138
Veda Navamani, 59, 60
Vedanayagam, Ammal, 25
Vedanayagam, Samuel Azariah, 33, 34, 47, 49, 60, 136
Veeragenthala, Periah, 15, 16
Vegesana, Vijaya Bhaskara Raju, 78, 138
Velayudam, 33
Vellalanvillai, 33
Vellikara, Mattai (Choti), 34, 37, 38, 40, 42, 123
Vellore, 59
Velpuru, 72
Veluvennu, 63
Vemagiri, 66
Venezuela, 30
Venkateswara, 112
Vennilingapuram, 11
Ventrapragada, 71
Vethamanikam, 14, 20
Victoria, 57, 59
Vijayaratnam, 82
Vijayawada, 17, 52, 56, 60, 61, 63, 66, 67, 69, 70, 71, 72, 73, 74, 75, 76, 78, 87, 88, 89, 92, 93, 94, 95, 97, 99, 101, 107, 120, 121, 126, 127, 134, 138, 139, 140
Vilasavilli, 75
Vinayaka, 112
Vinukonda, 16, 66
Virginia, 87, 94
Virginia Beach, 77, 78, 87, 89,

120, 121, 138, 139, 140
Visakhapatnam, 17, 52, 56, 60,
    61, 63, 66, 67, 69, 70, 71, 72,
    73, 74, 75, 76, 78, 87, 88, 89,
    92, 93, 94, 95, 97, 99, 101,
    107, 120, 121, 126, 127, 134,
    138, 139, 140
Visakhapatnam Central Jail, 68
Visions, 24, 25, 28, 30, 32, 33,
    64, 104, 115
Vizainagaram, 68, 75, 83
Voice of Good News, 83
Voice of World Missionary
    Evangelism, 66
Volbrech, Nagal, 44
Vongole, Abraham, 15, 16
Vootalanka, 66
V.R. Egbert, 58, 60
Vundrajavaram, 71
Vuyyuru, 59, 66, 69, 70, 71, 73,
    105, 124
V.V. Thomas, 34, 38, 49, 138
V.W. Newton, 44

Warangal, 65, 66, 67, 69, 70, 71,
    72, 73, 75, 77, 84, 85, 89, 92,
    106, 107, 109, 110, 120, 121,
    127, 138, 139
Water baptism, 43, 44, 45, 61,
    104
Welsh Revival, 31
Wesley, John, 28
West Godavari District, 63, 67,
    70
West Virginia, 79
W. Howell, 18
Wigglesworth, Smith, 60
Wings of Healing, 72, 80, 82
Winkle, Aldy, 35, 36, 49
Winter, Ralph, 5
W. McDonald, 49, 134
Wood Pet, 69
World Missionary Conference at
    Tambaram, 34
World Missionary Evangelism,
    66, 79, 80, 83, 89, 119, 134,
    139
W.S. Hunt, 48
Wyatt, Thomas, 80, 82, 83

Yalamanchili, 70
Yellamanchili, 30, 32
Yerneni, Estheramma, 83
Yesurathnam and Jogamma, 87
Yong, Amos, 118, 122, 126, 127,
    138

Zavet, 19
Zion Bible College (School), 63,
    66, 67, 69, 70, 72, 74, 75, 85,
    87, 92, 93, 94, 97, 98, 101,
    107, 120, 124, 125, 135, 140
Zion Bible Institute, 86

www.ingramcontent.com/pod-product-compliance
Lightning Source LLC
Chambersburg PA
CBHW021831300426
44114CB00009BA/400